Roman Jakobson

Roman Jakobson's work on poetry and poetics has always been overshadowed by his brilliant contributions to modern linguistics. His famous paper on 'Linguistics and Poetics', while acknowledged as central to the development of both linguistics and critical theory, has in the three decades since its publication been swept aside by the tide of poststructuralism. Richard Bradford reasserts the value of Jakobson's work, arguing that he has a great deal to offer to contemporary critical theory and providing a critical appraisal of the sweep of Jakobson's career.

Roman Jakobson: Life, Language, Art is an analytic guide to Jakobson's work: it includes practical demonstrations of Jakobsonian method; it considers his work within the broader context of structuralism and poststructuralism; and it argues for the relevance of Jakobson's methods in contemporary critical theory. In addition, the author discusses the problematical relationship between Jakobsonian poetics, literary history and modernism.

Richard Bradford re-establishes Jakobson's work as vital to our understanding of the relationship between language and poetry. By exploring Jakobson's thesis that poetry is the primary object language, a pathbreaking laboratory for insights into the structure and function of the sign, *Roman Jakobson: Life, Language, Art* offers a new reading of his work. This book will be invaluable to students of Jakobson and to anyone interested in the development of critical theory, linguistics and stylistics.

Richard Bradford is Lecturer in English at the University of Ulster at Coleraine, Northern Ireland.

CRITICS OF THE TWENTIETH CENTURY

General Editor: Christopher Norris,
University of Wales, College of Cardiff

Roman Jakobson

Life, language, art

Richard Bradford

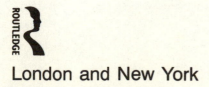

London and New York

First published 1994
by Routledge
11 New Fetter Lane, London EC4P 4EE

Simultaneously published in the USA and Canada
by Routledge
29 West 35th Street, New York, NY 10001

© 1994 Richard Bradford

Phototypeset in Baskerville by Intype, London
Printed and bound in Great Britain by TJ Press Ltd, Padstow, Cornwall

Printed on acid free paper

British Library Cataloguing in Publication Data
A catalogue record for this book is available from the British Library

Library of Congress Cataloging in Publication Data
Bradford, Richard, 1958–
   Roman Jakobson: life, language, art/Richard Bradford.
   p. cm. – (Critics of the twentieth century)
   Includes bibliographical references and index.
   1. Jakobson, Roman, 1896–. I. Title. II. Series: Critics of the
   twentieth century (London, England)
   P85.J3B7 1994   93–26943
   410'.92–dc20   CIP

ISBN 0–415–07731–1 (hbk)
ISBN 0–415–07732–X (pbk)

To Louie, Bill and Jan

Contents

Editor's foreword

The twentieth century has produced a remarkable number of gifted and innovative literary critics. Indeed it could be argued that some of the finest literary minds of the age have turned to criticism as the medium best adapted to their complex and speculative range of interests. This has sometimes given rise to regret among those who insist on a clear demarcation between 'creative' (primary) writing on the one hand, and 'critical' (secondary) texts on the other. Yet this distinction is far from self-evident. It is coming under strain at the moment as novelists and poets grow increasingly aware of the conventions that govern their writing and the challenge of consciously exploiting and subverting those conventions. And the critics for their part – some of them at least – are beginning to question their traditional role as humble servants of the literary text with no further claim upon the reader's interest or attention. Quite simply, there are texts of literary criticism and theory that, for various reasons – stylistic complexity, historical influence, range of intellectual command – cannot be counted a mere appendage to those other 'primary' texts.

Of course, there is a logical puzzle here since (it will be argued) 'literary criticism' would never have come into being, and could hardly exist as such, were it not for the body of creative writings that provide its *raison d'être*. But this is not quite the kind of knock-down argument that it might appear at first glance. For one thing, it conflates some very different orders of priority, assuming that literature always comes first (in the sense that Greek tragedy had to exist before Aristotle could formulate its rules), so that literary texts are for that very reason possessed of superior value. And this argument would seem to find common-sense support in the difficulty of thinking what 'literary criticism' could *be* if it seriously renounced all sense of the distinction between literary and critical texts. Would it not then find itself in the unfortunate position of a discipline that had willed its own demise by declaring its subject non-existent?

But these objections would only hit their mark if there were indeed a special kind of writing called 'literature' whose difference from other kinds of writing was enough to put criticism firmly in its place. Otherwise there is nothing in the least self-defeating or paradoxical about a discourse, nominally that of literary criticism, that accrues such interest on its own account as to force some fairly drastic rethinking of its proper powers and limits. The act of crossing over from commentary to literature – or of simply denying the difference between them – becomes quite explicit in the writing of a critic like Geoffrey Hartman. But the signs are already there in such classics as William Empson's *Seven Types of Ambiguity* (1928), a text whose transformative influence on our habits of reading must surely be ranked with the great creative moments of literary modernism. Only on the most dogmatic view of the difference between 'literature' and 'criticism' could a work like *Seven Types* be counted generically an inferior, sub-literary species of production. And the same can be said for many of the critics whose writings and influence this series sets out to explore.

Some, like Empson, are conspicuous individuals who belong to no particular school or larger movement. Others, like Jakobson and the Czech and Russian Formalists, were part of a communal enterprise and are therefore best understood as representative figures in a complex and evolving dialogue. Then again there are cases of collective identity (like the so-called 'Yale deconstructors') where a mythical group image is invented for largely polemical purposes. (The volumes in this series on Hartman and Bloom should help to dispel the idea that 'Yale deconstruction' is anything more than a handy device for collapsing differences and avoiding serious debate.) So there is no question of a series format or house-style that would seek to reduce these differences to a blandly homogeneous treatment. One consequence of recent critical theory is the realisation that literary texts have no self-sufficient or autonomous meaning, no existence apart from their after-life of changing interpretations and values. And the same applies to those *critical* texts whose meaning and significance are subject to constant shifts and realignments of interest. This is not to say that trends in criticism are just a matter of intellectual fashion or the merry-go-round of rising and falling reputations. But it is important to grasp how complex are the forces – the conjunctions of historical and cultural motive – that affect the first reception and the subsequent fortunes of a critical text. This point has been raised into a systematic programme by critics like Hans-Robert Jauss, practitioners of so-called 'reception theory' as a form of historical hermeneutics. The volumes in this series will therefore be concerned not only to expound what is of lasting significance but also to set these critics in the context of present-day argument and debate. In some cases (as with Walter Benjamin) this debate takes the form of a struggle for interpretative power among exponents or disciplines with sharply opposed ideological interests. Such controversies cannot simply be ignored for the sake of achieving a clear and balanced account. They point to unresolved tensions and problems which are there in the critic's work as well as in the rival appropriative readings. In the end there is no way of drawing a neat methodological line between 'intrinsic' questions (what the critic really thought) and those other, supposedly 'extrinsic' concerns that have to do with influence and reception history.

The volumes will vary accordingly in their focus and range of coverage. They will also reflect the ways in which a speculative approach to questions of literary theory has proved to have striking consequences for the human sciences at large. This breaking-down of disciplinary bounds is among the most significant developments in recent critical thinking. As philosophers and historians, among others, come to recognise the rhetorical complexity of the texts they deal with, so literary theory takes on a new dimension of interest and relevance. It is scarcely appropriate to think of a writer like Derrida as practising 'literary criticism' in any conventional sense of the term. For one thing, he is as much concerned with 'philosophical' as with 'literary' texts, and has indeed actively sought to subvert (or deconstruct) such tidy distinctions. A principal object in planning this series was to take full stock of these shifts in the wider intellectual terrain (including the frequent boundary disputes) brought about by critical theory. And, of course, such changes are by no means confined to literary studies, philosophy and the so-called 'sciences of man'. It is equally the case in (say) nuclear physics and molecu-

lar biology that advances in the one field have profound implications for the other, so that specialised research often tends
(paradoxically) to break down existing divisions of intellectual
labour. Such work is typically many years ahead of the academic
disciplines and teaching institutions that have obvious reasons of
their own for adopting a business-as-usual attitude. One important aspect of modern critical theory is the challenge it presents
to these traditional ideas. And lest it be thought that this is
merely a one-sided takeover bid by literary critics, the series will
include a number of volumes by authors in those other disciplines, including, for instance, a study of Roland Barthes by a
philosopher schooled in the American analytic tradition.

We shall not, however, cleave to theory as a matter of polemical
or principled stance. The series will extend to figures like F. R.
Leavis, whose widespread influence went along with an express
aversion to literary theory; scholars like Erich Auerbach in the
mainstream European tradition; and others who resist assimi-
lation to any clear-cut line of descent. There will also be authori-
tative volumes on critics such as Northrop Frye and Kenneth
Burke, figures who, for various reasons, occupy an ambivalent or
contested place in current critical debate. Meanwhile, there are
those – like Roman Jakobson, subject of the present study –
whose work has exerted a profound influence on our thinking
about language, literature and poetics, but whose sheer range of
interests and scholarly expertise creates problems for even the
best-willed reader. Without blowing the trumpet too loudly, let
me say that Richard Bradford has surmounted these problems by
deftly combining an account of the relevant cultural history with
passages of detailed textual exegesis. Above all, his book has
no truck with that current polarisation of attitudes that sees no
common ground of interest between 'literary criticism' and 'critical theory'.

CHRISTOPHER NORRIS

Preface and acknowledgements

This book has grown out of my own research and writing in the fields of poetry and poetics, and there are overlaps between elements of this volume and my books, *The Look Of It. A Theory of Visual Form in English Poetry* (1993, Cork: Cork University Press) and *A Linguistic History of English Poetry* (1993, London: Routledge): principally, my use of the two formulae, the double pattern and the sliding scale, as a means of documenting the interaction between the materiality and the signifying function of poetic language. It has also grown out of a sadness for the demise of poetry studies as an independent discipline. Poetry is at once made of language and about language: this was the driving force behind Jakobson's prolific output. I hope that this study will assist in the re-establishment of Jakobson's work as central to our understanding of the dynamic relation between language and art, an area of study that has been sidelined and colonised by the more powerful theories and theorists of context – situational, gendered, political, social, cultural, etc.

The writing of the book has been greatly assisted by a grant from the Leverhulme Trust, to which I owe many thanks. Gratitude is due also to the English Department and the Humanities Faculty of the University of Ulster, particularly Anne McCartney and my Head of Department, Robert Welch. Christopher Norris has been a patient and helpful editor. Nothing would have been possible without Bill and Louie Bradford, and Jan Elliott has, as usual, been irreplaceable.

Notes on the references and bibliography

Most of Jakobson's published work is now in his seven-volume *Selected Writings* (cited in the bibliography). This is referred to in the main text as *SW*. A compact collection of his work on language, semiotics and literature is *Language in Literature* (1987, ed. K. Pomorska and S. Rudy, Cambridge, Mass.: Harvard University Press). Where possible, I have quoted from this collection – referred to in the main text as *L in L*. Parts of Jakobson's 1921 essay 'Novejšaja russkaja poèzija' ('New Russian Poetry') are in English translation in Edward J. Brown's *Modern Soviet Writers* (1971, London: Oxford University Press). Where possible I have used this translation (cited as 'Brown'); elsewhere quotations are from the reprint in *Texte der russischen Formalisten II* (1972, ed. W. D. Stempel, Munich: Fink), cited as 'Stempel'.

There are no footnotes. Works cited in the main text will be found in the bibliography. 'Suggestions for further reading on context and influence' contains material which relates to the main points of the study but which has not been cited or dealt with specifically.

Introduction

Some facts. Born in 1896, he began his high school education in the Lazarev Institute of Oriental Languages in 1906. In 1914 he entered the historico-philological faculty at the University of Moscow, and the following year the 19-year-old Jakobson with six other students founded the Moskovskij Lingvističeskij Kruzok, the Moscow Linguistic Circle. Its stated aim was 'the study of linguistics, poetics, metrics, and folklore' (*SW II*, p. 530). Together with its Petersburg counterpart OPOJAZ, with which Jakobson was closely involved, the Moscow Circle was the founding moment in what has become the largest interdisciplinary growth industry of twentieth-century academe, variously known as critical theory, semiotics, structuralism, literary linguistics, cultural studies. . . . The parts have superseded the whole.

This, I realise, is a sweeping statement but while the published work of the Russian Formalists has largely been consigned to the critical history museum, its collective and individual identities continue to bear the stamp of originality. For example, it is often stated that since the late 1960s poststructuralism has succeeded in disclosing and unsettling the illusive distinction between 'creative' writing and its uncreative, analytical partner. Well perhaps, but the Formalists did it first. Jakobson's first major prose work, 'Novejšaja russkaja poèzija' (published in 1921, written during the preceding decade and variously translated as 'New . . .', 'Newest . . .' and 'Modern Russian Poetry'), concentrates upon the work of his friend and contemporary Velimir Xlebnikov. Xlebnikov was the most experimental and, it is argued, the most inaccessible of the Russian Futurist poets, but Jakobson, rather than treating his work as an object for cool analysis, regards it as a provocative contribution to the developing understanding of linguistics, semiotics and literature. Jakobson's argument, which will also be the principal subject of this study, is this: our experience of the formative elements of existence – perception, consciousness and communication – is inseparable from our encounters with language. Poetry is unique among the varied and often intermarried types and genres of linguistic discourse because it obliges the poet and the reader to confront the necessary but uneasy relationship between what language is (in Jakobson's post-Saussurean terminology, the signans) and what language does (the signatum and the referent). Poetry is about language, and as a consequence, the poet, as much as the linguist, the semiologist and the philosopher, is the pathbreaker in the realms of the sign, the system and the existential condition.

Jakobson's life and work bear an intriguing and rather eerie resemblance to his theory of the poetic function. Let us continue with a few facts and details: phenomena that Jakobson would characterise as the defining elements of the contiguity axis, the progress of units through the temporal continuum.

During the 1920s the Moscow and Petersburg groups suffered a theoretical and collective diaspora. The post-civil-war establishment of the Marxist–Leninist state was not conducive to work which gave roughly equal priority to the aesthetic and non-aesthetic dimensions of language, and the best known, and justly celebrated, marriage of Formalist principles and neo-Marxian ideology occurred within the so-called Bakhtin school of the late 1920s and 1930s. Jakobson moved to Prague in 1920 and was eventually given a full-time teaching post in 1933 at Masaryk University in Brno. But he did not sever his links with friends, colleagues and memories in the Soviet Union. His strange visit to his friend the poet Majakovskij in the besieged city of Moscow is recorded in his 1931 essay 'On a Generation that Squandered its Poets' and during the 1950s, 1960s and 1970s he made regular trips from his home in the USA to various academic institutions and individuals in the USSR and the then curtained-off Eastern Europe – any journey along the contiguity axis will always involve various, sometimes shocking excursions towards the originary code of the paradigm.

Jakobson played a major role in the founding of the Prague Linguistic Circle in 1926, a group which has had a significant influence upon European, primarily French, structuralism of the post-Second World War years and upon Anglo-American linguistics. Jakobson's own work in Czechoslovakia in the 1920s and 1930s appears to fall into two categories. Along with his fellow Russian Nicholai Trubetzkoy, whom he had known from his schooldays, he evolved a theory of phonology which, although often revised and criticised, is still regarded as at once the most radical and seminal of this century. His less well-known work from this period, on theories of literary history, film, Czech and Russian poetry, Puškin and Pasternak, seems only marginally related to his studies in phonology, but it draws upon the same network of associative-paradigmatic choices. His idea that speech sounds (phonemes) are not atomic entities devoid of further analysis but complexes of phonetic properties (distinctive features) inhabits the same sphere of perception and analysis as his studies of Puškin's obsession with statues, Pasternak's poetic prose and prosaic poetry, and his theory of the relation between poetry and history: all are founded upon the conviction that the material substance of the sign is never fully distinguishable from its signifying properties.

In 1939 the contiguity axis again intervened. The Nazi occupation of Czechoslovakia drove and indeed followed Jakobson first to Denmark, then to Norway and then, in 1940, to Sweden. During this brief period in Scandinavia, he began what during the 1950s would be recognised as his valuable and innovative work on child language and aphasia. It is almost as though, having proceeded without choice along the syntagmatic chain, his desire to resume command of the medium prompted him to project the axis of selection into the axis of combination. Aphasia and child language acquisition might seem only obliquely connected with his earlier concerns with the atomic phoneme and poetic form, but, as he would show, aphasics and children can tell us as much about the poetic function as the poet and the phonologist.

In 1941 Jakobson arrived in New York, and during the 1940s he taught at Columbia University and the French–Belgian Institute, the Ecole Libre des Hautes Etudes. Here he met and influenced the founding father of modern anthropological structuralism, Claude Lévi-Strauss. In 1949 he moved to a post in Harvard University and in 1957 was appointed to a second chair as Institute Professor at the neighbouring MIT. His years in the United States, from the 1940s to his death in 1982, can be regarded as the *magnum opus* of his mortal text. As he was to point out, 'poeticalness is not a supplementation of discourse with rhetorical adornment but a total re-evaluation of the discourse and all its components whatsoever' (*L in L*, p. 93). This re-evaluation involved the return to and the extension of his work on phonology, poetics, aphasia and semiotics.

In 1958 he gave a paper to a symposium on literature and linguistics at Bloomington, Indiana. Like the single stanza, the line or the phrase which lives in the mind of the reader and absorbs and reconstitutes the life and work of the poet, this paper on 'Linguistics and Poetics' is to many readers and theorists the essence of Roman Jakobson. This is neither an entirely inaccurate picture nor a particularly helpful state of affairs. Everything Jakobsonian is in this paper – Russian poetry, English poetry, Czech poetry, Slavic folklore, metonymy and metaphor, the projection principle, the six-part diagram of the communicative circuit, phonology, aphasia, metrical studies, Formalism, parallelism. Its density, complexity and brevity bring to mind Jakobson's declared preference for short poems 'which allow us to retain at the end of the poem a strong impression of its beginning; this brevity consequently makes us particularly sensitive to the poem's unity and to its effect as a whole' (*SW III*, p. 770). He adds a note of caution regarding the problems of adapting such responses to longer texts, and this could easily be directed at the reader who encounters 'Linguistics and Poetics' and goes no further: 'Any attempt to analyse fragments of such works without paying attention to the whole of the text is no less futile than a study of detached pieces of a vast fresco as if they were integral and independent paintings.' My objective in this study is to effect an introduction to the whole text, the vast fresco of Jakobsonian poetics.

Semiologists have for decades argued over the hierarchy of different sign systems, the most prominent distinction being between linguistic and non-linguistic structures. Jakobson regularly pays allegiance to the democracy of the sign but his true affiliation is clear: poetry is the ultimate object language, the fundamental touchstone against which we judge and analyse the relation between other communicative functions. This is Jakobson on the 'dominant': 'The dominant may be defined as the focussing component of the work of art: it rules, determines, and transforms the remaining components. It is the dominant which guarantees the integrity of the structure.'

He refers to the intrinsic, defining features of poems, but this model might just as easily be applied to the dominant function of poetry and poetics in his own work. His principal topic could be aphasia, the phoneme, shifters, or cubist aesthetics, but the anchor, the invariant point of comparison, will be the poem. 'The science of language . . . cannot rightfully neglect the *poetic function*, which together with other verbal functions participates in the speech of every human being from earliest infancy and plays a crucial role in the structuring of discourse' (*SW, III,* p. 765). Again, this might be a description of Jakobson's career as a writer. The years 1914–20 can hardly be regarded as his earliest infancy but it was during this period that he contributed a number of poems to Futurist anthologies, under the pseudonym R. Aljagrov (see below, pp. 68–70). He has often stated that encounters with Xlebnikov provided him with the original insights into the nature of language that would underpin his later work on phonology, but there is also a peculiar thread of continuity that plays if not a 'crucial' then at least an engaging 'role' in the structuring of his analytical discourse. The diphthong 'ja' (the Russian personal pronoun 'I') occurs almost obsessively in his best known poem 'Distraction', and indeed is carried from his surname to the pseudonym. In a commemorative collection, his widow Krystyna Pomorska picks up this thread. 'A striking feature of his discourse is a strong tendency to avoid the first person singular' ('Autobiography of a Scholar', in *Language, Poetry and Poetics*, ed. Pomorska *et al.*, p. 11). Even in his most candid, subjective discourse, his *Dialogues* with his wife, he maintains this impersonal stance.

> He is confronted with questions aimed directly at him. And yet he manages to use a similar strategy. Example: 'this was one of the main stimuli that *forced us* to overcome the separation between . . .'; or, 'the phonic analysis of Xlebnikov's poetic texture *prompted use* of linguistic data'.
>
> (p. 11)

Pomorska suggests that this habit originated in Jakobson's idea of poetic speaker, text and biography as a form of mythology in which life and work, or, more specifically, the referential and the textual function become intermingled. This would be consistent with the obsessive prominence of 'I' in his poetry. In a number of essays, Jakobson asserts that the addressee and the addresser of the poem are irreconcilably ambiguous figures, that the pronominal persona of the poem is at once present and absent. After 1920 he never again wrote in poetic form and, according to his wife, he assiduously excluded the first person singular from his non-poetic writing. This practice should not be dismissed as a mere eccentricity; rather it should be seen as silent testimony to his belief that the poetic function exerts a constant pressure upon our linguistic presence – he seems to have produced around 5,000 pages of prose while cautiously and self-consciously avoiding any trace of the lyrical first person.

The sense of mystery and ambiguity generated by the poetic seems also to have infused his work as a teacher. Paul Kiparsky, eminent literary linguist and pupil of Jakobson, comments:

> Jakobson was certainly the most captivating teacher I ever had. There was always a kind of mystery behind his teaching and writing. He explained what the problems were that interested him and why they were important, he dazzled you with his brilliant solutions to them, but if you wanted to try that kind of work yourself you had to figure out on your own how to do it. In his articles he would hide his tracks the way mathematicians do, presenting his results but not revealing how he discovered them. . . . As a result, while his leading ideas inspired several generations of linguists and entirely changed the field of phonology in particular, relatively few people truly learned how to apply his analytic techniques, so that there are not nearly as many 'Jakobsonian' studies extant as his enormous overall influence might lead one to expect. Many of his more original ideas have not yet been exploited, and perhaps not even been fully understood. This again, I think, applies particularly to his pathbreaking work in poetics.
>
> (1983, pp. 27–8)

Kiparsky makes two intriguing points. First, Jakobson has narrowed the distinction between poetry and writing about poetry. His articles, like poems, are in varying degrees challenging, evocative and revealing, and, again following the conundrum of the poetic, they demand the participation of the addressee in the untangling of the complex mesh of origins, influences and final conclusions. Second, it would seem that Jakobsonian poetics, unlike Jakobsonian linguistics, was a brief candle. In what follows I shall address both of these issues.

The study is divided into three sections: 'The Poetic Function',

'The Unwelcoming Context' and 'Space and Time'. The first deals with the nature of Jakobsonian poetics: his thesis, his methodology and his practice. The second continues to interrogate and decipher these arguments within the broader context of twentieth-century linguistics, semiotics and critical theory. It focuses upon Kiparsky's second point: how is it that 'Linguistics and Poetics' should remain as a kind of *locus classicus*, while its assumptions and propositions have been systematically discredited by the most influential figures in the post-1960s literary-theoretical world? The third considers elements of Jakobson's work that have been marginalised or ignored by the chroniclers of literary theory, most specifically the function of the linguistic sign as a determinant of our perceived relation between time and space. In this I shall argue that Jakobsonian poetics provides us with new insights into the form and function of modernist poetry.

I will end, and begin, with a conundrum. Jakobson's most cited remark is his quotation from Terence: 'Linguista sum, linguistici nihil a me alienum puto – I am a linguist and hold nothing that has to do with language to be alien to me.' In 1976 an interviewer remarked on his multilinguistic, well-travelled and somewhat rootless existence and asked, 'Who are you?' He answered, 'A Russian philologist. Period', and on his gravestone in Cambridge, Massachusetts, are the words, 'Roman Jakobson – Russkij Filolog'. After a lifetime of investigating practically every permutation of signans signatum, referent, genre and context this seems a rather parochial self-designation, but there is no contradiction. The Russian philologist found nothing that has to do with language alien to him, because if it has nothing to do with language it does not exist.

Part I

The poetic function

METAPHOR AND METONYMY

The bipolar opposition between metaphor and metonymy is crucial to our understanding of Jakobson's notion of language and literature as at once co-dependent and autonomous sign systems. We will begin with some basic descriptions and illustrations.

When we construct a sentence – the most basic organisational unit of any speech act or parole – we draw both upon the rules and conventions of the syntagmatic chain, in normative terms grammatical regulations, and upon the more flexible dimension of paradigmatic choices available at each stage in this process. I'll give an example:

His car moved along the road.

The syntagmatic chain consists of a main verb 'moved (along)', two nouns 'car' and 'road' and a pronoun and definite article, 'his', 'the'. If we wanted to offer another version of the same message we could maintain the syntagmatic (also known as combinative) structure but make different choices from the paradigmatic (also known as selective) pole at each stage in the sentence. For instance,

The man's motor vehicle progressed along the street.

The only substantive difference occurs in the substitution of street for road, suggesting as it does an urban environment; and indeed such changes as the above are generally made in order to clarify the message. To this end we might substitute 'sped' for 'moved' or 'progressed' to indicate that the car is moving faster than we would normally expect. So far we have drawn upon the paradigmatic pole and produced slight variations upon the same prelinguistic event. In short, we have attempted to employ language as a mimetic or transparent means of representation: the perceived speed of the car motivates alterations in our linguistic account. Jakobson associates the paradigmatic pole with the construction of metaphor, a linguistic device that is generally classified as a literary, or more specifically a poetic, figure, and this raises a question regarding the distinction between our 'ordinary' use of the paradigmatic pole and our use of it as a means of creating a metaphor. We might engage with the latter by stating that

His car flew along the road.

This is an, albeit unexciting, metaphoric usage because, although we have maintained the conventions of the syntagm ('flew' like 'moved' is a verb), we have also made an unexpected choice from the paradigmatic-selective bag. Cars do not fly, but, since the flight of birds and aeroplanes is generally associated with degrees of speed and unimpeded purpose, we have offered a similarity between two otherwise distinct fields of perception and signification. We have used the contextual relation between two classes of verbal sign to move beyond the mode of clarifying the event, have intervened as an active perceiver and offered an impression of the event – the movement of a car reminds us of the progress of a bird or aeroplane.

We should now consider the relation between the metaphoric dimension of the paradigmatic-selective pole and the metonymic dimension of its syntagmatic-combinative counterpart. Metonymy has usually been considered by conventional literary critics and theorists to be an element or subdivision of metaphor. It is also known as synecdoche, the substitution of part for whole or vice versa. Jakobson has not redefined metonymy; rather he has promoted it from the status of a decorative literary figure to a comprehensive, universal category as the 'other half' of all linguistic design, structure and construction: all sentences rest upon an axis between the metaphoric and metonymic poles.

A metonymic version of our sentence could be,

His wheels moved across the tarmac.

Here an element has been substituted for the whole (wheels for car, tarmac for road). This might seem metaphoric but in effect we have only deleted one element of the original semantic construct. To have metaphorically selected or substituted one for another we might have replaced 'wheels' with the phrase 'his last refuge' or with 'his heart's delight', which tell us something about, in our view, the man's relationship with his car, but which are not directly related to its physical or contextual dimensions.

Jakobson's distinction between the metaphoric and metonymic poles is a heuristic device, a tool which enables the analyst to dissect and categorise the structural and functional elements of language. As such it can run dangerously close to showing us the parts while obscuring or even falsifying the ways in which they actually combine and interrelate. Jakobson is, as we shall see, fully aware of this danger.

The principal problem with the two poles stems from their representation in explanatory texts in terms of visual diagrams. For example, the following columns are often used to illustrate homologous relations between the two halves of the linguistic process.

Paradigm	Syntagm
Selection	Combination
Substitution	Contexture
Similarity	Contiguity
Metaphor	Metonymy

These columns are frequently adapted to horizontal–vertical representations of the specific selections and combinations available in given sentences.

SYNTAGM

P	The	man	walks
A			
R	A	chap	strides
A			
D	That	fellow	wanders
I	This	woman	glides
G			
M	His	sheep	skips

In the second diagram any alternative combination of the given instances of article/pronoun, noun and verb is possible – 'His man wanders', 'That sheep strides', 'A woman walks', etc. In this respect the two diagrams are a useful means of illustrating how the two poles of language operate, but they are necessarily restricted by their self-determined contexts. For example, if we were to state that 'The tree wanders', we would maintain the relationship between the two abstract conceptions of the poles but in specific terms the statement would not make sense.

Jakobson's work on metonymy and metaphor is at its most detailed and intensive in his treatment, during the 1950s, of the linguistic disorders of aphasia. This work is summarised in the 1956 essay on 'Two Aspects of Language and Two Types of Aphasic Disturbances' (1956, in *SW II* and in *L in L*). Consider the problem raised by 'The tree wanders' in relation to Jakobson's thesis, which is as follows.

Jakobson relates combination and the syntagm to 'context'. This term is double-edged: it can refer to the internal linguistic context in which the meaning of a word is influenced by its relation to other parts of the syntactic pattern; or it can refer to the broader notion of a prelinguistic situation which in some ways affects the construction of a statement. Jakobson, in this essay, posits a necessary causal relationship between the contexture of the syntagm and the correspondence between language and its situation.

> ... selection (and correspondingly, substitution) deals with entities conjoined in the code but not in the given message. The addressee perceives that the given utterance (message) is a *combination* of constituent parts (sentences, words, phonemes) *selected* from the repository of all possible constituent parts (the code).
>
> (*L in L*, p. 99)

Note that the 'message', the particular statement which creates for the addressee or receiver a productive interface between word(s) and meaning, is linked with the combinatory, syntagmatic pole, while the 'code', the enabling system of relationships between classes and types of words, is linked with the paradigmatic, selective pole. So if we, as addressees, were to encounter the sentence 'The tree wanders', we would be able to decode it as a message because of its maintenance of a recognisable combinatory sequence, article–noun–verb. But in the process of decoding we might also be rather perplexed by the resulting paraphrase (what Jakobson refers to as the metalanguage, or 'language about language'). Trees do not by their own volition or motor power 'wander'. In short, we have made sense of a message that in any empirical or scientific context does not make sense. The 'code', the system which makes the verb 'wander' available as an alternative to more usual terms such as 'falls', 'sways' or even 'is moved', is clearly in conflict with the message. From this we might surmise that the syntagmatic, combinative pole is that which anchors language to the prelinguistic world of events and impressions, while its paradigmatic, selective counterpart is that which effects a more subjective and perhaps bizarre relationship between the mind of the addresser and the code of linguistic signs. Jakobson substantiates this thesis in a typically economic, and some might argue enigmatic, manner. 'Whether messages are exchanged or communication proceeds unilaterally from the addresser to the addressee, there must be some kind of continuity between the participants of any speech event to assure the transmission of the message' (*L in L*, p. 100). Note how the word 'contiguity', like 'context', is double-edged. It refers at once to the contiguous relationship between signs and the similarly contiguous relationship between addresser and addressee, speaker and hearer. In short, our most basic communicative interactions involve us in following the linear, combinatory movement from word to word; addresser to addressee cohabit within the syntagm, 'a kind of contiguity between the participants of any speech event'. But the selective pole, that which feeds more readily upon the code, is more closely associated with the individual addresser. 'Within . . . limitations we are free to put words in new contexts . . . the freedom to compose quite new contexts is undeniable, despite the relatively low statistical probability of their occurrence' (*L in L*, p. 98). This freedom to compose is exhibited by the addresser who states that trees can wander. He/she could also state that trees can shop, swim, weep, smoke, sail, fly, copulate. . . .

Let us now return to the diagrammatic representations of the two poles. They are at once useful and deceptive; useful in the sense that they graphically represent the binary opposition upon which our analysis of language is based, deceptive because they discriminate between and equalise two elements of the linguistic process that, for both addresser and addressee, are in practice in a constant state of interpenetration and sometimes conflict. The following is a revised version of the second diagram:

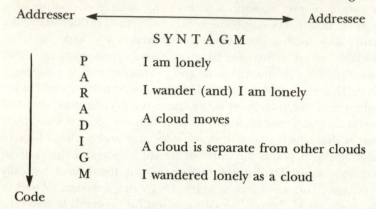

Addresser ⟵————————————⟶ Addressee

SYNTAGM

P
A
R   I am lonely
A
D   I wander (and) I am lonely
I
G   A cloud moves
M
    A cloud is separate from other clouds

    I wandered lonely as a cloud

Code

The final statement is, you will note, borrowed from William Wordsworth. I do not claim that the transformations and additions listed represent a record of Wordsworth's actual process of composition, but let us, for the sake of convenience, assume that they might. The addressee is led by the addresser along the syntagmatic chain and in this process they share the condition of cohabitants within this communicative dimension. It is likely that the addressee will have already encountered the phrases 'I am lonely' or 'I wandered', but it is less likely that he/she has encountered a comparison between these existential and active states; 'there must be a certain equivalence between the symbols used by the addresser and those known and interpreted by the addressee' (*L in L*, p. 100). But the concatenation of wandering, loneliness and cloud(iness) fractures this agreed consensual balance between the use and interpretation of the two poles. The addresser, standing at the axis between the poles (see diagram) disrupts the usual expectation of code in relation to message, paradigm to syntagm: a 'normal' substantive illustration of wandering or loneliness would be something like 'as a beggar' or some other isolated human presence.

Jakobson's use of the term 'equivalence' in the above sentence is another instance of the conflation of the internal mechanics of the linguistic system with the condition of its users. In the former case equivalence means the equation between the two poles: if two terms or words are equivalent they are substitutable in the same place in the syntagm. In the latter, this same equation is promoted to the context or the mental condition of expectations shared by addresser and addressee in their encounters with language and the prelinguistic world: 'the separation in space , and often in time, between two individuals, the addresser and addressee, is bridged by an internal relation' (*L in L*, p. 100). I mention this case because the term reappears in what must be the most widely quoted statement from Jakobson's work: 'The poetic function projects the principle of equivalence from the axis of selection into the axis of combination.' This statement occurs in his massively influential 1960 essay on 'Linguistics and Poetics'. Its meaning and its significance have been rigorously debated, but to understand it properly we must consider its origins in Jakobson's treatment of aphasia.

Jakobson identifies two types of aphasic condition, the similarity disorder and the contiguity disorder. The similarity disorder (also known as selection deficiency) involves the aphasic sufferer in a condition of enclosure within the syntagmatic, combinative chain, and as such this person becomes overdependent both upon the contexture of linguistic integers and upon concrete, non-verbal elements of his/her immediate situation.

> It is particularly hard for him to perform, or even to understand, such a closed discourse as the monologue. . . . The sentence 'it rains' cannot be produced unless the utterer sees that it is actually raining. The deeper the utterance is embedded in the verbal or nonverbalised context, the higher are the chances of its successful performance by this class of patients.
>
> (*L in L*, p. 101)

This condition of enclosure within the contextural, combinative dimension also restricts the aphasic's ability to distinguish between 'object language' (the actual message) and 'metalanguage', a circumlocution or equivalent version of the same intended meaning. The object language–metalanguage relationship is regarded by psycholinguists as a vital element in all forms of human dialogue, and is particularly important in child language acquisition. For example, if we are uncertain of the meaning of a statement we can request clarification. The speaker will then substitute equivalent terms from the agreed paradigmatic bag. To return to our original examples, if asked what we meant by the sentence 'The car moved along the road', we could substitute 'flew' as a means of specifying the unusual speed of the vehicle. A person with a similarity disorder will be unable to make such substitutions, and Jakobson gives an example of how such a person deals with this problem.

> When he failed to recall the name for 'black' he described it as 'What you do for the "dead" '. Such metonymies may be characterised as projections from the line of a habitual context into the line of substitution and selection: a sign (fork) which usually occurs together with another sign (knife) may be used instead of this sign.
>
> (*L in L*, p. 105)

Jakobson's statement is intriguing and, in relation to his definition of the poetic function, disturbing. In effect, the 'projection' achieved by the aphasic is virtually identical to that of the poet, albeit in reverse: the poet projects from the selective to the combinative axis, while the aphasic projects from 'the line of habitual context into the line of substitution and selection'. In both instances a disruption is caused between the matching of the two axes and the expected correlation between linguistic usage and context.

With the contiguity disorder, 'the patient is confined to the substitution set (once contexture is deficient) [and] deals with similarities, and his approximate identifications are of a metaphoric nature, contrary to the metonymic ones familiar to the opposite type of aphasics' (*L in L*, p. 107). The result of this condition is the diminishing of the coherent structure and variety of sentences; the usual grammatical order of words becomes chaotic, ties between co-ordinate and subordinate terms are lost. In short, the 'contexture-deficient' aphasic is confined within the paradigmatic dimension, a world in which signs relate primarily, sometimes exclusively, to other semantically connected signs and become resistant to the contextual dimension of the syntagm and prelinguistic circumstances. 'The type of aphasia affecting contexture tends to give rise to infantile one-sentence utterances and one-word sentences' (*L in L*, p. 107). Again we might be prompted to compare the condition of the contiguity disorder aphasic with that of the poet, particularly the modernist poet. The early modernist school of Imagist poetry is often characterised by lists or columns of phrases, sometimes individual words, which defy the normal rules of consecutive logic. The classic case is Pound's 'In a Station of the Metro':

The apparition of these faces in the crowd;
Petals on a wet black bough.

Pound does not state whether the faces of the crowd are like or unlike the petals on the bough; nor does he indicate the circumstances which prompted him to bring these two phrases together: did the petals on the bough remind him of the faces in the crowd or vice versa? In his essay Jakobson quotes Hughlings Jackson, a nineteenth-century pioneer of investigations into language disturbances: 'without a proper interrelation of its parts, a verbal utterance would be a mere succession of names embodying no proposition'. This seems an accurate summary of the effect created by Pound's poem. To return to the concept of metalanguage, we might claim that while the similarity disorder aphasic is excluded from the dialogic function of circumlocution or paraphrase, his contiguity disorder counterpart is enclosed within this same function to the extent that it isolates similarities between words and phrases from their usual relationship with the pre-linguistic context. The similarity disorder patient could continue endlessly to extend a sentence through sets of known and contiguous circumstances, and the contiguity disorder patient could reach further and further into his own repertoire of word connections, endlessly substituting one element of his personal paradigmatic repertoire for another.

We (he) could continue Pound's poem:

The train on the track
The blue pattern and the grey
The fish on the scales
The moment and the lifetime.

Jakobson's investigations of aphasic disorders seem to interpose linguistics and by implication mental abnormality with the condition of the poet. Such connections are by no means original nor even derogatory: Coleridge's mildly demented bard with 'flashing eyes and floating hair' has long been an accepted aberration from the norms of social behaviour and expression. What makes Jakobson's thesis different from previous conceptions of the poetic madman is that the Jakobsonian poet is someone who deliberately and consciously creates imbalances between the syntagmatic and paradigmatic chains, someone who steps joyfully and promiscuously between two linguistic-mental conditions which in isolation are regarded as an impairment. The question posed by Jakobson's thesis is why anyone should wish to engage in such activities. Jakobson never allows his investigations into language, other sign systems and their behavioural correspondences to come to rest upon a specific designation of the social, cultural, ideological or psychological motivations and effects of the poetic. Instead, he continually uses his model of the poetic function as an immutable point of comparison, against which the shifting patterns of other discourses and sign systems can be classified and analysed. In this instance the key is provided by Jakobson's use of the concept of metalanguage. Metalanguage is the ability, shared by addresser and addressee, to transfer the essence of a message, its content, from one form to another, and it is the command of this function which allows the poet to trespass in the tragically independent realms of the similarity and contiguity disorders. The similarity disorder aphasic is denied access to metalinguistic transformations; instead he/she progresses inexorably along the contextural, syntagmatic chain. The contiguity disorder aphasic cannot escape from an almost infinite duplication of metalinguistic substitutes. But the poet, like the addressee in the diagram on p. 14, stands at the corner of the axes of similarity and contiguity, able to release his/her verbal reflexes along both, yet capable of commanding and controlling the consequent effects. In short, the poet, at least when writing poetry, is a combination of the aphasic and the psycholinguist or commentator who both understands yet remains aloof from both aphasic conditions.

Jakobson's work on aphasic disorder involves elements of his Formalist legacy, elements he adapted, extended and revised, but never abandoned. There could hardly have been a more ill-matched or improbable marriage than that which occurred between Futuristic poetry and Formalist criticism. Futurist verse, particularly that of Jakobson's favourite Xlebnikov, is virtually unparaphrasable; it deliberately and self-consciously defies the metalinguistic capacities of its interpreters. Yet it provided the aesthetic counterpart to the dry analytic conceptions of literature as a deformation, a distortion of conventional communicative interchange. The paradox, which neither the Formalists nor the Futurists properly resolved, is this: If, as was clearly the case, the Futurist poets (indeed all poets) could communicate in normal, comfortably paraphrasable language, what sort of personal, mental or psychological transformation must they undergo in order to write the kind of supraconscious (*Zaum*) poems which remained enclosed within their own textual-linguistic sphere? Is poetry a means of access to a mental-linguistic condition which stands beyond the culturally and socially determined circumstances of normal exchange? Are we always, subconsciously, creating poetic texts which occasionally we find ourselves with the opportunity to write down? In short, how does the intrinsic difference between poetic and non-poetic language (a Formalist axiom cautiously preserved by Jakobson throughout his work) correspond with the motivations which differentiate poets from non-poets, poem readers from prose readers?

In a 1963 paper called 'A Linguistic Classification of Aphasic Impairments' Jakobson extended his distinction between similarity and contiguity disorder into the classification of encoding and decoding impairments. In basic terms the encoder is the speaker and the decoder the listener, and the terms generally used to identify the effects of aphasia upon these two types are, respectively, motor and sensory dysfunctions. Jakobson's model of the relationship between similarity–contiguity and encoder–decoder is mind-numbingly complex, but I shall attempt a summary. The essential difference between encoder and decoder, of both the aphasic and the normal type, arises from the order in which they deal with the two axes of language. For the encoder the paradigmatic axis (also known as the code) is the first building-block (in Jakobson's term 'antecedent'), followed by the combining and integrating of the chosen units along the syntagmatic chain ('consequent'). For the decoder, the initial encounter is with the combinative sequence, followed by its selected constituents: 'combination is the antecedent, selection is the consequent, that is, the ultimate aim of the decoding process' (*SW II*, p. 296). 'In [all] aphasic disorders the consequent is impaired, while the antecedent remains intact; combination, therefore, is deficient in the encoding types of aphasia, and selection in the decoding types' (*SW II*, p. 296). Jakobson goes on to explain how this formula translates into our distinctions between literary genres, specifically between lyric and epic poetry.

We may recall that metaphor is the inherent trope in lyric

poetry, and that metonymy is the leading trope in epic poetry. In this connection, the lyric poet, we note, endeavours to present himself as the speaker, whereas the epic poet takes on the role of the listener who is supposed to recount deeds by hearsay.

(*SW II*, p. 297)

In his 1956 essay Jakobson had further extended the denomination of the epic to include 'realism' or prose fiction, offering as an example Tolstoy's almost obsessive fixing upon synecdochic or circumstantial details (particularly the handbag) in his description of Anna Karenina's suicide.

With all of these combinations and binary pairings in mind, I shall now attempt to construct a Jakobsonian model of the motivating power of the poetic function.

The poet (particularly the lyric poet, since the lyric is the most intensely self-referential of all literary forms) is essentially an encoder, and the encoder is primarily involved in an encounter with the selective (metaphoric) axis. It could, of course, be argued that any user of language, most specifically the writer of prose fiction, is also an encoder, but what distinguishes these two classes of person is the concept that the poetic encoder is, as his title suggests, more concerned with the code (the vertical axis of the diagram on p. 14) than with the message or context (the horizontal axis). All this is so far consistent with the Formalist thesis, developed by Shklovsky and followed by Jakobson, that the essential quality of poetic language is its ability to defamiliarise or make strange (*ostranenie*) ordinary patterns of linguistic representation. But Jakobson's investigations of aphasic impairment provide him with an, albeit implicit, defence against the charges made against Formalist theory that it is a scientifically inclined offshoot of the 'art for art's sake' school, safely detached from the biases and conditions of the real world of language and events. If we accept that the selective axis is the initial encounter in any process of encoding (and Jakobson substantiates his case by citing the most respected research in psycholinguistics), then it follows that poets, who foreground the antecedent prominence of metaphor-selection above metonymy-combination, are the people who honestly confront the real phenomenal relation between language and referent, signans and signatum. Prose writers, epic poets or practically all users of non-poetic language are actually the true defamiliarisers or falsifiers of the linguistic process. They are the listeners, trapped like the selection deficiency aphasic (decoding type) on the deterministic axis of the syntagm. Think back to Jakobson's double use of the terms 'contiguity', 'context' and 'equivalence'. He suggests that there is a functional correspondence between the internal structure of language and its operations in the world of events and impressions. But in his 1963 essay he also suggests that this correspondence is a falsification of the actual relationship between human consciousness, language and prelinguistic experience. And think again about his monolithic pronouncement: 'The poetic function projects the principle of equivalence from the axis of selection into the axis of combination.' This act of projecting, examined in the context of the work on aphasia, is not a bizarre deformation of linguistic usage; it reinstitutes the axis of selection in its true role, as the primary, antecedent encounter with the code of language.

Jakobson, carrying with him the methodology of twentieth-century linguistics and semiotics, recalls the late eighteenth-century trend towards primitivism, a motivating influence upon the Romantic programme: poetry is the essence of the language–referent, signans–signatum relation; it predates prose, and indeed has been unseated from its genuine status by the falsifications of prose discourse. The prose writer, or to be more accurate the prose consciousness, receives the language–referent relation as a predetermined whole. The poet, however, remains faithful to the concept of the linguistic code as the initial point of contact between the self and whatever lies beyond the self.

This proposition, I admit, seems somewhat improbable. Jakobson, Formalist, structural linguist, a man who played a crucial part in bridge-building between the US and European sciences of the sign: what could such an individual have in common with the neo-mystical impulses of the pre-Romantics? We will return to the relation between Jakobson's theories and broader patterns of literary and aesthetic history in Part III but for the moment consider this quotation from Shelley.

A poem is the very image of life expressed in its eternal truth. . . . A story of particular facts is a mirror which obscures and distorts that which should be beautiful: poetry is a mirror which makes beautiful that which is distorted.

(see Abrams, p. 127)

Beneath the limpid prose style is a solidly structuralist axiom: language, both poetic and prosaic, is an enabling process, 'a mirror which obscures and distorts', 'a mirror which makes'. The relation between the story consisting of particular facts (metonymic-combinative axis) and the poetic function that super-adds the aesthetic to the already refractory index of language (metaphoric-selective) recalls Jakobson's comparison of the epic with the lyric. Jakobson's thesis that metaphor-selection precedes metonymy-combination is reminiscent of the pre-Romantic belief, shared by Herder and Rousseau (see Abrams, pp. 78–84), that all language is originally song-like, subjective and figurative.

In his preface to Ruth Weir's *Language in the Crib* (1962), Jakobson considers the significance of Weir's recordings of her 2-year-old son's soliloquies, uttered while in that grey area between consciousness and sleep.

> According to Ruth Weir's subtle observations, the lowering of the cognitive, referential function in Anthony's soliloquies brings to the fore all the other language functions. A typical property of children's speech is an intimate interlacement of two functions – the metalingual and the poetic one – which in adult language are quite separate.
>
> (*SW II*, p. 286)

Jakobson goes on to describe how the intimate interlacement of the poetic and the metalingual functions operates in Anthony's soliloquies, which resemble both Molly Bloom's similarly unstructured lowering of the referential function in the closing chapter of *Ulysses* and, if printed as a column, Imagist poetry. Jakobson's point is that Anthony demonstrates the originary, primal correspondence between the mental negotiation of the linguistic system and the intended point of reference. Often the affirmative predicate 'is' or the disjunctive 'or' is replaced by the conjunctive 'and' or, more often, any form of conjunction is missing. Anthony's initial encounter is always with the paradigmatic axis, more specifically that column of paradigms which relate to his own subjective experience rather than to the conventional, normative rules that govern the relation between paradigm and syntagm. But, unlike the contiguity disorder aphasic, Anthony is finally able to reintegrate his paradigmatic excursions with the combinative, syntagmatic chain.

> Members of a paradigmatic set (either lexical or grammatical), joined to each other by a conjunctive *and* or without any conjunctive at all, are open to selection: 'Hat for Anthony and Bobo – For Bobo – Not for Anthony – Hat for Anthony.' The desired choice is finally made: Anthony is the designated proprietor. . . . Grammatical alterations and purely phonemic minimal pairs are purposely strung together. . . . *Light* and *like* or *likes* and *lights* attract each other. *Black* and *wet* are blended in the portmanteau word *Babette*. Thus in the child's pre-sleep speech, lexical, morphological, and phonemic sets appear to be projected from the paradigmatic axis into the syntagmatic one.
>
> (*SW II*, pp. 286–7)

Jakobson's implication that there is an originary causal relation between the projection principle and linguistic patterns based upon the material, acoustic resemblances between signs is, as we shall see, of immense significance for his universal model of the poetic function.

THE SET

Jakobson's most widely quoted and discussed use of the term 'set' occurs in 'Linguistics and Poetics' : 'The set (*Einstellung*) toward the *message* as such, focus on the message for its own sake, is the *poetic* function of language.' This statement can easily be misunderstood. 'Function' is used by post-1950s sociolinguists to refer to what a statement is meant to achieve and to the circumstances which prompt, and for the addressee substantiate, this objective. The opposing term, 'structure', refers to the technique employed within a particular statement and to its salient features, all of which enable us to identify and classify the type of utterance or text involved (poem, question, letter, interjection, signpost, etc.). But Jakobson in 1960 remains faithful to his Formalist heritage: for him function involves both the external, socio-contextual and the internal, structural nature of the statement. The internal structure and the external effect of poetry are inseparable elements of its function. To understand the implications and significance of this conflation properly, we need to consider the concept of the 'set'.

It is a fact, acknowledged by those involved and pondered by later commentators, that OPOJAZ (St Petersburg) and the Moscow Linguistic Circle were influenced by the theories of ontology and perception currently being developed by Edmund Husserl. Husserl's *Logische Untersuchungen (Logical Investigations)*, the founding text of the philosophic school of phenomenology, was published in 1913, and almost simultaneously translated into Russian. The feature of Husserlian phenomenology that drew the attention of the Moscow and St Petersburg theorists was the concept of apperception – synonymous with 'set'. Jakobson (1915/16) took part in two seminars with the psychologist G. J. Celpanov, in which was considered the revolutionary effect of Husserl's notion of apperception upon traditional beliefs in the distinction between subjective and objective elements of apprehension. Crudely summarised, the theory of apperception begins with the assumption that the same object or objects can be differently apprehended, and that differences in perception depend largely upon the orientation, point of view or mode of apprehension of the perceiver. Ten years later, after his move to Prague, Jakobson included in a monograph on prosody and phonology (1923) an anecdotal account of how, for him, practically everyone in Czechoslovakia seemed to be either whining or preaching. This effect, he explained, was due to the fact that his conditioned expectations were grounded in Russian. In Czech the regular emphasis upon each syllable and the long qualitative pauses are conventions which foreground meaning differentiation, while in Russian these same patterns of intonation and emphasis have a particular expressive function. Thus, he implies, the object of attention and the intention of its creator is a stable, immutable phenomenon, upon which different perceivers are capable of imposing different interpretive significances. Jakobson's tale of apperceptive misunderstanding is itself potentially misleading, because it suggests that the 'set' primarily involves an act of perception. In fact Husserl uses two interrelated terms, *Einstellung* (set or point of view) and *Meinung* (that which is meant). In Formalist terminology and in Jakobson's work, set (or *Einstellung*) refers to the involvement both of the creator and the perceiver of the linguistic object in the act of signification. In his essay on

'Futurism' (1919) Jakobson considers the apperceptive conventions operating in traditional and in modernist painting.

> The set (in Russian, *ustanovka*) toward nature created for painting an obligatory connection precisely of such parts which are in essence disconnected, whereas the mutual dependence of form and colour was not recognised. On the contrary, a set toward pictorial expression resulted in the creative realisation of the necessity of the latter connection. . . . Line and surface attract the artist's attention; they cannot exclusively copy the boundaries of nature; the Cubist consciously cuts nature up with surfaces, introduces arbitrary lines.
>
> (*L in L*, p. 29)

Jakobson's use of the phrases 'in essence disconnected', 'the boundaries of nature', and 'cuts nature up' is deceptive in that he seems to imply that there is a natural, pre-representational continuum whose structural properties exist independently of the perceiver or painter. What he actually argues is that both realist and cubist painters are constructors of representational forms, the difference between them being that the former deceive themselves into believing that their work is a copy of objective reality while the latter self-consciously foreground the processes by which representation creates its apparent referent. If we translate this model of visual signs into its linguistic counterpart we achieve a reasonably precise idea of the Formalist concept of the set. The linguistic set involves speaker and hearer, addresser and addressee, in a mutually dependent engagement with a particular linguistic system. Language exists as a signifying medium only in terms of its use as a point of interaction between these two parties. Husserl argued that the material phenomena of language (graphemes, morphemes, lexies, phonemes, etc.) are indicative signs, literally 'lifeless' without the particular intentional force which endows them with meaning (*Bedeutung*). Husserl's thesis corresponds with Saussure's concept of the linguistic sign as a phenomenon composed of signifier and signified: both words indicate that the active participation of speaker and hearer is necessary for the linguistic unit to be transformed from substance to sign. In brief, the set refers to a specific instance, determined by time or a combination of cultural, social or emotional circumstances, in which an agreement is reached between addresser and addressee on the particular meaning of the utterance. It is in its emphasis upon the intrinsic qualities of literariness that we encounter divergences between Formalist theory and its phenomenological-philosophical counterpart. In Jakobson's first major work on language and poetry, 'Novejšaja russkaja poèzija' ('New Russian Poetry', first published in Prague in 1921, but conceived in Moscow and St Petersburg), we come upon a conception of poetry that is virtually identical to the model of the 'set' and the 'poetic function' offered in his 1960 paper.

> In emotional expression passionate outbursts govern the verbal mass. . . . But poetry – which is simply an utterance with a set toward expression – is governed, so to speak, by its own immanent laws; the communicative function, essential to both practical language and emotional language, has only minimal importance in poetry. Poetry is indifferent to the referent of the utterance, while, on the other hand, practical or more exactly object-oriented prose is indifferent to rhythm.
>
> (Stempel, p. 30)

The most significant correspondence between the 1921 and 1960 papers is the thesis that poetry possesses 'its own immanent laws'. It is significant because Jakobson, in both instances, is dealing not exclusively with Russian, Czech, French or English poetry, but with poetry as a cross-cultural, intralingual phenomenon. As he indicated in the account of his misperception of Czech intonational patterns, non-poetic ('passionate', 'practical' or 'object-oriented') utterances are subject to an almost limitless combination of circumstantial, geographical and cultural variations. Poetry, on the other hand, is governed by 'immanent laws' which transcend such variations. Jakobson's first book-length study of poetry was his survey of Czech prosody (1923, reprinted in *SW V*, pp. 3–130). In this he documents the relationship between quantity (syllabic length) and stress (accentual emphasis) in Czech verse and indicates the differences between this and the Russian system of versification, but he insists that such differences are variations upon a particular cross-linguistic, cross-cultural norm: the poetic utterance is determined by regular patterns of sound and intonation. In poetry there is a structural and functional dependence upon the material, non-signifying elements of language.

Think back to his consideration of metalanguage in his discussion of aphasic disorders. Metalanguage involves the translation of the content of a message from one form to another. This process of transference is, in ordinary non-poetic language, closely related to intentionality as a constitutive element of the set. If we do not understand the meaning of a statement we can, if the addresser is present, ask for clarification. The addresser will then offer a metalinguistic substitute for the original statement. The two statements might differ in syntactic, lexical or morphophonemic substance, but, in terms of the set occupied by addresser and addressee, their difference relates only to their agreed degree of accuracy or truth. However, 'poetry is indifferent to the referent of the utterance'. To illustrate this case Jakobson, in the 1921 essay, offers an example of prose entering the realm of the poetic.

> . . . 'when they cut off his [the saint's] head at last, he got up, picked up the head, and politely kissed it' (Dostoevskij). In this case a human being is simply a traditional semantic unit which retains all of its attributes; in other words the semantic unit has become fixed.
>
> (Stempel, p. 50)

It is, of course, impossible to offer a metalinguistic substitute for Dostoevskij's statement about the saint's activities. To attempt to do so would involve an admission that the original statement is absurd and self-contradictory. Not only is it impossible for a beheaded man to stand up (though in some fundamentalist systems of belief, saintliness might confer this privilege) but it is literally unimaginable that someone could kiss their own head, whether detached or still in place. In Jakobson's words the 'human being', the ideational referent, has been displaced by the 'semantic unit', a constituent of the 'message'. Hence, the poetic function involves 'the set toward the message as such, focus on the message for its own sake'. In the 1960 essay Jakobson curtails the more extravagant emphases of 1921: 'The supremacy of poetic function over referential function does not obliterate the reference but makes it ambiguous.' To obliterate totally the referential function would mean that the reader would be unable to recognise the contradictory tension between Dostoevskij's message and its referent. But what has been obliterated is the sense of there being a unitary, and consequently translatable, correspondence between the message and its referent.

A question raised by Jakobson's use of this prose quotation is that of whether the poetic function, identified as the 'set toward the message', is an element that is interchangeable between different literary and non-literary genres. Jakobson (1960) cites the election slogan 'I like Ike' as an example of how the message-focusing process of the poetic function can occur regularly in non-poetic contexts. The difference between Dostoevskij's paradox or Eisenhower's slogan and genuinely poetic language is that the former represent deviations from the textual and contextual norm. In a prose discourse the image of the headless saint kissing himself could be cited but would not be sustainable as a thematic or structural determinant. A novel or short story 'about' such an individual would be a contradiction in terms. As Jakobson states (*L in L*, p. 111), 'the Realist author [also known as novelist or prose writer] metonymically digresses from the plot to the atmosphere and from the characters to the setting in space and time'. In short, the message is largely dependent upon the referent, and if the referent is an unimaginable absurdity the message cannot be sustained and continued. With 'I like Ike' the message-focusing effect is generated by the repetition of phonemic elements (a conventional poetic device), but although its structural elements might be poetic, the phrase operates only in the functional sphere of non-poetic discourse. Its uses as a chant, as a citation on advertisements and billboards, or its quotation by commentators are all context-dependent, in the sense that the text or discourse that surrounds the phrase will not be structured by assonantal-alliterative repetitions. So what makes the poem 'different'?

> The principle of similarity underlies poetry; the metrical parallelism of lines or the phonic equivalence of rhyming words prompts the question of semantic similarity and contrast; there exist, for instance, grammatical and antigrammatical but never agrammatical rhymes. Prose on the contrary is foregrounded by contiguity. Thus for poetry, metaphor – and for prose metonymy – is the line of least resistance and consequently the study of poetical tropes is directed chiefly toward metaphor.
>
> (*L in L*, p. 114)

The key element of this distinction is the reference to rhyme. Rhyme, along with metrical patterning, is a primary constitutive element of most types of regular verse. As Jakobson states, its positioning along the syntagmatic chain can either supplement or distort the grammatical framework, but, crucially, the signifying function of grammar or syntax can never remain immune from its ability to create a secondary level of meaning. We will consider the interactive relationship between the metre-sound pattern and syntax more fully in Part II, but for the present we will look at the implications of such doublings of signification for the concept of the set.

Jakobson's work in phonology and phonetics is widely celebrated by other linguists as his most significant contribution to their discipline. But the correspondences between this sometimes very arcane and highly specialised work and Jakobson's theory of poetry are too often marginalised. The Husserlian notion of the set is a vital element of Jakobson's and Trubetzkoy's work on phonetics in Prague during the 1920s and 1930s, and the principle that sender–receiver, encoder–decoder, addresser–addressee are actually components of the linguistic phenomenon, rather than simply participants in a reducibly abstract process, is reiterated throughout the following forty years of Jakobson's writing. The following is from a 1960 paper on 'Linguistics and Communication Theory'.

> Language presents two considerably different aspects when seen from the two ends of the communication channel. Roughly the encoding process goes from meaning to sound and from the lexico-grammatical to the phonological level, whereas the decoding process displays the opposite direction – from sound to meaning and from features to symbols. While a set (*Einstellung*) toward immediate constituents takes precedence in speech production, for speech perception the message is *first* a stochastic process. The probabilistic aspect of speech finds conspicuous expression in the approach of the listener to homonyms, whereas for the speaker homonymy does not exist. When saying /sʌn/, he knows beforehand whether 'son' or 'sun' is meant, while the listener depends on the conditional probabilities of the context. For the receiver the message presents many ambiguities which were unequivocal for the sender. The ambiguities of pun and poetry utilize this input property for the output.
>
> (*SW II*, p. 575–6)

The implications of this model of production and reception for the perceived relation between poetic and non-poetic language are immense. Think back to Jakobson's classification of encoder and decoder and their antecedent–consequent use of the selective and combinative axes, and combine this with his discussion of sound and meaning. For the encoder the primary, antecedent encounter is with selection; the grammatical–lexical level is predetermined. When we choose to use the sign 'son' instead of, say, 'offspring' or 'child', we are not worried about its homonymous relationship with 'sun'. For the decoder such homonymous relations can, potentially, interfere with the transfer of the message; but this problem will in most instances be resolved by the priority given by the encoder to the combinative, contextual relation between signs in a particular syntagm. In regular poetry however this equation is disrupted at a number of levels. The poet-encoder, unlike his non-poet counterpart, gives primary consideration to sound patterns. Indeed, in strictly regular forms such as the closed heroic couplet, the process of selection is virtually overridden by the precondition that each sign must be accommodated within the abstract scheme of iambic regularity and rhyme. So when choosing the word 'sun' to end the first line of a couplet, we must be alert not only to the lexico-grammatical meaning but also to its phomenic relation with the word that will fill the corresponding syntagmatic space in the following line. For the poetry hearer-decoder the 'normal' hierarchy of antecedent–consequent encounters is similarly unbalanced. In normal linguistic exchanges similarities or dissimilarities of sound constitute the primary element of decoding – indeed, the much-quoted Saussurean example is of signifieds being dependent upon the phonic difference between signifiers. Once we intuit the difference between individual signs we can then tackle their relational function within the syntagmatic chain. But what happens when, in poems, the co-dependence between sound and the combinative axis registers as a complex interdependence? We will deal with the interpretive problems offered by specific poems in the third part of this book, but for the moment let us consider how the projection of the encoder–decoder relationship into the poetic sphere affects the concept of the set.

In the section covering 'Phonology and Phonetics' in *Fundamentals of Language*, Jakobson states: 'the auditory experience is the only aspect of the encoded message actually shared by the sender and the receiver since the speaker normally hears himself' (p. 46). By this he does not mean that sound is the only guaranteed norm in an otherwise chaotic experience of incomprehension; rather that what he calls the 'distinctive features' of a message, particularly at its morphophonemic level, are accorded different hierarchies of processing and decoding by speaker and hearer. The acoustic materiality of the message is, in Husserl's terms, 'lifeless' when cut off from the distinct but mutually vital motivating forces of intention and apprehension. This model of the communicative process has been extended and modified, but it remains essentially unchallenged as a description of what actually happens when human beings talk to each other. As such, poetry must be regarded not simply as the marshalling in a particular way of given linguistic resources and conventions, but as an outright subversion, even rejection, of the 'normal' practices of linguistic communication. The 'auditory experience' of the poem is that which effectively organises its lexical, morphological and syntactic constituents, and this hierarchy is pertinent for both sender and receiver. So we might rewrite Jakobson's statement: 'the auditory experience *of poetry* is the principal aspect of the encoded message shared by the sender and the receiver'. This does not merely involve a redistribution of terminology; it proposes that poetry is the only linguistic form in which both communicating participants are granted equal access to the complex architechtonics, the formal structuration, of the message. A number of paradoxes are raised by this thesis. A fact accepted by practically all commentators on poetry, and given particular prominence by the Formalists, is that the materiality of language is foregrounded in verse. This substantial dimension of the linguistic sign is most often cited as the cause of its refractory, arbitrary nature, but in the above formula its promotion becomes the vehicle for transparency, the unification of speaker and hearer in their shared apperceptive relation to the message. As Jakobson put it in 'New Russian Poetry', 'the link between sound and meaning is closer, more intimate [in poetry] insofar as the habitual associations based on contiguity retreat into the background'. And again we find a close symmetry between his 1921 entry into literary linguistics and his more celebrated performance of 1960. 1960: 'In referential language the connection between *signans* and *signatum* is overwhelmingly based on their codified contiguity', but poetry 'is a province where the internal nexus between sound and meaning changes from latent into patent and manifests itself most palpably and intensely' (*L in L*,

p. 88). The central paradox of this model of the poetic function, the set towards expression, arises from the conceptual and experiential centrality of the concrete sign. The linguistic sign is not an originary attribute of the human condition; it is acquired, and although we might subconsciously persuade ourselves that what we say corresponds with a priori perceptions of truth and similarity our medium of saying it is an autonomous system of rules and conventions indifferent to the particular human presence who might choose to make use of it. Or so we, in our post-Saussurean, poststructuralist condition, have been led to believe. The Formalists, for all their undoubted correspondences with Saussure's revolutionary theory of language, diverge from it in one crucial sense. Saussure gave slight acknowledgement to the structural distinctions between different types of linguistic exchange, but for the Formalists the designation of literary, particularly poetic, language in relation to its non-literary counterpart was as much an existential, philosophic issue as an aesthetic one.

The parallels between phenomenology and structuralism originate from the shared assumption that all forms of communicative exchange involve user and perceiver as agencies in the reconstitution of the sign as meaning, and meaning as, in turn, conjoined to referent. In both disciplines two levels of phenomena are required for an apperceptive act to take place: the phenomenon of the sign and the tangible or ideational phenomena mediated by the sign. The classic example of the contingent interdependency of these two levels is of the phenomenal continuum of the colour spectrum in relation to the very different divisions imposed upon this by different linguistic systems. In a 1932 essay Jakobson adapted this same model to the apperceptive conditions of music. 'For the [African] native and the European the same tone will mean completely different musical systems' (*SW II*, p. 551). In both instances the potential for confusion or misperception originates from the contingent relation between the phenomenon of the sign and its perceived relation to meaning and the referent, and from this basis one might go on to argue that all meaning is infinitely flexible and provisional, a function of the particular socio-cultural conditions of the apperceptive act. However, argues Jakobson, the enabling material of linguistic acts, sound, presents us with a more complex problem. Scholars of traditional (i.e. nineteenth-century) phonetics regard the system of distinctive features by which we construct phonetic alphabets as, like the relation between signifier and signified, an artificial, arbitrary imposition of a particular framework upon a chaotic flux of sound variations, and the objectives of the Prague phonologists, particularly Jakobson and Trubetzkoy, was to over-turn this belief in favour of a science of the phoneme based upon its identity as an immutable intralinguistic element. The sound structures of different languages would of course be related to different morphological, lexical and semantic systems, but the distinctive features of the phoneme would be a common element. In a 1956 essay (*SW I*, p. 475) Jakobson argues that the ideal linguist should be someone who suspends his/her reflexive command of the post-cognitive code and assumes the position of the cryptanalyst or even the non-native speaker, a person for whom unmediated phonemic integers occupy a primary pre-decoding role. The effects of this argument for the discipline of pure linguistics need not concern us here; of more significance is its bearing upon the relation between poetry and other sign systems. The regular poem effectively creates the conditions in which the listener becomes the cryptanalyst-translator. It is a text which engages with the sign-meaning relation of language but which is organised around and foregrounds an arbitrary pattern of sounds. In 'Linguistics and Poetics' Jakobson describes the effect of this.

> Ambiguity is an intrinsic, inalienable character of any self-focussed message. . . . Not only the message itself but also its addresser and addressee become ambiguous. . . . The supremacy of the poetic function over the referential function does not obliterate the reference but makes it ambiguous. The double sensed message finds correspondence in a split addresser, in a split addressee, as well as in a split reference . . . for instance, in the usual exordium of the Majorca storytellers: 'Aixo era y no era' (It was and it was not).
>
> (*L in L*, pp. 85–6)

If, as Husserl argues, the apperceptive set involves the creator, the act of communication and the recipient as co-dependent elements, it follows that each will also depend upon contextual conditions. In most instances any ambiguity can be rectified or at least explained. The addressee who has misheard a statement, who is unfamiliar with the circumstantial conditions which prompted it, or who is simply perplexed by its internal structure can ask for clarification. The European listener to African music, the non-native speaker who encounters an unusual spectrum of colours and signifiers, Jakobson himself, attempting to adapt the intonational patterns of Russian to Czech: each can ponder the factual circumstances of apperceptive dissonance. But poetry undermines the secure contextual perspective of the addresser and the addressee. For example, how would the addressee of a lyric poem go about asking the putative addresser why exactly a certain word is placed in a peculiar position within the metrical framework or what exactly is meant by the phonemic correspondence between two rhyme words? For one thing the actual addresser, the composer of the text, is unlikely to be present and, more significantly, the tension created between the syntagmatic chain and the systematic phonemic echoes of the text is not easily reducible to accurate paraphrase. The addresser and addressee of the poetic set are in the disorientating position of being elements of the communicative circuit while never being able to fully detach themselves from this state. Jakobson, in his famous six-part diagram of the communicative circuit, employs the ingenious device of having the message transposed with the poetic function so that the internal and the contextual elements of the set, including addresser and addressee, become like Siamese twins, at once autonomous and inextricable. I will deal with this in more detail in Part II, but for the moment I shall offer a summary of how Jakobson's notion of the set specifies the relationships between poet, reader, text and the circumstances inhabited by these presences and phenomena.

First of all it is evident that Jakobson perceives poetry not simply as a pattern of choices available to the literate, linguistically competent individual. Poetic composition, and indeed the reading of poetry, involves the individual in a process of personal, emotional and intellectual transformation. The sound pattern of a regular poem, its metrical framework and its rhyme scheme, shifts the encoding and decoding process away from the non-linguistic circumstances of the discourse towards the internal structure of the text. When we speak or write in non-poetic language, our command of the structural elements of language is compromised by our circumstantial condition and our intention. With poetry this hierarchy is reversed; the poetic function maintains supremacy over, but does not obliterate, its referential counterpart. The principle of equivalence is projected from the axis of selection *into* the axis of combination. This thesis guarantees the status of poetry not simply as a separate linguistic genre, but as an expressive, indeed an existential, condition that is structurally and functionally unique. Poetry is the only kind of linguistic discourse in which the encoder's command of the signans predetermines the relation between the signatum and the perceptual, experiential continuum of the prelinguistic world. It achieves this in two principal ways. First, the perceptual focus or set shared by addresser and addressee is primarily upon the nature of the medium: the selective, metaphoric axis supersedes its combinative, metonymic counterpart. Second, this shift in emphasis from the object of signification to its means is underpinned by the foregrounding of linguistic materiality. Jakobson concedes that rhythm, rhyme and alliterative-assonantal patterns can surface in non-poetic discourse, but it is only within the poem that this foregrounding of material elements constitutes a persistent, patterned structure that both governs the entire text and, as a consequence, creates an uneasy or, as Jakobson puts it, ambiguous relation between the text and the intrageneric flux inhabited by every other discursive structure.

THE DOUBLE PATTERN

The relationship between twentieth-century literary criticism and linguistics has never been a particularly comfortable one. The sense of unease is most pronounced in the literary-critical world, fuelled mainly by a reluctance to submit the mysteries and rarefications of an art form to the mechanical indifference of a science, but the relationship is sustained by a simple and undeniable fact: literature is the only art form whose raw material is drawn exclusively from language. Literary linguists have given roughly equal attention to prose fiction and to poetry, but the latter has a prior claim to the methodologies and perspectives offered by modern linguistics because, as Jakobson argues, the structural properties of poetic language are also, to a large extent, its subject. The meeting-point for the formal and the referential axes of poetry is versification, and Jakobson's investigations of this confluence form the core of his theory of poetry.

The study of versification can claim to be the oldest and most enduring branch of Western literary criticism. The language and methodology of George Gascoigne's 'Certayne Notes of Instruction concerning the making of verse or rhyme in English . . .' (1575) might superficially seem to have little in common with Paul Kiparsky's 'Stress, Syntax and Metre', published, neatly enough, in 1975, but they share the same objective of determining how the stress patterns of ordinary language can be organised into the phenomenon known as metre. The interchangeable topics of metre, prosody, versification featured prominently in the debates and published work of the members of OPOJAZ and the Moscow Linguistic Circle. Prosody is an ancient science; it is a discipline whose focus and objectives have rarely been disturbed by the shifting contours of the post-sixteenth-century European literary landscape. But the creative and interpretive circumstances in which Jakobson's earliest literary and linguistic affiliations were forged involved such a disturbance. The alliance between Futurism and Formalism is grounded upon a shared belief in the structural and functional significance of the concrete linguistic sign. Xlebnikov's poems involve a centripetal concentration upon phonic patterns and repetitions almost to the exclusion of the linear, referential patterning of normal language and Jakobson-Aljagrov's own poetic work (see 'Razsejanost', 'Distraction' below, pp. 68–70) follows this same emphasis upon linguistic materiality. Such foregroundings of the physical means of representation at the expense of the represented object were also the central compositional tenets of cubism and Dadaism, both of which were enthusiastically endorsed by Jakobson. The principal difference between poetic Futurism and its visual counterparts was that in promoting the material sign as central to the structural and signifying patterns of their work poets such as Xlebnikov and Jakobson-Aljagrov were not rejecting or overturning the methods of their traditional forebears – and the cubists and Dadaists certainly were – but re-emphasising the dominant and definitive element of all poetic composition. Regular or traditional poetry involves the repetition of metrical and rhyming patterns, and what the Futurists did was to shift the perceived balance away from the referential structure of poetic language towards the process by which this referential pattern is compromised by a secondary structure of phonic and metrical parallels. This creative act of reintegrating and refocusing was mirrored by the analytical work of the Formalists, particularly Ejxenbaum, Jakobson and Tynjanov (1922, 1923, 1924). All three published lengthy studies of Slavic prosody and their shiftings of perceptual and structural hierarchies were very similar to those of the Futurists. The traditions of post-Renaissance prosodic theory were, in the early years of this century, kept alive in the work of the Germans Saran (1907) and Sievers (1912), the Frenchman Verrier (1909), and in Britain by George Saintsbury (1906–10). For all the more obvious distinctions between the native poetic traditions upon which these works were focused, they shared an important common feature: each critic regarded versification as an autonomous disciplinary and compositional system. They recognised that the construction of metrical and phonic patterns must involve the use of morphological and syntactic continua drawn from the governing system of non-poetic language, but they maintained that the study of metre could remain aloof from the non-poetic investigation of how linguistic structure creates meaning. In short, they held that form could be classified and analysed separately from content. To borrow Victor Erlich's terms, the Formalists moved from traditional or 'phonetic' prosody, the study of sounds and structures as autonomous phenomena, to their own method of 'phonemic' prosody, the study of the relationship between sound patterns and their meaning-generating functions in the morphophonemic structures of language. This shift from the investigation of sound to the relation between sound and meaning might not seem to be a particularly astounding or revolutionary act, but it involved a recognition that in poetry the correspondence between the referential, refractory nature of language and its material substance was a complete reversal of its counterpart in non-poetic language. To clarify this point and to enable us properly to investigate and extend Jakobson's theories of poetry I shall introduce the concept of the double pattern. A brief definition is required.

In all forms of linguistic discourse some kind of pattern emerges. At its most basic it is the pattern of comprehensibility, a function of grammar, syntax, semantics, phonetics, and the interlocking of the syntagmatic and paradigmatic axes. We understand and create linguistic statements because we can distinguish between individual words and we know that some words should and some words should not follow one another in order to create intelligible meaning. To use a term made famous by Noam Chomsky, it is the deep structure, the abstract framework of rules and conventions, that allows us to encode and decode the specific and complex meanings of a chain of individual words, the surface structure. Occasionally, and often by accident, this referential pattern of discourse will create supplementary surface patterns of rhythm and sound which draw upon the materiality of language but which do not relate directly to its conventions of meaning and signification. The double pattern occurs when this secondary, surface pattern is deliberately deployed as a regular and persistent feature of the text. The unit by which we measure and classify this secondary pattern is the poetic line.

This concept of the double pattern provides a diagrammatic template into which we can fit the apparently disparate elements of Jakobson's theory of language and literature. His work on phonemics in Prague – the phoneme as a 'bundle' of distinctive features, the concept of morphophonemics, the teleology of linguistic exchange, the opposition of marked and unmarked features in phonology, morphology and syntax – focuses upon and originates from the overarching relationship between sound and meaning. Jakobson gives an account of these interconnections in 'The Phonetic and Grammatical Aspects of Language and the Interrelations' (1949, *SW II*, pp. 103–4).

> Any intended comprehensive study of a phonemic pattern invariably runs into the problem of partial patterns mutually distinguishing and specifying the diverse categories of a given language. . . . And vice versa . . . the study of the grammatical pattern inevitably leads up to the problem of phonemic means utilized for the expression of the diverse grammatical categories.

In short, the phonemic and the grammatical patterns of language are causally related, and it is the duty of the linguist to devise methods and schema which stabilise the apparent slides between the two continua. The premise upon which this programme is based is the belief that the two constituent elements of the sign, the signans and the signatum (in Saussure's terms signifier and signified), are separable only in theory. In the practical sphere of linguistic interchange, in the set, they are interdependent elements of the same process: sound is meaning and meaning is sound (*SW II*, pp. 103–4). The most significant point to be made regarding this problematic relation between phonemics and grammar, sound and meaning, signans and signatum is that it holds the key to the fundamental distinction between poetic and non-poetic language. The dangerous potential for a rift between the two patterns of language originates in the unpredictable circumstantial and temporal conditions of linguistic usage. The unfamiliarity of the addressee with the personal or institutional idiom of the addresser, the difference between the native dialect or language of addressee and addresser, diachronic shifts in agreed or perceived usage – all of these factors can destabilise the interface between signification and linguistic materiality (for an accessible account of these issues see Jakobson's *Six Lectures on Sound and Meaning*, 1978). But in poetry the double pattern is a deliberately and purposively integrated network of sounds and meanings. Even for the reader of a poem who has no knowledge of its origin as a speech act, of the condition of the poet or the circumstances of the act of creation, phonic patterns will create an interface between sound and meaning that is intrinsic to the poetic artefact, creating interchanges of effect and signification that will remain safely detached from the unstable conditions of non-poetic exchange. In the 'Retrospect' to *Selected Works* vol. I Jakobson tells of how his early encounters with Futurist poetry provided the impetus for all of this later work on the relation between sound and meaning in language.

> Xlebnikov's poetry became the topic for my first 'onset' upon the analysis of language in its means and functions. . . . Poetic language, disregarded by the neogrammarian doctrine but presenting the most patently, deliberate, goal-directed, and integrated linguistic species, was a field that called for a new type of analysis and particularly required us to study the interplay between sound and meaning. . . . It was on poetry that the initial phonemic concepts were tested. In my essay on Xlebnikov I suggested that phonic texture 'does not deal with sounds but with phonemes, i.e. with acoustic representations capable of being associated with semantic representations'.
>
> (*SW I*, p. 633)

The progress and the results of this programme are available in Jakobson's *Selected Works* and their significance for the discipline of linguistics has been assessed by, amongst others, Holenstein, Waugh and Sangster. What has not been given proper attention is his continual emphasis on poetry as the 'most patently deliberate, goal directed and integrated linguistic species'.

The principal issue to be addressed is this: Jakobson argues that poetry involves the organisation of phonetic material not simply as a decorative overlay upon signifying structures shared by poetic and non-poetic language, but as signifying structure in itself. Hence the traditional opposition of form (metre, rhyme, etc.) to content (what the text actually means) is an inaccurate model of the poetic function. How then does poetry work? The following is from 'Linguistics and Poetics'.

> Equivalence is promoted to the constitutive device of the system. One syllable is equalised with any other syllable of the sequence, word stress is assumed to equal word stress, as unstress equals unstress, prosodic long is matched with long, and short with short, word boundary equals word boundary, no boundary equals no boundary; syntactic pause equals syntactic pause, no pause equals no pause. Syllables are converted into units of measure, and so are morae or stresses.
>
> (*L in L*, p. 71)

The key to our understanding of this formula is Jakobson's use of the word 'equivalence'. We have already encountered what might be termed its general meaning: equivalent elements of language are substitutable in the same place in a syntagm. Here equivalence represents the point of interchange between the two continua of the poetic double pattern. The poet, like all users of language, faces the choices available along the syntagmatic chain – which verb? which connective? which adjective? But in the writing of poetry these choices are supplemented, and to an extent governed, by an abstract pattern of regulations that do not operate in the production of non-poetic statements. If the poem adheres to the pattern of the heroic couplet or to a particular stanzaic formula, the poet's choice is limited by considerations of whether a particular word or syntactic construction can be accommodated by particular rules of stress, boundary, pause and measure. So far this thesis corresponds with the broadly accepted perception of poetry as an artistic game, not serving any important referential purpose, but providing its participants with an engaging and mentally taxing distraction from the usual imperatives of life and language. But this is not what Jakobson meant. The following is from his 1961 essay 'Poetry of Grammar and Grammar of Poetry'.

Any unbiased, attentive, exhaustive, total description of the

selection distribution and interrelation of diverse morphological classes and syntactic constructions in a given poem surprises
the examiner himself by unexpected, striking symmetries and
antisymmetries, balanced structures, efficient accumulation of
equivalent forms and salient contrasts.

(SW III, p. 92)

The examiner, or to be honest the informed analyst, of non-
poetic speech or writing might well encounter deviations from
the consensual norm, but none of these could be regarded as
unexpected or the cause of surprise – illiterates, aphasics, drunks,
eccentrics, non-native speakers are all fully documented sources
of shifts between the variant and invariant forms of linguistic
usage. But poetry can create surprise and disruptions of expectation even for the 'unbiased attentive, exhaustive' reader. It can
do this because the poetic use of equivalence operates as the axis
between two patterns of form and signification. Each of these is
available for 'exhaustive' codification and analytical dissection,
but the effects created by their interrelation and often their
conflict are particular to the text in question, and, in the abstract,
normative sphere of analysis, unpredictable. Think back to Jakobson's classification of the sound–meaning relationship in non-
poetic exchanges: 'Roughly the encoding process goes from
meaning to sound and from the lexico-grammatical to the phonological level, whereas the decoding process displays the opposite
direction – from sound to meaning and from features to symbols'
(SW II, p. 575). In each instance sound is subservient to the more
powerful, normative patterns of lexico-grammatical structure and
context. But in the sound pattern of a poem, equivalence, the
interlocking of the syntagmatic and the paradigmatic chains, is
determined by patterns of phonemic matching, stress, pause and
syllabic measure. The entire system of causal and temporal hierarchies which governs the process of non-poetic exchange – enco-
der-paradigm, decoder-syntagm, sound as consequent for speaker
and antecedent for hearer – is thrown into a state of disarray.
Hence the equivalences, the balances, the symmetries, the salient
contrasts are tangible, but in terms of the a priori model of how
non-poetic language is created and received, they are surprising
and unexpected. So how does the linguist-critic go about reas-
sembling some kind of analytical structure from these disorderly
interweavings of the double pattern?

The two essays which contain the most detailed accounts of Jakobson's strategies for dealing with the sound–meaning nexus of the double pattern are 'Poetry of Grammar and Grammar of Poetry' (1961) and 'Grammatical Parallelism and its Russian Facet' (1966). The complex procedures of these works are, like practically all of Jakobson's theories of the poetic, summarised in 'Linguistics and Poetics'. In this he offers an example from a Russian wedding song.

> A brave fellow was going to the porch
> Vasilij was walking to the manor
>
> Dobroj mólodec k séničkam privoráčival,
> Vasílij k téremu prixažival.

Jakobson points out that in both lines of this couplet the predicative verbs, the subjects (common name and proper noun) and the modifiers of place 'correspond to each other syntactically and morphologically' (*L in L*, p. 84). He adds that in the oral folklore tradition this couplet is usually preceded by:

> A bright falcon was flying beyond the hills
> A fierce horse was coming at a gallop to the court
>
> Jasjón sokol zá gory zaljótyval
> Retív kon' kó dvoru priskákival.

The negation 'ne' ('Not a bright . . .', 'Not a fierce . . .') is optional, suggesting that the relationship between falcon-horse and brave fellow-Vasilij exists primarily within the textual sphere of signification. The text *suggests* connections between these objects and activities, irrespective of their actual, simultaneous presence at a particular place and time. Jakobson's explanation of how the four lines of these couplets interact is precise and detailed, and the following is a summary. The metonymical relation between falcon–hills, horse–court, brave fellow–porch, Vasilij–manor is transformed into a complex fabric of metaphoric–metonymic intersections. Vasilij is a brave fellow who appears like a bright falcon from the hills. He is also metaphorically related to both the primal nature of the horse image (Jakobson points out that 'retív kon'' is a 'latent or even patent phallic symbol' in Russian erotic lore) and, metonymically, to the idea of possession: horseman possesses horse, horse approaches and will be possessed by courtyard, both images carrying resonances of spatial, physical and legal possession. The overarching metonymy–metaphor interconnection is, of course, the traditionally pre-scribed relationship between the prospective groom and bride, the possessor and the possessed, approach and entry, journey and destination, active and passive.

Jakobson's principal point is that, having naturalised this poetic structure, transformed it into a prose paraphrase, we have only touched the surface of what is a 'thoroughgoing, symbolic, mul-tiplex, polysemantic essence'. Prose is dominated by the linear, contiguous relationship between signs and their referents. We could state that: Vasilij is like a fierce horse. Vasilij is the owner of a fierce horse. Vasilij walked to the court like a fierce horse. Vasilij is like a bright falcon. . . . This list of potential, actual and figurative connections could continue, and their relation to one another would create a consecutive pattern of ideational, referen-tial images. But in poetry the parallelism of syntax and mor-phology with metre and rhyme creates patterns of correspondence that are both consecutive and simultaneous, con-tiguous and selective, metonymic and metaphoric: 'the "fierce horse" emerging in the preceding line at a similar metrical and syntactic place as the "brave fellow", figures simultaneously as a likeness to and as a representative of this fellow' (*L in L*, p. 84). Again we encounter the re-emergence of the Formalist notion of the poetic as a kind of violence done to the balanced conventions of ordinary language. Jakobson: 'In poetry, where similarity is superinduced upon contiguity, any metonymy is slightly meta-phoric and any metaphor has a metonymic tint' (*L in L*, p. 85). The dominant axes of all linguistic usage and exchange, meta-phor and metonymy, selection and combination, paradigm and syntagm are not simply reversed or reordered; they are effectively destabilised as discrete, formulaic models of how language works.

We are confronted with the image of poetry as a self-indulgent deviation from the normal, rational patterns of linguistic exchange, and Jakobson counters this in a number of ways. His choice of an example from a Russian folksong is significant. The following is from 'Grammatical Parallelism and its Russian Facet'.

Traditional types of canonical parallelism offer us an insight into the various forms of relationship among the different aspects of language and answer the pertinent question: what kindred grammatical or phonological categories may function as equivalent within the given pattern? We can infer that such categories share a common denominator in the linguistic code of the respective speech community.

(*SW III*, pp. 98–9)

What he suggests is that in linguistic-anthropological studies of different tribal or national communities, the double pattern of their respective poetic traditions provides us with a far more fruitful comparative index than their non-verbal rituals or conventions or their non-poetic linguistic conventions. The latter are essentially unidimensional codes, whose structural and functional conditions are determined by a vast number of political, historical, economic, even climatic variables. Poetry, however, returns each communicative instance to the binary features of phonology. In the field of non-literary linguistics Jakobson's most influential work involved the identification of the variant and invariant features of speech sounds (begun in Prague and continued in the USA with the assistance of spectrographic recording equipment). He demonstrated that the two oppositional pairs compact/diffuse and grave/acute are invariant structures common to vowels and consonants, and, more significantly, that these physical-acoustic features are intralingual, the common ground of verbal communication. Consequently the study of poetic parallelism, which involves the pairing of these intralingual features with the far more diffuse and variant elements of syntax and morphology, provides us with the universal element of the long-sought notion of a natural language. In short poetry, far from being the deviant, eccentric, linguistic form, is that which perpetuates and articulates the interlingual relation between life and language. In 'Poetry of Grammar and Grammar of Poetry' Jakobson compares the effects achieved by parallelism in the folk poem with 'dynamic cutting in film montage': 'a type of cutting which . . . uses the juxtaposition of contrasting shots or sequences to generate in the mind of the spectator ideas that these constituent shots or sequences do not carry' (*L in L*, p. 128). This comparison is intriguing in that it transposes the conventional notion of pictoral and narrative mimesis with the concentrated self-referential function of localised poetic devices. This is Eisenstein on the concept of montage juxtapositions in film:

> . . . each montage piece exists no longer as something unrelated, but as a given *particular representation* of the general

theme that in equal measure penetrates all the shot pieces. The juxtaposition of these partial details in a given montage construction calls to life and forces into the light that *general* quality in which each detail has participated and which binds together all the details into a whole, namely, into that generalized image, wherein the creator, followed by the spectator, experiences the theme.

(*The Film Sense*, pp. 163–4)

Eisenstein offers the example of the hands of a clock and the events (tea, the rush hour, late afternoon light) that the viewer might associate with this image. These are essentially metonymic correspondences in that the process of association is founded upon a pre-existing pattern of circumstances and events. A metaphoric association is suggested when two images with no prior causal or circumstantial relationship are juxtaposed: associative meaning is generated rather than recalled (Eisenstein's juxtaposition of Kerensky and a peacock is one example of this). Hence, in film the distinction between metonymy and metaphor is clear and straightforward. In poetry this relationship is far more complex. As Jakobson demonstrated with the two couplets from the folk song, metonymic and metaphoric effects can be simultaneously generated from the same image complexes. Poetry is able to create a continuous metonymic–metaphoric interface because the double pattern is exclusive to language. If the images of the falcon, the horse, the courtyard, the porch, etc. were filmed, their relation to one another would be determined by the spatial limitations of the screen: the stillness of the mountains and the manor would provide a spatial background to the movement of the horse and the falcon. What film could not do is to capture the verbal intercutting of Vasilij as at once on a horse and walking, and more significantly it would not allow for the optional shift between 'Not a bright falcon', 'Not a fierce horse' and their positive counterparts while maintaining the same interconnections between image, event and meaning: in language the presence of a sign is necessary for the specification of its referential absence (see Jakobson's work on the relation between marked and unmarked linguistic structures, Holenstein, pp. 129–36). How would the film-maker portray the 'semantic' image of the saint kissing his own severed head? (see above p. 27). In the terminology of C. S. Peirce, whose work was promoted and extended by Jakobson, visual or cinematic signs are iconic, imparting a direct physical resemblance between sign and referent, while linguistic signs are symbolic, involving an interface between the arbitrarily related continua of prelinguistic perception and the system of language. Consequently parallelisms or resemblances between linguistic signs can at the same time follow their metonymic counterparts in the 'real' prelinguistic world (part for whole, time and circumstance, cause and effect, etc.) and also suggest correspondences which depend upon phonemic, semantic, syntactic echoes within the same text. This is the essence of Jakobson's double-edged use of the word equivalence. In non-poetic texts an unusual or unexpected substitution of a term from the paradigmatic axis involves a conspicuous departure from the dominant and parallel progression of syntagm and referential continuum. In poetry the intrinsic, textual parallelism of syntax, metre and sound pattern literally destabilises this compositional and interpretive relationship. In non-poetic language the distinction between metaphor and metonymy is secured by the extratextual, ideational images created by the text: in poetry material, textual figures and devices create a constant interplay between the structural features of the text and their referential counterparts.

> We have learned the suggestive etymology of the terms *prose* and *verse* – the former, *oratio prosa* < prosa < proversa (speech turned straightforward), and the latter *versus* (return). Hence we must consistently draw all inferences from the obvious fact that on every level of language the essence of poetic artifice consists in recurrent returns. Phonemic features and sequences, both morphologic and lexical, syntactic and phraseological units, when occurring in metrically and strophologically corresponding positions, are necessarily subject to conscious or subconscious questions of whether, how far, and in what respect the positionally corresponding entities are mutually similar.
>
> ('Grammatical Parallelism and Its Russian Facet', *L in L*,
> pp. 145–6)

Here Jakobson focuses upon what is the most obvious difference between poetic and non-poetic discourses, yet which, as we shall see in much post- and anti-Jakobson theory, can cause empirical and interpretive blind spots for the most sophisticated linguistic or literary commentator. I refer to the poetic line. Jakobson: 'Measure of sequences is a device that, outside of the poetic function, finds no application in language' (*L in L*, p. 72). This proposition might sound straightforward and unproblematic, but unless it underpins and anchors all discussions of poetic structure and the poetry–prose distinction, these become effectively invalid.

Flick through Brogan's bibliography of *English Versification 1570–1980* and you will find that not a year, indeed hardly a month, of the last four centuries has passed without there being some attempt to define, redefine or extend our structural perceptions of the poetic line. But you will rarely encounter attempts to specify the means by which writing in lines draws upon and transforms all other relations between language, perception and communication. This was Jakobson's principal objective, and his most famous, some would say infamous, attempts to transform theory into critical practice occurred in two essays: 'Baudelaire's "Les Chats" ' (1962, with Claude Lévi-Strauss) and 'Shakespeare's Verbal Art in "Th' Expence of Spirit" ' (1970, with L. G. Jones).

SONNETS AND EVERYTHING ELSE

The sonnet has exercised a peculiar fascination on Jakobson. Apart from his work on Baudelaire and Shakespeare he has devoted lengthy studies to individual sonnets by Dante (*SW III*, pp. 176–92), du Bellay (*SW III*, pp. 239–74) and Sidney (*SW III*, pp. 275–83). This degree of concentration has led some of his more sceptical critics (see Fowler, 1981) to accuse him of cautiously choosing his material in order to validate his method. Indeed, the emphasis upon sixteenth- to seventeenth-century Renaissance literature in his studies of non-slavic poetry prompts comparisons with the similar exclusivity of the New Critics: they too found ample justification for their 'general' theories of tension, paradox and ambiguity in the work of the metaphysical poets. Such charges are to a degree valid, but what are too often ignored are the correspondences between his attraction to the sonnet and his early associations with Formalism and Futurism.

The sonnet can claim to be a uniquely independent, or to borrow Jakobson's term 'invariant', element in the shifting and uncertain domains of intralinguistic poetics, literary history and genre. The vast majority of post-sixteenth-century Anglo-European poets have at some point attempted to accommodate their particular stylistic voices within the tight and merciless symmetries of the sonnet form. Innovators such as William Carlos Williams and e. e. cummings have done violence to its pristine formal architecture, and the concrete poet Mary Ellen Solt has validated its claim to being the ultimate formal abstraction by offering a silent, wordless sonnet. The sonnet is the structure which foregrounds the uneasy relationship between the two elements that enable us to distinguish between poetic and non-poetic discourse – the sentence and the line. The sentence is the meeting-point between what might be termed micro-linguistics (the focus upon the nature and composition of the sign, phonemics, phonetics, morphology, lexis), and macro-linguistics (discourse theory, pragmatics, the organisation of individual texts or speech acts, the relation between these and the broader continua of non-linguistic sign systems, ideology, behavioural instinct and conventions, etc.). The poetic line is the monkey wrench thrown into the otherwise comfortable workings of linguistic theory and practice. In its regular formal dress it consists of a predictable relation between a specific number of syllables, their accentual/stress pattern and rhyme scheme. These features can be overlaid with alliterative and assonantal patterns (and sometimes 'internal' rhyme). Premodernist variations upon this formula (primarily in English poetry) consist of varied line length, usually anchored by rhyme, or blank verse, a form in which the unrhymed iambic pentameter is counterpointed against interlineal syntax. The free verse line presents problems that will be examined in Part III. So much for what the line is. What does it do? One could claim that it is the principal organisational element of poems, but this could be countered by pointing out that poems also consist of sentences. At a more localised level the abstract structure of the line can be said to compromise the choices available within non-poetic syntax, and here we face a problem. Freedom in linguistic construction is a relative term: we can say or write what we like, so long as the finished communicative product is accommodated by the decoding procedures of the listener or reader, and for both participants units of encodable and decodable meaning are governed primarily by the nature of the sentence. If we supplement these abstract preconditions with yet another level of organisational conventions and regulations, what happens? Syllabic regularity, iambic metre and rhyme scheme do not obliterate ordinary meaning, but they set up a tension between what most literate human beings have come to regard as linguistic transparency and something else, a pattern of echoes and repetitions which might be found in other poetic texts but which, unlike the transformational relation between the deep and surface structures of sentences, draws us into the particular substance of the message and text in question. In 'Linguistics and Poetics' Jakobson designates this tension as between the 'referential' function (governed principally by the sentence) and its 'poetic' counterpart (governed principally by the line). Parallelism allows us to identify the points of intersection between the line and syntax. For example, the repetition of a similar grammatical structure in the two lines of a couplet cannot be accounted for in the same way as recurrent structures in a prose discourse. In the preceding sentences the recurrence of similar verb phrases, 'to identify' and 'be accounted for', is not an instance of poetic parallelism, because the structure and the individual constituents of each sentence do not adhere to the abstract regulations of stress, syllabic number or rhyme scheme. If they did, the relationship between their respective noun phrases would not only be syntactic: the relative positions of the four syntactic components within the verse form would create a secondary level of structure and signification. There are two major problems with this model of parallelism. The first, which has drawn the attention of the anti-Jakobson camp and which we will consider in Part II, is this: if two systems of linguistic organisation and signification are in a continuous state of interpenetration, how does the reader/critic know which points of contact are the most significant generators of that elusive entity, poetic meaning? The second is an extension of the first: assuming that we can identify the most prominent and relevant interfaces between the two lines of a rhymed couplet, we then face the much more complex problem of relating the internalised functions of this unit to those of preceding and succeeding couplets. To complicate matters even further, how do we deal with the relation between blocks of two, three or four consecutive couplets and the broader thematic and narrative shifts in a poem consisting of more than a hundred couplets?

In the *Dialogues* with Krystyna Pomorska Jakobson is disarmingly honest about the specialised and somewhat partial nature of his poetic investigations. In the chapter on 'Parallelism' he concedes that in his work on Czech and Russian couplet poetry he had succeeded more in establishing the nature of the pertinent critical questions than in offering final and conclusive answers.

> The perception of similarities and contiguities within the couplet united by parallelism leads automatically to the need to find an answer to the unconscious questions: what links the two lines? Is it an association by similarity or by contrast? Or is it an association through contiguity, and, if so, is its contiguity in time or in space? All of which leads to the essential question for the comprehension of the verse: what is the hierarchical relation between the parallel units? Which of them is subordinated to the other? How is the relation in question actualized – by the internal content of the verse, or by the fact that one of the lines simply dominates the other, or finally by the position that the couplet occupies in the whole?
>
> (*Dialogues*, pp. 103–4)

This passage recalls Jakobson's almost paradoxical proposition in 'Poetry of Grammar and Grammar of Poetry': an exhaustive unbiased investigation of a poem can disclose 'surprising' effects. The abstract formulae of syntax and versification are the instruments of analysis and their continuous interrelation is the premise upon which the analysis is based, but the results of the investigation depend entirely upon the particular poet and poem in question.

Later in the *Dialogues* Jakobson offers rather enigmatic answers to the major questions that had been raised by his work (pp. 112–17). Why, for instance, does he focus mainly upon isolated fragments of long narrative poems or upon short lyrical pieces? He answers that the complete narrative poem 'requires a different, more complex presentation than the devices that allow us to disclose the structure of a short integral text' (pp. 113–14). The sonnet is the ultimate integral text. It is like a stanza in the sense that its enclosed structural mechanism is determined primarily by a rhyme scheme. But unlike the stanza it is a complete text, rather than a unit of a longer consecutive pattern. In all other regular poetic structures the poetic function, whose primary organisational unit is the line, shares with its syntactic, referential counterpart an allegiance to structural contiguity, the progressive consecutive pattern. The blank verse line, the closed couplet, the stanza, constitute the framework of the poetic function but they are unlimited in number: a poem might consist of three or three hundred stanzas. The sonnet, however, is the structural enactment of Jakobson's general principle of the poetic function. Similarity is superimposed upon contiguity in the sense that none of the parts that constitute the progressive, sequential movement of the text ever remains immune from the parallelisms of syntax, metre and sound pattern that constitute its integrated architechtonic structure.

I $_1$Th' expence of Spirit | in a waste of shame
     $_2$Is lust in action, | and till action, lust
     $_3$Is perjurd, murdrous, | blouddy full of blame,
     $_4$Savage extreame, rude, | cruel, not to trust,
II $_1$Injoyd no sooner | but dispised straight,
     $_2$Past reason hunted, | and no sooner had
     $_3$Past reason hated | as a swollowed bayt,
     $_4$On purpose layd | to make | the taker mad.
III $_1$Mad[e] In pursut | and in possession so,
     $_2$Had, having, and in quest, | to have extreame,
     $_3$A blisse in proofe | and provd | a[nd] very wo,
     $_4$Before a joy proposd | behind a dreame,
IV $_1$All this the world | well knowes | yet none knowes well,
     $_2$To shun the heaven | that leads | men to this hell.

In his analysis (with Jones) of Shakespeare's 129th sonnet Jakobson describes how the grammatical and metrical parallelism of the text not only organises but effectively absorbs the referential shifts between mortal instinct (metonymic) and the notion of life as a mirror-image of heaven and hell (metaphoric). In Section III, 'Interpretation', Jakobson paraphrases each of the most prominent formal units of the poem, the three pentameter quatrains and the concluding heroic couplet, but this procedure should not be mistaken for naturalisation. Jakobson does not offer these prose transformations as a model of how the text signifies; indeed, their temporal, consecutive relationship is a model of the way in which the text does not signify. What the essay demonstrates is that it is impossible, or more accurately incorrect, to regard any of the signifying structures of the sonnet as immune from each other. For instance, when he considers the phonemic parallelism of the closing couplet, he is aware that the repetition of *heaven* / hɛvn / *men* / mɛn / *hell* / hɛl / draws upon and intensifies the broader thematic subjects of the sonnet and that the position of each phoneme within the syntactic structure cannot be fully analysed without giving equal attention to the surrounding metrical formula of the iambic pentameter and the couplet.

Sections V–IX of the essay concentrate on patterns of binary oppositions which manifest themselves within and across the various syntactic and metrical structures of the sonnet: 'Odd Against Even', 'Outer Against Inner', 'Anterior Against Posterior', 'Couplet Against Quatrains', 'Centre Against Marginals'. His point is that the sonnet is finally and irretrievably multidimensional. We are aware of course that multidimensional signification is regarded by most schools of criticism as the defining feature of literary and, more specifically poetic, texts: ambiguity, paradox, the interpenetration of syntagm and paradigm, etc. But the levels, folds, intersections and collisions of pattern that occur in sonnet 129 attain such a degree of complexity that we begin to suspect that we are no longer dealing with language as a communicative medium. For example in Section IV, 'Pervasive Features', Jakobson identifies 'a conspicuous alliteration or repetition of sound sequences and entire morphemes or words' in each of the sonnet's fourteen lines. This pattern of phonemic foregrounding further specifies the tension between the line and syntax, and the reader might be prompted to investigate the semantic interplay between these foregrounded elements. But it is not as simple as that because we have also to take into account the rhyme scheme, which sometimes interacts with and sometimes remains separate from the internal pattern of assonance and alliteration. So far we have only touched the outer skin of the textual system. The rhyme scheme divides the sonnet into four strophes. The syntactic structures of the even strophes present us with 'a motion picture of merely straightforward development, whereas the odd strophes introduce a retrospective and generalising approach: I_2 *In action, and till action*; III_2 *Had, having, and in quest, to have extreame*' (*L in L*, p. 205). As if this binary distinction between odd and even strophes were not sufficient to occupy the attention of the average reader/critic, we also find that the inner strophes (II and III) exhibit a tendency towards 'minor clauses deprived of finites and acting effectively in an independent function' (p. 209), while their outer counterparts (I and IV) are each dominated by one 'finite clause which occurs twice in the coordinate clauses linked by a conjunction' (p. 208). Tired? Don't lag behind because we have yet to consider the internal alternation of definite and indefinite articles in the anterior strophes (I and II) versus the strict division between indefinite (four in III) and definite articles (two in IV) in the posterior strophe (p. 210). Not to mention the density of 'pure substantive' nouns in the couplet versus the relational dependence of substantive nouns on verbs in the three preceding quatrains (p. 211). And we should not forget that a shift occurs from the grammatical parallelism of the opening 'Marginal', six lines to the non-parallelism of the two 'Centre' lines and back again to the 'grammatical (morphological) and, save III$_2$ and IV$_2$, syntactic parallelism of hemistichs' of the six closing 'Marginal' lines.

One is prompted to compare this sonnet, as discussed by Jakobson, not with other collections of words but with a piece of baroque architecture or a Renaissance painting (Brueghel for instance) in which the whole consists of parts whose relation to one another is not progressive or linear but determined by a vast number of intrinsic cross-references and extrinsic, perceiver-oriented, levels of cognition and interfusion. Even then we will not have done proper justice to the uniqueness of this artefact and its manner of signification. Our perception of visual complexity is atemporal: the parts of a building or a painting intersect at once, although the procedure of mentally negotiating and recording them might well be determined by the linear patterns of rational thought and language. In this sonnet the distinctive elements of the spatial and the temporal, structure and cognition, are perversely yet systematically entangled. As we read the sonnet and move from syllable to syllable, word to word, clause to clause, line to line, our sense of linear progression is virtually eliminated by the patterns of correspondence, echo, subversion, reiteration, doubling, trebling and exclusion that attend practically every unit (metrical, syntactic, phonemic, morphological, semantic, etc.).

At the beginning of the essay Jakobson distinguishes between the centripetal nature of the first seven lines of the sonnet, as they move toward its centre, and the centrifugal nature of the concluding seven. He refers to the internal structure of the text, but if we expand the terms of reference to the relation between the text and the levels of linguistic and prelinguistic continua outside the text the poem must be regarded as the ultimate centripetal device. All attempts to disentangle a sign or a sign sequence from their closed, internalised patterns of interpenetration will result in an unequal struggle between what, in a general, paraphrasable sense, the words mean and their far more prominent function as constituents of a single operative sign – sonnet 129. In practically all our encounters with language or linguistic exchanges a large amount of any residual uncertainty regarding the meaning of an utterance or the intention of its creator can be resolved by some form of external, contextual reference. The direction on the matchbox, 'Please keep away from children', will rarely be interpreted as a philosophical or existential statement because the apparently ambiguous subject–object reference of the sentence (keep what away from children? yourself? something else?) is effectively specified by its placing on a box of dangerously ignitable instruments. In spoken exchanges our uncertainties can be clarified by our knowledge of who the speaker is. We can either contextualise the speaker's utterance in terms of our a priori knowledge of his/her condition, allegiances, idiosyncrasies, or we can move towards this state of awareness by asking for a clearer statement of what they mean (in Jakobson's terms a transposition of language and metalanguage). With poetry this process of clarification is unsettled in two principal ways. First, the poem as speech act is always detached from the presence of its creator and from the circumstances and conditions which might have prompted it. Second, practically all poems, particularly regular poems, are self-referential – 'the set toward the message as such, focus on the message for its own sake'. The procedure through which we bring poems back into line with the concrete, referential certainties of the 'normal' language–world interface depends largely upon the interpreter's identification of deictic features. *Deixis*, the Greek word for 'pointing', refers to the orientational features of a particular statement. The principal deictic features of a statement will refer to the condition of the speaker (first- or third-person pronoun) and will involve the use of locatives, the time, place or circumstances of the utterance (the use of second-person pronouns, the indication of objects and concepts and their spatio-temporal relation to the speaker). Deictic features enable us to generate a stabilising, metalinguistic counterpart to the acontextual, internalised mechanisms of the text. In Section IV of the essay Jakobson, without using the term 'deictics', considers the elements of sonnet 129 which create an interface with the non-textual world – or rather, he savours their absence.

> It is the only one among the 154 sonnets of the 1609 Quarto which contains no personal or corresponding possessive pronouns.... Sonnet 129 avoids epithets.... Except for the word *men* in the final line, only singular forms occur in the sonnet. The poem admits no other finites than the third person singular of the present tense.
>
> (*L in L*, p. 203)

We have absolutely no clues as to the condition of the speaker, the circumstances of the speech act or dramatic relation between addresser and addressee. In 'Linguistics and Poetics' Jakobson considers the potential for tension between 'the inalienable character of any self-focused message' and everything else. 'Besides the author and the reader, there is the "I" of the lyrical hero or of the fictitious storyteller and the "you" or "thou" of the alleged addressee of dramatic monologues, supplications and epistles' (*L in L*, p. 85). But in sonnet 129 the conditions allowing for such a tension are effectively removed: 129 is the pure self-focused message. The following is Roger Fowler's summary of the 'critical limitations' of Jakobson's writings: 'Jakobson's "exhaustive" analyses of Baudelaire and Shakespeare are notoriously shallow, formalistic, dominated by mechanical and perhaps spurious patterns in phonology and syntax, absolutely uninformative when the analyst comes to interpretation or to placing in history' (1981, p. 167). This is an economic and largely accurate synopsis of the anti-Jakobson school of the 1960s and 1970s. We will consider this in more detail in Part II, but for the moment let us consider the charge that Jakobson's analysis is 'absolutely uninformative'. In the final section, 'Concluding Questions', this case is effectively conceded: 'An objective scrutiny of Shakespeare's language and verbal art, with particular reference to this poem, reveals the cogent and mandatory unity of its thematic and compositional framework' (*L in L*, p. 215). To go against the intrinsic, centripetal 'unity' of the text would involve a metalinguistic distortion of its effect. However, there is one part of the essay, ignored by its critics, in which the mask of objectivity is allowed to slip – Section X, 'Anagrams?' The question mark is significant because Jakobson offers a tentative and by no means provable explanation of why sonnet 129 is Shakespeare's most anonymous, self-focused text. Jakobson points out that in a number of the sonnets the name 'Will' is inserted as a pun, citing 'every word doth almost tell my name' (sonnet 76), which 'might be applied in its literal meaning to the poem under discussion'.

> The letters and sounds of the first line seem to disclose the family name of the poet, written in his own and contemporaneous spellings as *Shakspere, Shakspeare, Shackspeare, Shaxpere.* I, *expence* (xp) *of Spirit* (sp.r) *shame* (sha), while the terminal couplet with its thrice iterated /w/ and particularly with the words *well* (w.ll) *yet* (y) *men* (m) could carry a latent allusion to *William.* Since in wordplays Shakespeare was prone to equate the vocables *will* and *well,* the entire concluding couplet could – perhaps! – conceal a second, facetious autobiographical reading: 'All this [is] the world Will knows, yet none knows Will to shun the heaven that leads men to this hell'. The omission of the copulative verb would be consistent with the ellipses used in the rest of the sonnet; moreover, the contraction of 'this is' to 'this' was current during the Shakespearean era.
>
> (*L in L*, pp. 213–14)

One must admire Jakobson for the cool and laboriously detailed way in which he makes this observation. To return to the text–picture analogy the effect of this suggestion upon, in Fowler's words, the 'formalistic, mechanical and uninformative' tone of the essay is comparable to that of the art historian who at the close of his lecture on the seventeenth-century practices of painting upon another painting, takes out a knife, chips away the surface and discloses the face of the artist beneath the dense, refractory layers of representational signs and material (it should be noted that Jakobson makes a similar 'discovery' in a sonnet by Sidney, *SW III*, pp. 282–3).

The curious absence of those deictic keystones, the pronouns linking addresser to addressee, is suddenly explained – though Jakobson leaves it to the reader to make the connection. The pronoun shifts the focus from text to communicative participants: here the principal participant, Will, is literally inscribed within the text. Sign and referent (will) (y) (m) (she) (xp) (sp.r) rest at the opening and the closing of the sonnet, but these disguised signatures are not marginal to the substance of the text. As Jakobson demonstrates, no single element of its form can remain immune from the complex and self-enclosed interlacing of pattern and substance that constitute its 'cogent and mandatory unity'.

The sonnet represents for Jakobson the vortex of linguistic usage. It is capable of offering the reader a complex network of extratextual representational patterns while at the same time never allowing any of these to escape from the closed symmetries and tensions between the material structure and the signifying function of the sign, the signans and the signatum. In the study, with Claude Lévi-Strauss, of 'Baudelaire's "Les Chats" ' Jakobson discloses an interaction between text and poet very similar in operation, though dissimilar in substance, to that of Shakespeare's sonnet 129. This essay has been summarised and criticised by a number of people (most cogently by Michael Riffaterre in 1966), and in effect, Baudelaire's and Shakespeare's sonnets are both treated as perfect realisations of metonymic and metaphoric infolding. In 'Les Chats' the metonymic relation between the cats, the human beings and the house that they share is constantly expanded and intercut with metaphoric images of cats as gloomy coursers, grand sphinxes, and living manifestations of earthly and cosmic signs (sand and stars); the overarching metonymic–metaphoric interplay being between the cats as female, and the 'fervent lovers', 'austere scholars' (and by implication the speaking presence) as male. This gestalt of traces, resonances and specific references is achieved primarily by the structural mechanisms of the sonnet; phonemes, morphemes, syntactic patterns, metrical emphases are effectively the catalysts for the shifts between metaphoric and metonymic levels. Described in this way the essay would again seem to satisfy Fowler's judgement of it as formalistic and mechanical, but at its conclusion Jakobson quotes from Baudelaire's *Foules*.

> Multitude, solitude: terms equal and interchangeable by the active and fertile poet. . . . the poet enjoys the incomparable privilege that he can, at will, be both himself and another. What men call love is very small, very restricted and very weak compared to that ineffable orgy, that blessed prostitution of the soul which gives itself in its entirety, its poetry and charity, to the unforeseen which emerges, to the unknown one who passes.
>
> (*L in L*, p. 197)

This piece of prose is itself a disorientating mixture of metaphor and metonymy, but it finds a clearer echo in Jakobson's 'Linguistics and Poetics': the 'I', the speaker, the fictitious storyteller of the poem shifts continuously between a real or imagined presence and a less tangible construct of textual figuration – in Baudelaire's terms he becomes 'both himself and another'. In most poems this relation between a tangible speaking presence and a confluence of textual devices becomes evident mainly through shifts either towards the metonymic or towards the metaphoric dimension of language and reference. For example, a poem densely packed with deictic references to a particular place, time or event which might exist independently of their poeticisation (the funeral elegy on a well-known person, for instance) invokes a metonymic continuum of specific processes and connections and the poetic persona becomes more closely allied with the prose fiction author. Jakobson: 'Following the path of contiguous relationships, the ... [prose] author metonymically digresses from the plot to the atmosphere and from the characters to the setting in space and time' (*L in L*, p. 111). In all types of poetic writing we encounter a complex network of tension between the constituent parts of the communicative process – sound and meaning, paradigm and syntagm – and this set of uneasy relationships will involve a shift either towards the controlling presence of the encoder or towards the extratextual context shared by encoder and decoder. But the sonnet is different. Let us remind ourselves of the formulaic model of linguistic communication presented in Jakobson's work on aphasia.

The encoding process goes from meaning to sound, from the lexico-grammatical to the phonological level, while the decoding process goes from sound to meaning, from features to symbols. For the encoder the paradigmatic axis is the first building-block of composition (antecedent) followed by its syntagmatic counterpart; and for the decoder this hierarchy is reversed. This means that encoder, decoder, speaker and listener must negotiate the impersonal mechanisms of language to effect communication, but at each stage they are positioned at opposing points. This process of mutual exclusion can even manifest itself within the divisions between poetic genres – according to Jakobson the epic poet (emphasis upon the combinative syntagmatic axis) takes on the role of the listener while the lyricist (emphasis upon the selective, paradigmatic axis) presents himself as the speaker. The sonnet succeeds in levelling these hierarchies of creation and perception. Its structure ensures that meaning and sound, syntagm and paradigm are continuously interfused, and as a consequence the antecedent–precedent distinction, which dislocates encoder from decoder, becomes invalid. The effects created do not offer us the long-sought and regularly demolished ideal of linguistic transparency – we are still dealing with the impersonal materiality of signs – but the participants in this process of encoding and decoding achieve a state of cohabitation, a parallel interface between the sensory and the intelligible faculties of each person.

With this in mind let us return to the apparent anagram inserted in Shakespeare's 129. Jakobson's most prominent debt to the work of Saussure is manifest in his adaptation of signifier–signified to signans–signatum, of the all-language designation of langue–parole to its literary counterpart, and we will consider his revisions of the Saussurean concepts of synchrony and diachrony in Part III. With specific regard to literature, the most intriguing connection between the two theorists is their interest in the anagram. Saussure filled many notebooks with remarks on anagrams, mainly of the poet's name, that he had found in Latin verse (for discussion and quotations from this unpublished work, see Starobinski, 1979). He said in a letter that he remained uncertain about 'what one should think of the reality or fantasy of the whole business' (Starobinski, p. 138). His problem is this: these anagrams are clearly real in the sense that the poet has offered them as a supplementary level of linguistic organisation to be perceived by the reader, but this apparently slight aberration from the normal conventions of poetic design has serious consequences for the orthodox model of form and content in poetry. In one sense the anagram is an extension of the use of the double pattern – precedence is given to the material nature of the sign rather than to its signifying function. At the same time an act of signification is achieved which effectively short-circuits the entire signifier–signified-based model of communication: we decode a sign which is clearly inscribed within the complex patterns of syntagm and paradigm, phoneme and morpheme, but which in the normal sense does not register. The phonemes of the name William Shakespeare are at once present and absent. Every time we read or listen to the sonnet we will hear them, but it is possible that these sound patterns will not register as a sign – they also function as meeting-points in an entirely separate complex of sounds and meanings. Since the anagram is a continuation of the system of the double pattern, what other levels and registers of structure and meaning might be released in our encounters with poetry?

Jakobson cites Saussure's 'daring studies on poetic anagrams' on a number of occasions and their significance for his own work becomes most evident in his essay on 'Subliminal Verbal Patterning in Poetry' (1970). In this he addresses the following question: 'Are the designs disclosed by linguistic analysis deliberately and rationally planned in the creative work of the poet and is he really aware of them?' (*L in L*, p. 250). He does not offer a straightforward answer; rather, he subdivides the question. The vast majority of the patterns that become evident during the reading of a poem are conscious and deliberate strategies of the poet. What is uncertain is whether the effects and meanings generated by these patterns draw upon the conscious manipulation of the linguistic raw material or whether some kind of interface between subconscious interiority and the external nature of the sign is responsible. Jakobson considers an example from the work of Xlebnikov, recalling a conversation during which the poet admitted that only after several years did he realise that the sounds, *k, r, l* and *u* occurred five times in the opening sentence of the poem 'The Grasshopper' 'without any wish of the one who wrote this nonsense'. Jakobson goes on to point out that the number 5 was particularly important in Xlebnikov's non-poetic writing on the nature of language, and he extends this to a consideration of fivefold patterns and symbols in biology – fingers, toes, starfish, honeycombs, bubbles, etc. – many of which feature as images in Xlebnikov's verse. His point is that the poetic function is sometimes capable of short-circuiting the conventional relationship between signs and concepts.

There are a number of models of this relationship, but the most widely accepted is the one which draws upon Saussure's notion of the binary nature of the sign and Jakobson's work on the fundamental axes of syntagm and paradigm. The poetic function is seen to reverse the normal hierarchy of non-poetic relations between these elements: material signifiers are promoted as organisational and structural elements above and beyond their bonding with specific signifiers; the paradigmatic axis, the code, is drawn upon and reintegrated with its syntagmatic, contextual, counterpart in a way that unsettles orthodox parallels between language and experience. Designated as such, poetry becomes a deviation from the 'norm' of non-poetic language, obscure, mysterious and surprising but at the same time reconcilable with the more familiar patterns of non-poetic exchange. In short, a poem can be naturalised, brought into line with its accessible metalinguistic substitute. But subliminal patterns of the sort disclosed in Xlebnikov's and indeed in Shakespeare's verse create for poetry an independent function, a release from its reliance upon governing systems of non-poetic discourse. The conventional method of explaining poetic signification is to regard devices such as metre, rhyme and sound pattern as supplements to the fundamental structures shared by all types of discourse, and as capable of extending or intensifying these intrageneric levels of meaning. The anagram or the fivefold patterns of Xlebnikov's verse are signs which correspond with discursive or mythological patterns outside the text, but their function within the text renders them uniquely immune from the normal processes of transformation, metalinguistic paraphrase or, in critical terms, naturalisation. To appreciate this distinction properly we should consider what the activity of naturalisation involves. We naturalise literary texts by firstly identifying their formal features and specifying their operation and then by considering how this particular form of linguistic organisation can absorb and restructure meaning. One major difference between poetic and non-poetic writing exists in the relation between the textual object and the metalanguage of criticism and understanding. When we engage with prose, either in discursive critical language or by employing the precise, descriptive formulae of transformational and generative linguistics, we are closer to the stylistic and referential pattern of the text than we can be with poetic writing. With poetic writing there is an uneasy relationship between the structure of the text, the mental register of our initial response and the subsequent process, either internalised or discursive, of explanation: rhymes stay in the mind and interfere with the progress of the syntagm, metrical patterns foreground individual words or sequences in a way that would not occur in non-metrical language. In short, we are dealing with the simultaneous interplay of the two elements of the double pattern, and when we naturalise or demystify poems we effectively translate one form of linguistic organisation into another. When we decode, analyse or interrogate non-poetic forms of signification we participate in a shared condition of composition and understanding. For instance, when I state that NP (noun phrase) plus VP (verb phrase) underlies all English sentences I should be aware that this formulaic concept of deep structure underlies the sentence that I'm using to describe it, all other sentences that I might use to clarify my statement, and any sentences that my addressee might use to enquire about my statement. But the relationship between poetry and the process of understanding poetry fractures this state of intertextual cohabitation. It is possible, of course, to address the subjects and nature of poems in poetic language but in doing so we will be perpetuating and extending the isolation of poetry from non-poetic explanation rather than addressing their uneasy relationship. Jakobson regards the anagram and the sonnet, in Shakespeare's case both, not as whimsical aberrations from the more accessible types of poetic discourse, but as explicit foregroundings of the essential nature of all poetic discourse: in crude terms its untranslatable distance from every other type of linguistic usage. If we stated that 'Xlebnikov has written a poem that addresses the mythological significance of the number five' or that 'Shakespeare has added his signature to a poem about lust, mortality and death' we would be offering a grossly inaccurate account of what actually happens within the perceptual registers of both texts. We would desensitise the actual, multidimensional relation between reader and text in which the sign 'William Shakespeare' and the image of 5 are both present and absent, and convert this experience into a syntagmatic, consecutive register.

ZAUM

Jakobson's theory of poetry is obviously motivated by the belief, in his case the verifiable certainty, that poetic structuration and signification are intrinsically different from any other form of linguistic discourse, and it might seem rather odd that his generally impartial, scientific methods of analysis could accommodate the pseudo-mystical notion of supraconscious, subliminal exchange. The essay on 'Subliminal Verbal Patterning' was published in 1970, and a short, related piece called 'Supraconscious Turgenev' in 1979, but the questions raised by both take us back again to the Russia of half a century before, to the unlikely collaboration between Futurism and Formalism. The *zaumnye* or supraconscious/transrational poem was one of the more wildly revolutionary gestures of the Futurist ethos. In the broader context of modernism correspondences can be found between *Zaum* and stream of consciousness or the Imagist notion of an object or experience captured in an instant of time. All share the desire to transcend the refractory mechanics of conventional language, literary and non-literary, and to uncover more instinctive, primal relations between consciousness, experience and signification. The principal difference between *Zaum* and its modernist relatives is that, while the latter maintained the irritating, indeed self-contradictory, belief that language, in all its forms, is a barrier to or falsification of true consciousness and experience, the *Zaum* poets dealt with language as a constituent element of all aspects of the human condition. Xlebnikov and Kručenyx (see Pomorska, 1968, pp. 93–118), the two most prominent *Zaum* poets, believed that their new method of writing would bring poet and reader closer to an encounter with language *as* experience. Many of Xlebnikov's poems share with concrete poetry (of which Marinetti was the principal Futurist exponent) and sound poetry an emphasis upon the materiality of the sign at the expense, and virtually to the exclusion, of conventional linguistic organisation. But unlike most of his graphicentric or phonocentric counterparts Xlebnikov also concentrated upon the systems and subsystems by which we classify and analyse linguistic material. In short, he shifted the balance of the double pattern as far as possible towards poetic convention. He did not, however, create formless, unstructured collections of sounds and rhythmic sequences; rather he allowed correspondences between rhyme, assonance and alliteration to effectively supersede syntactic structure as the generator of meaning. This foregrounding of intersections between the material elements of language was the principal topic of Jakobson's 1921 essay on 'New Russian Poetry'. For example, when dealing with the deployment of neologisms Jakobson stresses that the bringing together of different roots, prefixes, suffixes, affixes will create 'dissociations' 'in the given structure of language as a whole', but that in Xlebnikov's poems this deformation of the structural norm is countered by an internal pattern 'within the framework of a particular poem, which as it were forms a closed linguistic system' (Brown, p. 74). This secondary pattern consists of phonemic parallelism.

It is possible to produce verses characterised by an emphasis primarily on euphony. But is this sort of emphasis equivalent to the accentuation of pure sound? If the answer is yes then we have a species of vocal music, and vocal music of an inferior kind at that. . . . Euphony operates, however, not with sounds but with phonemes, that is, with acoustical impressions which are capable of being associated with meaning.

(Brown, p. 77)

This brief statement anticipates much of Jakobson's groundbreaking work in linguistics. The phoneme is the tactile collusion of the intelligible and the sensory, the meeting-point of language as a system of arbitrary conventions and language as sound. In Xlebnikov's poems this unit is promoted from its conventional, functionary role as the acoustic marker of abstract signifying structures to the principal organising feature of a given text. 'The language of poetry strives to reach, as a final limit, the phonetic, or rather – to the extent that such a purpose may be present – the euphonic phrase – in other words, a trans-sense speech' (Brown, p. 82). So Xlebnikov's work achieves a form of irretrievable linguistic deformation. First it violates the autonomy of individual signs and creates two levels of signification. Second, by enclosing these syntactic contractions and neologisms within a textual pattern of semantic–acoustic interpenetrations, it disallows the normative procedures through which we might make sense of them.

The unlikely connection between Jakobson's early associations with Futurism and Formalism and his later concentration upon the sonnet should by now have become more plausible, in fact, logical. Xlebnikov's *Zaum* poems and the regular sonnets by Shakespeare and Baudelaire involve, in Jakobson's words, the creation of 'a closed linguistic system'. Jakobson demonstrates that in the latter there is 'a cogent and mandatory unity' between the two definitive elements of poetic form, the constituents of the syntactic unit and the constituents of the line; in the former this process is taken a stage further. When, in sonnet 129, we encounter an individual word as the catalyst for phonemic echoes from one part of the poem and semantic-thematic echoes from another, we also encounter the pre-modernist prototype for Xlebnikov's concentrated neologisms, the enforced collision of two or three morphonemic elements, which are themselves tied into a system of phonemic–semantic parallels.

Both techniques succeed in detaching the poem from any clear or reliable correspondence with its metalinguistic surrogate. The effects created are transrational or *zaumnye*, in the sense that each term describes a condition in which signs, carrying their representational import, are present but the relation between them is not accommodated by the rational, consensual systems through which we document experience. The question raised by the concept of a continuum of signs which operates separately from its rational counterpart is twofold: first, what motivates such acts of (mis)representation; second, if such continua disclose alternative patterns of association or cognition what purposes, for both encoder and decoder, do these serve? The possible answers to these questions can be similarly divided into two distinct classes. The dominant theory of subconscious activity has been provided by Freud. In the classical Freudian model of the psyche, the subconscious (or unconscious, since the terms are largely interchangeable) is seen as a dynamic subsystem of instinctual drives, repressions, desires and fears. These manifest themselves in the world of concrete signs as 'compromise formations', symptoms, dream images and narratives, jokes, verbal slippages. They are regarded as a compromise because they achieve a level of explicitness and coherence that is half-way between what our intrinsic psychological restraints do not allow us to disclose or express and the terms and conditions of conventional, public systems of expression and representation, the most significant of these being language. Classical Freudian critics approach the literary text as a means by which the compromise formations become evident: in short, repeated stylistic patterns or images will be interpreted not as conscious literary strategies but as the linguistic equivalent of dream symbols.

A second school of thought, while by no means contradicting Freudian principles, shifts the emphasis from symbols to the function of phenomenologically or even biologically discrete units and patterns. The disciplinary origins of this model are more closely linked with psychology and neurology than with psychoanalysis, and Jakobson's use of the term 'subliminal' rather than 'unconscious' or 'subconscious' signals his allegiance to this school. Much of twentieth-century linguistics focuses on some element of the relation between subliminal and external consciousness. For example, the distinction between deep and surface structure in transformational–generative grammar involves the acceptance that some individuals who are linguistically competent (i.e. they can encode and decode coherent statements) remain completely unaware of the existence or the nature of the deep structures that enable them to participate in the communication process.

Freudian notions of the unconscious and the models of subliminal activity presented by gestalt psychology are not opposing theses but in literary theory there exists a potential for conflict. In the section on *Zaum* in *Russian Formalism. A Metapoetics*, Peter Steiner documents the often chaotically conflicting opinions on supraconscious Futurism developed by contemporary critics. For instance, in a 1921 essay called 'Where Does Verse Come From?', Jakubinskij offers an early adaptation of classical Freudianism to literary theory; he classifies the self-focused message of poetry as the mature equivalent of 'infantile babble' and suggests similarities between the unconnected tirades of the mentally ill and the non-referential, metrical patterns of verse ('Otkuda berutsja stichi', *Kniznyj ugol*, 7, 1921). In contrast, Jakobson, in 'New Russian Poetry', quotes from Xlebnikov:

> My first idea in dealing with language is to find . . . a touchstone for the transformation of all Slavic words one into another, for the free fusion of all Slavic words. . . . Such is the self valuing word without relation to life or use. And seeing that all roots are simply phantoms behind which stand the living alphabet, the discovery of a general unity of all world languages . . . such is my second purpose. This is the way to a discovery of a transworld trans-sense language.
>
> (Brown, p. 81)

This conscious, deliberate programme of disclosing patterns of signification that lie behind, indeed transcend, the conventions of rational language is echoed in Jakobson's preamble to his 1970 essay on subliminal patterns: these, he argues, 'cannot be viewed as negligible accidentals governed by the rule of chance'. Nor, he suggests, are subliminal patterns condensations or displacements of some internalised discomfort of which the poet is not completely aware. 'Any significant poetic composition, whether it is an improvisation or the fruit of long and painstaking labour, implies a goal oriented choice of verbal material.' He goes on to quote a riddle from Russian folklore,

| Šlá svin já iz Pítera | A pig was coming from St Petersburg |
| vsjá spiná istýkana | [its] back is pierced all over. |

(*L in L*, pp. 254–5)

The answer to this riddle is Napërstok (thimble), and Jakobson's point is that the relation between problem and solution registers at two levels. At the referential, ideational level we encounter the implied metonymic suggestion that the metal object which, like the pig, has a rough pitted surface represents an ironic reversal of the usual flow of trade between city and country. At the supraconscious, textual level we find that the answer is anagrammatised in the phonemic patterns of the riddle: the suffix /na/ occurs in spiná and istýkana; istýkana echoes the consonant sequence in the final syllable of the answer, stok, etc. The similarities between this two-dimensional effect and Shakespeare's hidden presence in sonnet 129 are clear enough, but Jakobson does not argue that all poems contain a specific encoded riddle; rather he uses the example of the riddle as a means of emphasising that the process of understanding poems involves an interweaving of the specific and irretrievable elements of the text and those features of the text which can be transposed as paraphrase or naturalisation. The former involve what he refers to as the subliminal verbal patterns. Subliminal, in Jakobson's model, does not mean subconscious or repressed; a more accurate definition would be 'untranslatable'. In a discussion at Cologne University, following his paper on Yeats's 'The Sorrow of Love', Jakobson addresses the problematical concept of poetic 'substance'; that which is intrinsic to the text, but which is lost when the text is transformed into paraphrase:

[C]ould you tell me, just tell me without bothering about verse, what could be preserved as the substance of this poem by Yeats? Hardly anything remains. Tolstoj's famous answer applies here as well. Upon being asked what he had meant to say with *Anna Karenina*, he said one should simply read out *Anna Karenina* from the beginning to the end.... It is the external and internal form of language that makes a poem a poem.

(*Verbal Art*, p. 72)

Napërstok is the paraphrasable substance of the riddle (its external form) yet at the same time it contains tangible elements of its unparaphrasable substance (its internal form). In an economical and perhaps enigmatic way the riddle provides an explanation of Jakobson's mechanistic, impersonal dealings with the sonnets: it is the duty of the critic to disclose the means by which the internal and external, the subliminal and the conscious, dimensions of the text intersect, but by shifting the focus from text to biographical, historical or cultural context, this curious sense of presence and absence, internal and external interfusion will be lost.

The value of preserving this sense of the text as a living, self-generating artefact is that it maintains the status of poetry as the uniquely intrapersonal medium. All other forms of communication are elements of a contextual dialogic process and each speech act or written message necessitates clarification, extension or response, but the poem integrates the internal and external functions of language, it draws addresser and addressee into a continuous pattern of interrelations between meaning and the creation of meaning.

The validity of this model of the poetic function has, particularly in an era governed by poststructuralist scepticism, generated a large number of dismissive responses, but before considering these let us examine the origins of the model in Jakobson's brief career as a poet.

In 1916 a slim volume entitled *Zaumnaja gniga* and edited by Kručenyx was published in Moscow. The title suggests itself as *A Zaum Book*, but, in the *Zaum* manner, the substitution of 'g' for the 'k' of 'kniga' (book) invokes the image of 'nit' (gnida). Jakobson's contribution to this insect-size volume was a poem called 'Razsejanost' ('Distraction') and the text is printed beneath his poetic pseudonym of Aljagrov.

ALJAGROV
mzglybžvuo jix"jan'dr'*ju* čtlěščk xn fja s"p skypol*z*a
a Vt*a*b-dlkni t'japr*a* kak*a*jzědi evreec černil'nica

RAZSEJANOST'.
*u*duša *ja*nki ark*a*n
kank*a*n arm*ja*nk
duša*ja*nki kita*ja*nki
k*i*t y t*a*k i n*i*kaja
arm*ja*k

ètikètka tĭxaja tk*a*n' t*ĭ*k
tk*a*nija k*a*ntik
a o oršat kj*a*nt i tj*u*k
t*a*ki mj*a*k
tmj*a*nty xnj*a*ku škj*a*m
anmj*a* k*y*k'
atr*a*ziksiju nam*e*k um*e*n tamj*a*
mj*a*nk – ušatja
ne avaopostne peredovica
perednik gublicju stop
tljak v vago peredavjas'

This text is certainly untranslatable into English and it continuously and systematically evades any attempt to translate it into
a naturalised metatext in any language. The most useful and
illuminating readings of it are by Rudy and Vallier in *Language,
Poetry and Poetics* (ed. Pomorska *et al.*, 1987). I shall neither
attempt a qualitative judgement nor assess it as a contribution to
the Futurist-modernist canon; its value, for this study, lies in its
intriguingly accurate prediction of how the stylistic and temperamental idiosyncrasies of the 19-year-old poet would become the
agenda of the world-famous literary linguist.

The name Aljagrov preserves the diphthong 'ja' 'Я' of Jakobson – this being the first-person singular of the personal pronoun
'I'. In the original printing the letter 'Я' in the name Aljagrov
is given visual and thematic prominence: АЛЯГРОВ. This foregrounding of the concrete sign is echoed in the repetition of 'ja'
in the title and throughout the complex alliterative-assonantal
structure of the poem, and it is more than likely that Jakobson
would have been reminded of his own work when he detected
anagrammatised traces of 'Sidney' and 'Shakespeare' in their
sonnets. One might also speculate on the relation between his
critical emphasis on centripetal–centrifugal forces in the sonnets
and the inner–outer tensions exhibited in 'Razsejanost'. The centripetal focus of the latter is 'ja'. Each of the most prominent
nominative references – janki (yankee), arkan (lassoo), kankan
(cancan), kitajanki (Chinese), kit (whale), armjak (cloak), ètikètka (label), tkan (textile), tik (tree or twill), tkanija (cloth),
kantik (small edge), tjuk (parcel) – either incorporates the diphthong or echoes some component of a word that does so. These
deictic references to people, items or conditions are in themselves

specific but their alignment along the chaotic syntagmatic chain creates a montage of juxtapositions and random associations. This represents the centrifugal axis of the text. The overall effect is not unlike that created by sonnet 129. In the latter the personal pronoun, the anchoring keystone of centripetal-textual and centrifugal-referential tensions, is absent but implied (someone must have created the observations on lust and mortality). In 'Razsejanost' this uneasy relation between the presence and absence of the speaker is sustained by the reiteration of the sound 'ja' ('I') which at the same time becomes disposed through the montage of deictic and morphophonemic elements. In both texts we experience the incipient feeling of a speech act, a personal gesture which invites response and demands contextualisation but which is continuously unsettled by the acontextual autonomy of its textual features: 'It is the external and internal form of language that makes a poem a poem' (Jakobson).

THE SLIDING SCALE

These two concepts of the internal and the external, foregrounded and set in conflict by Jakobson's poem and by his reading of Shakespeare's sonnet, migrate and metamorphose through Jakobson's entire programme of literary-linguistic writing.

To close this part I shall introduce the concept of the sliding scale. This will serve a number of purposes. It will provide us with a summary of Jakobson's theories of poetic language considered so far and it will enable us to test the validity of his distinction between poetic and non-poetic language. We will employ it in engagements with texts and critical issues that have not featured in Jakobson's writings, and we will use the techniques and strategies of anti-Jakobson theorists to explore its potential flaws and inconsistencies. The following columns of binary oppositions represent the salient features of Jakobsonian poetics.

Internal	External
Textual	Referential
The line	The sentence
Paradigm	Syntagm
Metaphor	Metonymy
Centripetal	Centrifugal

Signans	Signatum
Versus	Proversa
Himself	Another (Baudelaire)
Sound	Meaning

In all types of non-poetic discourse the right-hand column occupies the centre of gravity. All types of internal grammatical deviation are classified or normalised in relation to the governing conventions of the external system. Paradigmatic choice only becomes available within the external specifications of the syntagm. Prose metaphor is effectively governed by the broader circumstances of the text and its metonymic context. The foregrounding of the signans in non-poetic discourse (rhyme or rhythm in prose, alliteration in speech, 'I like Ike', etc.) is reified by the governing imperatives of the prelinguistic context or perceived intention of the text – the signata. But in poetry the relationship between the two columns is equalised – or in Jakobson's terms their mutual interpenetration creates 'equivalence'. Parallelism ensures that grammatical structures – including abnormalities and deviations – become as much a function of the sound patterns of the text as a conspicuous aberration from external convention. Paradigmatic choices are closely interwoven with internal textual echoes and are less dependent on the abstract regulations of the syntagm – Jakobson's theory of the poetic predicates a state of tension between these sets of binary oppositions, and to qualify as a poem a text must maintain, from beginning to end, a productive, interactive tension between two or more of them. The sliding scale can best be represented by drawing a line between the two columns and considering the extent to which a particular text integrates and causes tensions between the binary pairings.

Consider the following line from Wordsworth's 'Resolution and Independence'.

The sky rejoices in the morning's birth.

This involves a classic example of the projection principle. The axis of selection is projected into the axis of combination. The sky and the morning are not human figures but they are given human attributes, and several patterns of tension are created. The external-referential notions of the rejoicing sky and the infant morning are tenable only in relation to the internal-textual mechanisms that have created them (recalling the saint kissing his severed head). But does this short extract enable Wordsworth's complete text to qualify as a poem? For example, it is possible to create a similar effect with a sentence that might open a novel.

The sky seems to rejoice in the birth of the morning.

The most obvious difference between the two statements is that Wordsworth's line satisfies the regulations of metrical regularity that governed most pre-modernist poems, while the prose sentence is, in traditional terms, unmetrical. But, argues the sceptic, what is so important about metricality? Indeed, it is possible to convert Wordsworth's entire text into prose, preserving its metaphoric excursions and maintaining the tale of the Old Man, the pond, the landscape and their effect upon the speaker. The effect, the referential substance of the text, is preserved; all that has changed is its metrical structure. But this is not the case. The sentences that would surround our extract in the prose form would bear primary allegiance to the right-hand column. In the metrical text the stress pattern foregrounds those words which govern the workings of the projection principle – sky, rejoices, morning's, birth – and although each preceding and succeeding line might shift the thematic and referential emphasis away from the image of the morning each will incorporate a parallel version of its metrical–syntactic formula. So even if we could reproduce in prose the referential, narrative structure of 'Resolution and Independence', we would not be able to reproduce the continuous state of tension between key elements of both columns. The prose version would fracture the continuous interdependencies of the sliding scale. In the poem our centre of attention might shift towards the ideational circumstances of the speaker, the pond and the Old Man, but at the same time this referential pattern will never become completely detached from the patterns of repetitions and echoes that govern the internal structure of the text. The sliding scale is a system of retrievals that guarantees an ever-present 'set toward the message as such, focus on the message for its own sake'. At the end of 'Linguistics and Poetics' Jakobson offers a curious anecdote.

A missionary blamed his African flock for walking around with no clothes on. 'And what about yourself?' they pointed to his visage, 'are not you, too, somewhere naked?'. 'Well but that is my face'. 'Yet in us' retorted the natives, 'everywhere it is face'. So in poetry any verbal element is converted into a figure of poetic speech.

(*L in L*, p. 93)

This analogy inadvertently discloses the two principal challenges to the universal validity of the sliding scale. First, is it valid only for specific, cautiously chosen texts? Clearly the sonnet, the anagram and the *Zaum* poem belong on the left-hand side of the scale; each of these forms minimalises the drift towards the external-referential column. But problems arise with forms such as blank and free verse in which syntactic structure and external reference can often supersede the self-focusing functions of the line and structural integrity. Second, the phrase 'Yet in us, everywhere it is face' shifts the focus from the textual object to the a priori conditions and expectations of the perceiver. This is the premise upon which most of the anti-Jakobson strategies are based. We will examine the first problem in Part III and the second in Part II.

Part II

The unwelcoming context

THE SHIFTING PARADIGM

The affiliations and fashions of the literary-critical world are prone to unpredictable and often merciless changes, and it is ironic that the most popular current explanation for these changes should focus on the concept of the paradigm. T. S. Kuhn, historian and philosopher of science, has argued that the 'horizon of expectations' or the paradigm of concepts and assumptions shared by scientists at a particular time will inevitably exhaust itself. The new paradigm will be precipitated as much by the proliferation of unanswered, perhaps unanswerable, questions as by innovative, groundbreaking discoveries. The irony for Jakobsonian poetics is that the celebrated linguistic theorist of the paradigm was to fall victim to a clear manifestation of Kuhn's notion of paradigm shift. The 1958 Indiana University conference on literature and linguistics presented Jakobson with the opportunity to offer the Anglo-American literary-academic establishment his life's work on 'Linguistics and Poetics'. Prior to this the strikingly similar objectives of the New Critics and the Formalists had, with the assistance of Erlich (1955) and Wellek (1949), existed as a tantalising, but somewhat marginal, possibility. The final sentence of Jakobson's paper was like eyes meeting across a crowded room. 'All of us here, however, definitely realise that a linguist deaf to the poetic function of language and a literary scholar indifferent to linguistic problems and unconversant with linguistic methods are equally flagrant anachronisms' (*L in L*, p. 94). The scientists of literary raw material (the linguists and their theoretical forebears, the Formalists) suddenly found themselves consulting the same agenda of objectives and potential techniques as the scholars and aestheticians (the American New Critics and their slightly eccentric British cousins).

Read through Thomas Sebeok's (1960) volume on the Indiana conference and you will encounter an air of heady enthusiasm. The literary linguists (Jakobson, Stankiewicz, Hill, Chatman, etc.) and the critics (Wimsatt, Beardsley, Wellek, I. A. Richards, Hollander, etc.), if not exactly speaking with the same voice, were at least addressing the same questions and objectives: what is literature and how does it work? These would be pursued and interrogated throughout the following three decades by the conference contributors and by many others, but rather than signalling the sublime realisation of the contemporary paradigm's 'horizon of expectations' the conference was effectively its curtain call. The new paradigm was about to arrive. The poststructuralists were waiting in the wings, and within a decade the notion of the literary text as something whose structure and function was distinguishable from practically everything else was no longer on the agenda. The energies and motivating forces of critical writing shifted from a centripetal emphasis upon the constitution of the literary text to the centrifugal forces that sweep such artefacts into the diffuse and untidy world of deconstruction, gender studies, psychoanalysis, historicism. The effect of all this was to lend a degree of consensual authority to those who wished to disclose the flaws and inconsistencies of Jakobson's thesis. His detractors could lean comfortably on the shifted paradigm: it was not just that Jakobson's answers were invalid; more that his questions were grounded upon discredited and irrelevant premises.

Attacks on Jakobson's ideas and methods have come from a number of sources – he even appears with Saussure in Derrida's seminal deconstructive text, *Of Grammatology* – but the best known literary critical demolitions occur in Riffaterre (1966), Culler (1975) and Pratt (1977). The agenda and the techniques of these sceptics are varied, but the Introduction to Pratt's *Toward a Speech Act Theory of Literary Discourse* provides their effective manifesto.

Over the past decade there has developed a growing consensus among Anglo-American critics that the traditional structuralist opposition between poetic and non-poetic language is an inadequate foundation on which to construct a linguistic theory of literature. Theoretically, there is no reason to expect that the body of utterances we call 'literature' should be sys-

tematically distinguishable from other utterances on the basis
of intrinsic grammatical or textual properties.

(1977, p. xi)

As a self-appointed advocate for Jakobsonian theory, I can quite
easily unsettle Pratt's thesis. Poetry, good or bad, is intrinsically
different from other discourses, because it uniquely consists of
two structural continua, the line and the sentence. The title
of that rare and briefly fashionable phenomenon, the prose
poem, testifies to the validity of my definition – the text calls
itself a prose poem in order to warn the reader of its claims to
be something that, in verifiable empirical and formal terms, it is
not. Jakobson: 'Measure of sequences [the line] is a device that,
outside the poetic function, finds no application in language' (*L
in L*, p. 72). However, a problem arises when we attempt to state
how the poetic double pattern creates effects that are essentially
different from those generated by other linguistic discourses. The
double pattern and the sliding scale exist, but what exactly do
they do? We will begin the investigation of this problem with a
critic who, in most respects, dwells in the pro-Jakobson camp. In
1962 Samuel Levin published a short monograph called *Linguistic
Structures in Poetry* and this can be regarded as the first attempt
to apply Jakobson's so-called projection principle ('the poetic
function projects') to a wide variety of English poems. Levin
recategorised Jakobson's notions of metonymic–metaphoric projection and metrical–grammatical parallelism within the general
poetic activity of 'coupling'. Coupling is what occurs when the
two elements of the double pattern intersect. In a later essay,
'The Conventions of Poetry' (1971), Levin named the two axes
of the double pattern as the cognitive and the conventional
features of poetry. The cognitive features of any text or speech
act – in short, the meaning-generating elements shared by all
linguistic discourses, i.e. syntax, lexis, semantics, phonemics, etc.
– are the salient structures which enable us to attain a basic level
of understanding. The conventional features are those that poetry
does not share with other discourses, essentially the division of
text into lines, with subdivisions consisting of metrical pattern,
rhyme scheme, interlineal sound pattern, etc. Consider again the
closing couplet of Shakespeare's sonnet 129.

All this the world well knows yet none knows well,
To shun the heaven that leads men to this hell.

The cognitive features of the couplet are determined primarily by its correspondence with lexico-grammatical rules, while its conventions are determined by the abstract formula of two rhyming iambic pentameters. The most problematic element of this structural model is the question of how these two dimensions of language intersect. For example, the regulations of the conventional element specify that the seventh syllable of an iambic pentameter should receive a lower stress value than the sixth or the eighth. If the reciter or interpreter were to ignore this rule and give principal accentual and thematic value to either 'men' or 'this' rather than 'to', we would therefore encounter an instance of what Levin refers to as coupling, the intersection of the cognitive and conventional dimensions of the text. Alternative rhetorical emphases are, of course, made available in prose discourses, but in the sonnet any disturbance of the balance between the cognitive and the conventional structures reverberates through the entire text. By choosing between 'men', 'to' and 'this' we are not simply judging which foregrounded nexus of meaning is most appropriate to the perceived intentional or situational context, because each choice will register differently in relation to the intrinsic textual pattern of conventional features. A stress reversal in the final line will either complement or subvert the stress patterns, and as a consequence the meaning, of the preceding lines. And we should here be reminded of Jakobson's double-edged use of the term the 'poetic function': the functional (cognitive) status of the text can never remain immune from its structural (conventional) dimension. The problem referred to above arises from a disagreement between Levin and Jakobson on the relative signifying or enabling roles of the cognitive and conventional features, and, as we shall see, this lies at the heart of the pro- and anti-Jakobson debate. Consider Levin's definition of poetic conventions.

> . . . the essential fact about the conventions is that even though they comprise patterns or structures of language elements, the patterns or structures so constituted have no *linguistic* significance. Another way to put this is to say that a structure has linguistic significance if it figures in a grammatical or phonological rule, and that the structures entered into by the conventional features figure in no such rule.

(1971, p. 177)

In the abstract, Levin has a case, since neither an iambic pentameter nor a rhyme scheme can be regarded as a grammatical formula, but the actuality of the sonnet makes his distinction more uncertain and problematic. Following Levin's formula, we could claim that the foregrounding of 'men' or 'this' causes no violation of a grammatical rule. But Jakobson would claim that in the sonnet there is no clear distinction between the grammatical rule and the metrical rule: the syntactic structure of the text is determined by its conventional structure to such a degree that any disturbance of this parallelism becomes just as apparent and has the same effect upon signification as an instance of grammatical deviation.

This disagreement between Jakobson and Levin on the role and status of cognitive and conventional features might seem to involve only a slight adjustment to the otherwise stable concepts of the double pattern and the sliding scale, but Levin's approach to linguistic and poetic structures is the thin end of a theoretical wedge which, from the 1960s to the 1980s, was driven into the methods and objectives of those critics who attempted to specify the intrinsic nature of literary and non-literary texts.

To understand properly the premise upon which Levin's model is founded we should return to the concept of critical naturalisation. The conventional features of poetry are naturalised when we translate our initial impression of the multidimensional effects of a poem – its rhyme scheme or its metrical pattern in conflict with its syntactic movement for instance – into a prose description of how these effects occur and of the variety of meanings generated from them.

Consider the opening lines of Pope's 'Epistle to Dr Arbuthnot'.

Shut, shut the door good John! fatigued I said
Tye up the knocker, say I'm sick, I'm dead.

Reading these lines, we can discern a peculiar tension between the progressive, syntactic movement of the couplet and the extra-syntactic echo of 'said' in 'dead'. Logically there should be no correspondence between Pope's straightforward order to his servant and the potentially disruptive juxtaposition of life (speech) and death. We could naturalise or demystify this tension by pointing out that Pope's ability to vocalise his own posthumous condition imbues what would otherwise be an unengaging problem of domestic order with a degree of irony and dark comedy. Levin would argue that in doing so we have effectively subjugated the conventional element, rhyme, beneath the overarching determinism of the cognitive dimension: rhyme has no intrinsic 'linguistic significance'; it only becomes significant when we translate it into its explanatory, cognitive counterpart. Jakobson states that 'In poetry, any conspicuous similarity in sound is evaluated in respect to similarity of dissimilarity in meaning' (*L in L*, p. 87); that 'the phonic equivalence of rhyming words prompts the question of semantic similarity or contrast' (*Fundamentals*, p. 96). The problematic terms here are 'evaluated' and 'prompts'. In non-poetic discourse the need or the desire to evaluate the relative signifying properties of two words or statements is prompted primarily by external, circumstantial factors. If someone were to ask for an explanation of the semantic difference between 'said' and 'dead', irrespective of their use by Pope, it would be pointed out that their phonic similarity is an accident whose potential for misapprehension is cancelled by their consonantal/vocalic difference. We distinguish 'buck' from 'puck' because the opposition of 'voiced/unvoiced' makes it possible to distinguish between two 'plosives' (/p/ is unvoiced, /b/ is voiced). As Jakobson stresses (see *Fundamentals of Language, passim*), in non-poetic discourse sameness of sound is a subelement of the activating principle of phonic difference. 'A phoneme, as Sapir remarked, "has no singleness of reference". All phonemes denote nothing more than mere OTHERNESS' (*Fundamentals*, p. 22). Indeed, the mechanism of the syntagm, the primary mechanism of linguistic constructions, depends upon our ability to distinguish between the sounds and consequently the meanings of successive words. By foregrounding the phonic similarity between 'said' and 'dead' Pope has projected the principle of equivalence from the axis of selection (sameness or different) into the axis of combination (continuous difference). Jakobson and Levin agree on the fact that the conventional features of poetry (based on phonic echoes) interfere with the principle of sign differentiation upon which non-poetic discourse depends. They disagree on the relation between the internal textual devices that create such effects and the normative power of the evaluative processes that enable us to make sense of them. Levin (1971): 'I would suggest that rhyme interacts with the phonetic remainders or unrhyming parts of the rhyming words – thus in *room/foam*, the rhyme interacts with the non-rhyming opposition between *r* and *f*' (p. 189).

Thus, to make sense of rhyme, and by implication all types of phonic correspondences, including metre, the reader must, paradoxically, ignore their constituent features – in effect re-establish the differential power of the sign above its contingent sameness. Jakobson, as we have seen in the previous part, maintains that while the poetic function can be documented and analysed, it cannot, or rather it should not, be translated, naturalised, returned to the differential sphere of non-poetic discourse that it patently rejects. Such a belief presents literary theorists, of whatever designation, with a variety of problems. Most significantly it places severe limitations on what can legitimately be said about poems: on the one hand we should be aware that poetry draws upon the same raw material as all other kinds of linguistic discourse; on the other it deploys this material in such a way as to render its signifying function just as immune from comprehensive, normative translation as the statue or the picture. In short, we can talk about the structural means by which poems create their effects, but these effects are enclosed within a private, intuitive interaction between text and reader. Jakobson's thesis echoes what most people would regard as the New Critical manifesto, John Crowe Ransom's 'Criticism Inc.' (1938).

> The poet wishes to defend his object's existence against its enemies, and the critic wishes to know what he is doing and how. The critic should find in the poem a total poetic or individual object which tends to be universalised, but is not permitted to suffer this fate.
>
> (p. 238)

During the two decades between 'Criticism Inc.' and the Indiana conference Anglo-American critics had wandered uneasily between a respect for the untranslatable poem and the more pressing disciplinary and educational prerogative of explaining it – a condition reflected in Wimsatt and Beardsley's precise yet indecisive account of 'The Intentional Fallacy' (1946). Jakobson, in the 'Linguistics and Poetics' paper and in subsequent employments of its principles, seemed to offer an impressive technical framework for the investigation of the mysterious otherness of the poetic, but the mood of the new paradigm was very different from that of the old.

Michael Riffaterre's 'Describing Poetic Structures: Two Approaches to Baudelaire's "Les Chats" ' (1966) offered two counter-arguments to Jakobson's and Lévi-Strauss's treatment of Baudelaire's sonnet. Riffaterre acknowledged that Jakobson's and Lévi-Strauss's approach was precise and in purely empirical terms correct, and that they had successfully identified the essential grammar of the sonnet, but he claimed that their structural model was an entirely inaccurate account of the reader's experience. He argued that by giving roughly equal attention to how each conventional element of the double pattern, primarily metrical structure and sound pattern, interacts with its cognitive counterpart in syntax, grammar or metaphorical play, they had disclosed what he called a Superpoem, which exists but which bears no resemblance to the real experience of reading it. He insisted that, although textual foregroundings could be identified in practically any part of the poem, only a small number of these will register as functions of the reader's understanding of what the poem means. He answered Jakobson's disclosure of the Superpoem with his own disclosure of the Superreader. This individual would be able to step outside the intense text–reader relation of the communicative circuit and select those elements of the poem's structure which, to him, seem to intersect with such elements as his knowledge of the conditions and circumstances of the text's composition, the ex-cathedra beliefs and practices of its creator, its position within the intertextual langue of poems and non-poetic texts, and the interpretive disclosures already made and discussed by friends and colleagues. This hypothesis was by no means a recipe for subjectivist chaos, although one might be forgiven for recalling a similar set of interpretive conditions which Jakobson, and his fellow Formalists, had rejected as a useful basis for literary critical work. Russian scholarship, at the turn of the century, 'obeyed all the laws of causerie, skipping blithly from topic to topic, from lyrical effusions on the elegance of forms to anecdotes from the artist's life, from psychological truisms to questions concerning philosophical significance and social environment' ('On Realism in Art', 1921, *L in L*, p. 19). Riffaterre's 1960s Superreader might be prone to pluralistic, interdisciplinary tendencies, but he/she is more the cool polydidactic processor than the blithe *fin de siècle* dilettante. A more familiar and recent manifestation of this presence has emerged from the theories of reader-response criticism. The post-1960s Superreader is a member of Stanley Fish's 'interpretive community', a person whose 'literary competence' will guide him/

her through the dense jungle of textual patterns, contextual interfaces and interpretive strategies. Before proceeding into a detailed consideration of how Jakobson's theories can be defended against such a well-equipped individual, we need to specify the terms and conditions of combat.

What Levin's, Riffaterre's (and, as we shall see, Fish's) interpretive models have in common is an emphasis upon context rather than text. Levin defers to the normative context of cognitive linguistic features. These are supplemented in poems by their conventional counterparts, but in the sphere of naturalisation the latter are marginalised by the desire to make sense of the nonsensical. Riffaterre's notion of context involves the reader as a casuistic middleman between what the poem is and what is known about the poem. The potential for irrelevance or perverse subjectivity – whether, for instance, there is a correlation between the prevalence of cat fleas in late nineteenth-century France, Baudelaire's laundry bills (if extant) and his poetic engagement with 'les chats' – is curtailed by the general rule that only the obvious thematic emphases of the text should determine the corresponding features of its contextual orbit. 'Each point of the text that holds up the superreader is tentatively considered a component of the poetic structure' (p. 204). By 'holds up' Riffaterre refers to the points of intersection between a priori or contextual perceptions of what the text is and does and its corresponding internal features. Riffaterre does not differ from Jakobson on the validity of the latter's method of analysis; rather, he argues that the relevance of disclosed features should be partly determined by the right-hand column of the sliding scale – the contextual dimension.

THE DIAGRAM

Jakobson's model of the relation between text and context has been widely debated (see Scholes, pp. 24–7 and Hawkes, pp. 85–6), and usually misinterpreted. Jakobson's two six-factor diagrams of the communicative circuit emerged into the arena of critical theory through their appearance in 'Linguistics and Poetics', but, like most of that paper, they had been a vital constituent of his lifetime programme of linguistic investigation. His principal objective was to provide a methodological framework within which the intrinsic properties of poetic and non-poetic texts can be discussed.

CONTEXT
(referential)

MESSAGE
(poetic)

ADDRESSER ————————————————————— ADDRESSEE
(emotive)   (conative)

CONTACT
(phatic)

CODE
(metalingual)

The format reproduced above is the one that Jakobson used in his 1956 paper on 'Metalanguage as a Linguistic Problem' (*SW III*, pp. 113–21). In 'Linguistics and Poetics' he offers two separate diagrams (one consisting of the higher-case words, the other of their bracketed, lower-case counterparts). The 1956 format is in my opinion the more effective since Jakobson's intention is to consider the interactive relation between elements of each six-part framework, but I shall refer to the higher-case elements as diagram 1 and the lower-case as diagram 2.

Diagram 1 is a relatively straightforward model of any act of linguistic communication. Consider our present circumstances. The assumed context of this discourse is the field of linguistics and literary criticism, a field whose oral and written exchanges are usually limited to the more specific context of higher education. The context will often determine the code and in this instance I (addresser) assume that you (addressee) have become inured to the stylistic and interdisciplinary codes of talking and writing about literature. Contact is a further subdivision of context and code, referring specifically to the means by which a particular communicative act is effected: in this case it is written rather than oral, with the likely and probably unfortunate condition that you cannot interrupt me to seek further clarification of my message. The message is the substance of the information transferred from addresser to addressee. These six designations could easily be adapted to, say, the purchase of a railway ticket. I, addresser, will speak (contact) to the addressee within the usually self-determined context of the station. The code is variable within a number of agreed limitations – 'Ticket, return, London' would preserve the message, but would deviate sufficiently from the usual locutionary format to indicate impoliteness or urgency on the part of the addresser.

Diagram 1 is effectively a means of describing the general circumstances and mechanisms of linguistic communication – the right-hand column of the sliding scale. Diagram 2 refers to the intrinsic properties of the text itself ('text' in this sense incorporates the oral speech act) and to the immediate effects created by these properties. And here we encounter the startling, and some would say disturbing, thesis embodied in this model: the poem is the only independent, self-determined textual object. In fact, if we define text as an autonomous structure whose inherent properties separate it from other texts and from the incursions of linguistic and non-linguistic contexts, then the only real texts are poems.

Consider the pairing of message with poetic. This is consistent with the principle of the poetic function as the 'set toward the message as such, focus on the message for its own sake'. One might argue that Jakobson pairs these two elements simply as a means of promoting, rather than validating, his own model of the poetic function (see Pratt, pp. 30–2), and we can test this charge by examining the precise relationship between the two diagrams. For example, the code is paired with the metalingual function, which means that within any given linguistic code it is possible to refer to the same thing in two different ways. In the opinion of most structural and sociolinguists and cultural theorists poetry represents a single dimension of the broader linguistic code and, like its generically separate counterparts, is subject to metalinguistic substitution or paraphrase. However, in Jakobson's model our assumption that we can translate a poem into a surrogate metatext is invalid because of the intrinsic, non-transferable substance of the double pattern. Similarly, we could argue that the contact function displaces the autonomy of its poetic counterpart: the oral performance of a poem demands the presence of addresser and addressee (even if the latter is an externalised version of the former, in the case of reading to yourself). Jakobson describes the phatic function as 'serving to establish, to prolong or to discontinue communication, to check whether the channel works ("Hello do you hear me?")' (*SW VII*, p. 115).

Hence the phatic-contact function enables the addresser effectively to suspend the information-carrying elements of the circuit
(context, message and code), and speak directly to the addressee.
In poetry, however, any phatic interjection remains an element
of the double pattern. Jakobson uses the example of Antony's
'Lend me your ears!' Such a channel-checking enquiry might
appear in any discourse but only in blank verse is it bound within
the extra-syntactic pattern of the iambic pentameter.

The pairing of context with referential corresponds with Jakobson's double-edged use of context as an element both of the
combinatory, syntagmatic chain and of the prelinguistic situation
which in some way affects the construction of a statement (see
Part I, pp. 12–13). In all types of discourse the former can never
remain immune from the influence of the latter, but in poetry
the contextual-referential dimension is more a construct of the
internal textual pattern. In non-poetic discourse the latter will
defer to the former.

To summarise: In diagram 1 the message is the primary focus
of the linguistic exchange, and its substance can be affected,
often determined, by the co-present functions of context, contact
and code. With diagram 2 this hierarchy is reversed. The poetic
function is the dominant, organising feature of context-referential, contact-phatic, code-metalingual: each of these is interwoven
with the double pattern. Consequently, in non-poetic exchanges
the message is a potentially diffuse, transformable entity, at the
mercy of a variety of linguistic and prelinguistic determinants,
while in poems the poetic function of the double pattern binds
these same determinants into the message. One could argue that
diagram 1 corresponds to the right-hand column of the sliding
scale and diagram 2 to the left.

The transposition of the addresser–addressee relation with
emotive and conative effects can be explained in terms of this
integrating function of poetic language. If I were to ask for my
rail ticket in metre and rhyme I would displace the practical,
utilitarian, transparent elements of context, contact and code and
shift the focus towards a more personal, enclosed circuit in which
the emotive (addresser-oriented) and conative (addressee-
oriented) functions bind the two presences together as elements
of the message. The real presences of traveller and ticket-seller
are at once present and absent in the same way that the real
John Donne, apparently addressing his lover, is also the creator

of an autonomous structure which itself creates another addresser and another addressee. Jakobson:

> The supremacy of the poetic function over the referential function does not obliterate the reference but makes it ambiguous. The double sensed message finds correspondence in a split addresser, in a split addressee, as well as in a split reference. . . .
>
> (*L in L*, p. 85)

It is this notion of the 'split addressee' which features most prominently as the point of division between Jakobson and his critics. Riffaterre correctly points out that many of the structural constituents detected by Jakobson and Lévi-Strauss 'cannot possibly be perceived by the reader; these constituents must therefore remain alien to the poetic structure, which is supposed to emphasize the form of the message, to make it more "visible", more compelling' (p. 195). In short, the average, or even the above-average, reader of 'Les Chats' does not possess a sufficient level of cognitive and ratiocinative competence to process all of the multidimensional effects of the sonnet. As a consequence the 'Superreader' must draw upon his/her awareness of the broader context of the poem (the poet's biography, his other works, contemporary stylistic convention, etc.) and balance this against its most obvious internal correspondences. In doing so the Superreader re-establishes the dominance of diagram 1 (non-poetic) over diagram 2 (poetic). Similarly, Levin argues that the conventional features of the text (diagram 2) can only be properly naturalised when subordinated to the normative capacities of the cognitive, linguistic elements (diagram 1). However, there are a number of intrinsic flaws in these arguments. If, as Riffaterre and Levin contend, the putative, constructed presence of the listener is but one element of the broader perspective commanded by the reader-critic, then the consequent model of the poem as speech act must involve a similar conflation of poet and speaker – indeed Riffaterre refers to 'the speaker – the poet' (p. 202). The speaking presence of any poem, particularly a poem which employs such an intense formal structure as the sonnet, is, as Jakobson states, an ambiguous figure. Just as the mental equipment of the average reader is incapable of decoding in an instant every element of the poem's formal design, so the creative faculties of the poet are incapable of encoding, in a single speech act, this same complicated artefact. Riffaterre claims that any interpretation 'depends on elements exterior to the act of communication' (p. 203), by which he means that pronouns, spatio-temporal shifters and deictic references to objects and circumstances enable us to construct a context for the poetic speech act. But he should also be aware that there is a constant shift between the stability of these circumstantial conditions and their contrived unreality. On the one hand, we might visualise the type of individual and the kind of situation which would produce a short disquisition on the similarity between cats and human beings; on the other, the validity of such a real-world construct is cancelled by the self-focused nature of the text.

In Jakobson's model addresser and addressee are at once textual devices, serving a similar purpose to such impersonal devices as metre, rhyme and metaphor, and tangible human presences. When we interpret, naturalise or demystify a poem, we necessarily attempt to reconcile the effects created within the text with those that the referential features of the text enable us to construct, and Jakobson maintains that throughout this process we should not allow one element to override the other. In their attempts to invalidate his methods, Jakobson's detractors have cunningly allowed these elements to do just this.

CULLER AND 'THE FLEA'

The most effective critique of Jakobson's theory of poetry occurred in Jonathan Culler's *Structuralist Poetics* (1975). Its effectiveness is due more to the timing of this publication than to its comprehensive validity. By the mid–1970s the literary studies faculties in Anglo-American higher education were undergoing what is often referred to as a crisis. Structuralism was half a century old and poststructuralism was already well established: what was required, both by students and by the majority of academics, were texts that provided reliable guides to these bizarre continental practices. Sadly, most readers' encounters with 'Jakobson' are via Culler (and others) rather than through a direct reading of Jakobson's own work. Jakobson himself, perhaps sensing Culler's status as a trusted spokesman for the new paradigm, was displeased. Culler's writings are 'equally as pretentious as amateurish, demonstrate an inability to catch the essence of . . . the general structuration of a poem. Critics of Culler's mold conceive their only task to be one of criticising and discarding any rudiments of analytic enquiry into poetic works, without undertaking any positive steps themselves' (*SW III*, pp. 787–8).

This might sound like the embittered complaint of an unseated elder statesman, but, as I shall show, Jakobson has a point.

There is a curious inconsistency in Culler's book, which will become apparent to the reader who moves directly from Chapter 3 on 'Jakobson's Poetic Analyses' to Chapter 8 on 'Poetics and the Lyric'. Reading the former, one can only assume that Culler has precategorised Jakobson as a particular type of structural linguist and has subsequently ignored what Jakobson's work actually involves. For example:

> If one assumes that linguistics provides a method for the discovery of poetic patterns, then one is likely to blind oneself to the ways in which grammatical patterns actually operate in poetic texts, for the simple reason that poems contain, by virtue of the fact that they are read as poems, structures other than the grammatical and the resulting interplay may give the grammatical structures a function which is not at all what the linguist expected.
>
> (p. 73)

This passage combines blatant misinterpretation with an unquestioning trust in the dogma of the new paradigm. Jakobson's entire programme of literary linguistics is based on his belief that poems do indeed consist of structures that are 'other than' grammatical and that the 'resulting interplay' will produce unexpected effects. Culler cites the passage from 'Poetry of Grammar and Grammar of Poetry' in which Jakobson claims that an 'exhaustive, unbiased, total description' of the poem's constituent features will enable the critic to disclose unpredictable patterns from predictable data (*SW III*, pp. 92–3), but he seems to think that it refers only to the mechanical documentation of grammatical structures, when in fact it celebrates the unforeseeable results of the interplay between the material and the signifying functions of language. A clue to the reason for Culler's misreading is his statement that poems contain structures other than the grammatical only 'by virtue of the fact that they are read as poems'. This is the pronouncement of an extremist version of Riffaterre's Superreader: nothing is intrinsic, all is conferred by the power of interpretive competence. Culler compounds this disclosure of critical correctness in his assault upon Jakobsonian method, or at least upon what he believes to be Jakobsonian method. He quotes from the opening page of the 'Postscriptum' to Jakobson's *Questions de poétique*, renames the four sentences as 'strophes', sets about charting the distribution of grammatical and morphological figures (in the same way that Jakobson treated the sonnets of Baudelaire and Shakespeare) and concludes that 'this sort of numerical symmetry cannot in itself serve as a defining characteristic of the poetic function of language' (p. 65). True, it accounts for only one dimension of the double pattern. He then claims that 'the same kind of problem is encountered at the level of sound patterns' and argues that the sound patterns within any given text only constitute a purposive structured framework when they are 'authorized' to do so by the particular method or disposition of the analyst. What Culler does not mention is that the abstract structure of the sonnet form effectively foregrounds and specifies the interpretation of grammar and sound pattern. If he had, he would not have gone on to 'give proper value', 'put a different construction on Jakobson's definition of the poetic function'. Which is: 'as will be obvious in the light of Jakobson's analytical procedures, repetition of similar constituents may be observed in any text and thus cannot in itself serve as the distinguishing feature of the poetic function' (p. 66). Culler argues that it is the 'orientations with which one approaches' a text which give 'phonological repetition [the] function of posing the question of semantic relationship'. Apparently, it is only because we are oriented to the text as poem that we are prompted to investigate the semantic properties of rhyme words at line endings, and this same orientation prevents us from doing so with random sound patterns in prose. Culler's presiding assumption is this: 'The work has structure and meaning because it is read in a particular way, because these potential properties, latent in the object itself, are actualised by the theory of discourse applied in the act of reading' (p. 114). The particular way of reading poems, validated and promoted by the late twentieth-century Western critical establishment, is described by Culler in 'Poetics of the Lyric'. He concedes that the formal patterns of poems exist, but he insists that they function as signals, enabling factors which set in motion the reader's sophisticated mechanisms of literary competence. Deictics, for instance, 'do not refer us to an external content but force us to construct a fictional situation of the utterance'

(p. 166). The organic whole or totality of a poem is not an objective, empirical fact; rather it is a 'literary version of the Gestaltist law of Prägnanz: that the richest organisation compatible with the data is to be preferred ... that the reader will not feel satisfied with an interpretation unless it organises a text according to one of these formal models of unity' (p. 174).

I give so much space to Culler's thesis because he serves as a respected spokesman for the collective wisdom of the new paradigm (*Structuralist Poetics* remains in print and features as a recommended introductory text in most courses on critical theory and history), and more significantly because he exposes the dangers of a biased and selective reading of Jakobson. For Culler the poetic addresser is a construct, a result of the reader's careful reconstitution of a persona and a situation from an arbitrary pattern of effects and devices. For Jakobson the addresser is both a real and an unreal presence.

A test case is called for and I shall use Donne's lyric 'The Flea'. I have chosen this poem because it poses uncomfortable questions both for Jakobson's two-diagram model of the poetic function, and for Culler's thesis that the latent properties of a text are 'actualised' by the applied theory of discourse.

The Flea

Marke but this flea, and marke in this,
How little that which thou deny'st me is;
Mee it suck'd first, and now sucks thee,
And in this flea, our two bloods mingled bee;
Confesse it, this cannot be said
A sinne, or shame, or losse of maidenhead,
    Yet this enjoyes before it wooe,
    And pamper'd swells with one blood made of two,
    And this, alas, is more than wee would doe.

Oh stay, three lives in one flea spare,
Where wee almost, nay more than maryed are:
This flea is you and I, and this
Our marriage bed, and marriage temple is;
Though parents grudge, and you, w'are met,
And cloysterd in these living walls of Jet.
    Though use make thee apt to kill mee,

> Let not to this, selfe murder added bee,
> And sacrilege, three sinnes in killing three.

Cruell and sodaine, has thou since
Purpled thy naile, in blood of innocence?
In what could this flea guilty bee,
Except in that drop which it suckt from thee?
Yet thou triumph'st, and saist that thou
Find'st not thy selfe, nor mee the weaker now;
> 'Tis true, then learne how false, feares bee;
> Just so much honor, when thou yeeld'st to mee,
> Will wast, as this flea's death tooke life from thee.

To appreciate fully the relation between this text and Jakobson's theory of the poetic we should consult his 1956 paper on 'Shifters, Verbal Categories and the Russian Verb' (*SW II*, pp. 130–47). Shifters occupy the same linguistic category as deictic features, the elements that enable us to specify the conditions and circumstances of a speech act when these are not immediately apparent – the most obvious instance of this being the poem, which is encountered in the absence of the original addresser and beyond the time and place of its creation. Jakobson draws up an ontological plan of the events and participants of any speech act.

> In order to classify the verbal categories two basic distinctions are to be observed:
> 1) speech itself (^{s}), and its topic, the narrated matter (^{n});
> 2) the event itself (E), and any of its participants (P), whether 'performer' or 'undergoer'.
> Consequently, four items are to be distinguished: a narrated event (E^n), a speech event (E^s), a participant of the narrated event (P^n), and a participant of the speech event (P^s), whether addresser or addressee.

> (*SW II*, p. 133)

Donne's poem creates a very unsettling relationship between these four items. We, as readers, are at once the participants of the narrated event and participants in the speech event, in the sense that the personal pronouns and the present tense oblige us to become participants in order to become interpreters. This is consistent with Jakobson's notion of the 'split' poetic addresser and addressee. Now let us proceed with a reading of the text according to Jakobson's principle of the poetic function.

The most prominent and distinctive deictic features of this lyric are its interpersonal references – the dense and almost obsessive emphasis upon personal pronouns, I, thee, you, me – and its use of very specific locative phrases – this flea, it sucked, now sucks. The locative phrases are temporal as well as spatial determinants in that they consistently relocate the immediate past and future in the present; everything done both by the flea and the addressee takes place within seconds of the addresser's response to them. By identifying the main deictic features of the poem we provide ourselves with a framework to chart the interwoven metaphoric–metonymic strategies of the addresser. The two people, male addresser and female addressee, and the flea function as the three principal components of the figure. Stanza 1 maintains an allegiance to the metonymic rather than the metaphoric axis. The key phrase is 'our two bloods mingled be'. This statement of verifiable fact allows the speaker to propose a daring but somehow logical connection between one form of physical union, the flea-bite, and the sexual act – synecdoche in action. In stanza 2 metaphor replaces metonymy, with the flea proposed as at once a token and symbol of their relationship: 'marriage bed and marriage temple', 'living walls of jet', and, more disturbingly, as a kind of contractual joining of their fate, 'three sins in killing three'. In stanza 3, after the woman has succeeded in swatting the vehicle of the metaphor, the male voice has to reinterpret his own metaphoric propositions and return to a more metonymic pattern – the flea bite and the death of the flea are physical acts which neither harm nor dishonour their participants; nor, he argues, would the proposed sexual act.

Donne deliberately and self-consciously foregrounds the apparently improvisational and spontaneous nature of the utterance and in doing so he creates a paradox. On the one hand, the entire text seems to defer to the contextual, referential function of the communicative model. The verbal shifts between metonymy and metaphor are responses to prelinguistic events, and we should note that this imagined existential continuum is given greater psychological plausibility by the addresser's almost desperate deployment of extravagant metaphor in stanza 2, the point at which the substantive premise for his pseudo-logic (the flea) is most seriously threatened. On the other hand, it is entirely implausible to imagine that the deployment of such a complex structure in rhyme and metre is spontaneous. This further complicates the relationship between a narrated event and a speech event, since both the participants and the related matter become constructs of the pattern of textual devices.

For example, in stanza 2 we encounter an instance of grammatical deviation.

> Though parents grudge, and you, w'are met,
> And cloysterd in these living walls of Jet.

The second-person pronoun and its connective, 'and you' are shifted outside the more conventional grouping of second- and third-person forms antecedent to the verb, 'though you and your parents grudge'. We might explain this as a mimetic effect, a paratactic slippage betraying the sense of pressure felt by the speaking presence as he attempts to rescue his linguistic strategies from the woman's act of rejection. In doing so we would have drawn upon the contact–code–context functions of diagram 1 to explain one element of the message. But we would then have to remind ourselves that this real-world continuum is interwoven with its textual counterpart: the grammatical deviation is syntactic (real), but it is normalised by its maintenance of the metrical (textual) pattern. 'And you' fits easily into the iambic-octosyllabic structure of the line (we can assume that 'w'are' is, in contemporary fashion, elided as a single, unstressed syllable). This tension between elements of the poem anchored to the contextual situation of the utterance and elements that function as constituents of the text is continuous and unremitting. Consider the rhyme scheme.

The semantic–phonemic–referential syntheses are quite dazzling. On two occasions the locative term 'this' rhymes with the emphatic 'is', and there is a habitual, almost urgent configuration of the speaker's projected ideal, 'be', and the pronouns that allow the reader to construct the situation of the utterance: 'sucks thee' – 'mingled be'; 'kill me' – 'added be' – 'killing three'; 'fears be' – 'to me' – 'life from thee'. The pattern is complicated by the use of 'flea' as an internal counterpoint to 'be', 'me' and 'thee'. The centripetal-textual and centrifugal-referential forces identified by Jakobson in Shakespeare's sonnet are here set against each other with cunning precision. In the essay on 'Shifters' Jakobson isolates personal pronouns as a special type of semiotic unit (pp. 131–2). Like all other words they are symbol; a term borrowed from C. S. Peirce, which specifies the sign as associated with its referential object only by a conventional rule. But they are also indices (another of Peirce's terms) which are in existential relation to the objects they represent – the most widely used example being the painted, pointing finger on the signpost. So personal pronouns (in Jakobson's terms 'indexical symbols') require a physical presence or its imagined counterpart (its existential relation) yet cannot properly function without the conventional system of symbols: it is impossible to imagine an 'I' or 'you' without also connoting a specific physical presence, and it is impossible to make this signifier–signified connection without also prefiguring a relation between presence and condition, I am . . . , I want . . . , I feel . . . etc. In the rhyme scheme of 'The Flea' we encounter a continuous tension between the indexical function of pronouns – that which further validates the presence of addresser and addressee – and their material function as symbols. The former specifies the contingent actuality as the speech act while the latter binds them into a contrived, unspontaneous system of phonic correspondences.

Even the stanzaic structure of the poem seems specifically designed to unsettle the relation between the communicative circuits of Jakobson's two diagrams. The non-verbal space between each stanza emphasises the dependence of the argument upon unpredictable circumstances and events (diagram 1) while the internal structure of each stanza foregrounds preplanning on the part of the addresser: the complex system of three couplets of eight and ten syllables terminated by a triplet of two octosyllabic lines and one pentameter is anything but circumstantial and spontaneous (diagram 2, poetic = message).

To summarise, we as readers are shifted between these two separate yet interwoven models of the communicative circuit. We have to situate ourselves, at least partly, in the position of the addressee whose non-verbal gestures determine the structure of the message, while at the same time we are confronted with an addresser whose self-conscious disclosure of preplanning transforms the addressee into an unreal textual figure. And we should here recall Jakobson's claim that it is 'the external and internal form of language that makes a poem a poem'. 'The Flea' does indeed disrupt all normal rules of the dialogic process and draws addresser and addressee into an unsettling pattern of interrelations between external referential meaning and the internal structures that create meaning.

Now let us return to Culler's assertion that the 'literary' qualities of a text are conferred upon it by the reader's theory of discourse.

> Anyone wholly unacquainted with literature and unfamiliar with the conventions by which fictions are read, would, for example, be quite baffled if presented with a poem. His knowledge of the language would enable him to understand phrases and sentences, but he would not know, quite literally, what to *make* of this strange concatenation of phrases. He would be unable to read it *as* literature – as we say with emphasis to those who would use literary works for other purposes – because he lacks the complex 'literary competence' which enables others to proceed. He has not internalized the 'grammar' of literature which would permit him to convert linguistic sequences into literary structures and meanings.
>
> (p. 114)

I would argue that anyone with a basic 'knowledge of language' would experience, to borrow the Formalist term, *ostranenie* in his/her reading of 'The Flea'. This person would be sufficiently, if only intuitively, familiar with the morphophonemic conventions of signification to recognise that the extraordinary density and configuration of sound patterns is not what normally happens during the dialogic process. He/she would recognise that the speech act is generated by a chain of unpredictable circumstances and would also recognise that the phonic patterns of this act are preplanned and predictable. What would happen next is the crux of Culler's, and others', argument with Jakobson. It is true that our hypothetical non-literary reader would not possess the vocabulary to describe exactly how the poem creates its effects, but I would contend that such effects are nevertheless intrinsic to his/her experience of it and not, as Culler claims, due 'to the type of attention which poetry receives by virtue of its status within the institution of literature' (p. 164).

SPEECH ACTS AND 'THE RAVEN, NEVERMORE'

Mary Louise Pratt in *Toward a Speech Act Theory of Literary Discourse* (1977) shifts the emphasis from Culler's reader-oriented theory of interpretive practice to the general question of the relation between speech acts, their participants and their context. She argues that the Formalists, particularly their late twentieth-century representative, R. Jakobson, base their methods and assumptions upon the limiting and restrictive concept of autonomous textuality. In short, the signifying abilities of poetic language are rescued from intrageneric collusion with those of non-poetic language by the uniquely depersonalised nature of the poetic artefact. She notes that 'the overriding tendency to disguise all notions of intention, perception, and value by converting them into textual attributes has a conspicuous stylistic effect on almost all formalist and structuralist writings' (p. 74). The poem is an 'it' with 'its' own characteristics, intentions, impositions, derivations, purposes, possessions, effecting the apparent exclusion of the poet (his/hers) and the reader (ours, yours, etc.): the left-hand column of the sliding scale subjugates the right; diagram 2 encroaches upon diagram 1. Pratt's overall objective is to refocus the attention of critic and linguist upon the continuum of expressive and receptive cohabitation in which literary and non-literary texts share 'context-dependent' features.

> The poetic text, which 'forms itself' and 'orients itself' according to its own intentions and values, is every bit as mechanistic, as divorced from the reality of human communication as the 'ordinary' utterance that 'transmits merely information about the outside world'.
>
> (p. 75)

She quotes from Mukarovsky's (1932) paper on 'Standard Language and Poetic Language', but her extension of his text-based orientation into a general condemnation of Formalist practice is unnecessarily metonymic – the parts do not necessarily conform to the whole. Jakobson states that 'the supremacy of the poetic function over the referential function does not obliterate the reference but makes it ambiguous' (*L in L*, p. 85) and he would seem to be in agreement with Pratt on the necessary co-dependence of text and context. The true nature of their disagreement exists in whether poetry creates a relationship between text and context which is intrinsically different from that created by non-poetic discourses.

In 'Linguistics and Poetics', shortly after his designation of the 'supremacy' of the poetic function, Jakobson examines the final stanza of Poe's 'The Raven'. His discussion (of paronomasia) is brief but it originates in an illuminating and arguably ground-breaking piece, written in 1949 as an introductory chapter to a planned, but sadly never finished, book on *Sound and Meaning* (the 1978 book bearing this title consists of Jakobson's lectures and should not be mistaken for the planned project). The essay was eventually published in 1964 and entitled 'Language in Oper-ation' (*L in L*, pp. 50–61). The opening of the essay (pp. 50–2) is Jakobson's most effective, and indeed pre-emptive, parry against the 'context-dependent' arguments of the new paradigm. Jakob-son tells the story of how recently, on a train, he had overheard a conversation between a man and a woman, from which he quotes: 'They were playing "The Raven" on the radio. An old record of a London actor dead for years. I wish you had heard his *Nevermore*.' Jakobson ponders the contextual journey of this single word. The literary quotation by the male addresser might well allude to an emotional experience shared with his female interlocutor. The source of the quotation is a transposition of contextual circumstances: it is recited by a (dead) British actor and addressed to a diffuse and unspecific audience. This addresser had reproduced Edgar Allen Poe's 'message' of 1845. Poe had been transmitting 'the confession of a "lover lamenting his deceased mistress" – perhaps the poet himself, perhaps some other man, real or imaginary'. To complicate matters further, the word 'nevermore' is attributed in the poem to a non-human addresser, the talking bird, which had '*caught from some unhappy master*' the '*melancholy burden* of his customary laments' (italicised quotes from Poe's text).

> This is a chain of actual and fictitious senders and receivers, most of whom merely relay and to a large extent intentionally quote one and the same message, which, at least to a few of them, was familiar beforehand. Some of the participants in this one-way communication are widely separated from each other in time and/or space, and these gaps are bridged through various means of recording and transmission. The whole process offers a typical example of an intricate process of [poetic] communication.
>
> (*L in L*, p. 51)

Jakobson's point is that the single word 'nevermore' is a charged particle, transferable and potentially subject to all manner of contextual reinterpretations and usages, but, when offered to an addressee familiar with its particular textual origin, capable of subjugating context to text. The means by which it achieves this returns us to what actually happens within Poe's poem.

> And the Raven, never flitting, still is sitting; *still* is sitting
> On the pallid bust of Pallas just above my chamber door;
> And his eyes have all the seeming of a demon's that is
>   dreaming,
> And the lamplight o'er him streaming throws his shadow on
>   the floor;
> And my soul from out that shadow that lies floating on the
>   floor
>   Shall be lifted – nevermore!

Jakobson's discussion of this closing stanza and its relationship with other parts of the poem is typically precise and complex and I shall offer a crude summary of his principal objectives and disclosures.

'Nevermore' is a focal point and a catalyst. It is repeated by the bird throughout the poem, and in each instance it gathers echoes of assonantal, alliterative and rhyming patterns. In this stanza, 'more' rhymes with 'door' and 'floor', the two principal deictic locatives of the sequence; the 'Raven', the focus of these spatio-temporal deictics, 'is simply an inversion of the sinister "never"'. No element of the semantic, grammatical or morphological make-up of the stanza can remain immune from some correspondence with the concluding word. For example, the phrase 'the Raven, never flitting' reverberates at three interrelated levels: 'flitting' double-rhymes with 'sitting'; the alliterative pattern of the /l/ consonant recurs in 'still', 'pallid' and 'Pallas'; the /r/ of Raven and never is cautiously suspended, until 'chamber door'; and it is from above the door that the bird casts its shadow on the floor and repeats, literally and textually, the inverted echo of its own name, 'nevermore'.

Such density of semantic–phonemic configurations is not an unusual feature of regular poems but for two reasons Jakobson regards 'The Raven' as a special case. First, one of the participants of the speech event is not a human being: the pseudo-dialogue between the bird and the lover involves the exchange of linguistic signs but for only one of them does the signans 'nevermore' also register as a signatum. Jakobson finds a parallel for this one-sided dialogue in Poe's letters, in which he writes of his response to the death of his wife, Virginia Clemm, and refers to 'the psychological reality of the image of the enlarged self confronting the notself'. The 'notself' is at once the externalised self of the soliloquy and its potential, imagined addressee. 'Talking' with the bird is a gothic enactment of what happens when the bereaved husband addresses the memory of a speaking presence – Poe's wife had 'ruptured a blood vessel *in singing*'.

Second, Jakobson classifies 'The Raven' as a poetic manifestation of the linguistic concept of 'regressive action': 'If in a sequence a prior moment depends upon a later one'. A widely quoted example of this is the slip by the radio announcer in which 'the convention was in session' becomes 'the confession was in session', with the regressive image of the final word exerting an assimilative influence upon 'convention'. In a similar but more complex way the word 'nevermore' infects and to an extent predetermines the grammatical and phonemic patterns that precede it. A prelinguistic counterpart to this effect is provided in Poe's letters, where he describes the horrific progress of his wife's fatal illness. For a year she 'clung to life with . . . desperate pertinacity' and each time 'the vessel broke again', Poe 'felt all the agonies of her death'. 'I had indeed nearly abandoned all hope of a permanent cure when I found one in the *death* of my wife' (*L in L*, p. 57). Jakobson comments:

> Not only the questions propounded by the desperate lover but in fact the whole poem are predetermined by the final rejoinder *nevermore* and are composed in distinct anticipation of the denouement, as the author disclosed in 'The Philosophy of Composition' (1846), his own commentary to 'The Raven': 'the poem may be said to have its beginning – at the end'.
>
> (*L in L*, p. 55)

Jakobson's point is this: When the man on the train says to the woman 'I wish you had heard his *Nevermore*', he refers at the same time to the single word and to the sense in which the word constitutes and internalises the entirety of the poem. An extract from non-poetic discourse can, as politicians often remind us, be taken 'out of context', and context in this sense refers both to the other constituent parts of the text or speech act and to the circumstances and conditions which prompt and are effected by the discourse. 'Nevermore', like the anagram or the solution to the riddle of the thimble, is at once an element of the material structure of the text and of its referential function: it carries with it its textual and its prelinguistic context. Jakobson's scholarly disclosures of its biographical correspondences are enlightening, but they do not tell us anything more than we already know of the signifying structures of the poem, only of a likely connection between these structures and the experiences of its creator. Our understanding of Poe is enriched by these disclosures, but they do not alter our understanding of his poem. Poetry, in Jakobson's opinion, is uniquely capable of preserving its own self-focused contextual function (in Jakobson's two diagrams – see p. 84 – once 'message' is aligned with 'poetic', so 'context' is aligned with 'referential'). Pratt disagrees.

> With a context-dependent linguistics, the essence of literariness or poeticality can be said to reside not in the message but in a particular disposition of speaker and audience with regard to the message, one that is characteristic of the literary speech situation. This view has more explanatory power than the view that asks us to regard 'poetic resources' as 'concealed in the morphological and syntactic structure of the language'.
>
> (p. 88; Pratt's quotations are from Jakobson)

'Context-dependent linguistics' is founded upon the assumptions and propositions of modern speech act theory, developed in the 1960s by a group of British language philosophers, most importantly J. L. Austin, and extended by John Searle (1969). The two necessary preconditions for any speech act are that the speaker must perform a locutionary act, the act of producing a recognisable grammatical utterance in the given language, and an illocutionary act, an intentional, goal-directed act of promising, warning, asking, informing, commanding, etc. Consequently speech act theory shifts the emphasis from the relation between unit and system, parole and langue – the traditional focus of linguistic discovery procedures – to a broader consideration of the conditions and circumstances within which the speech act takes place. For example, Searle argues that an illocutionary act of promising can only be properly understood if we are aware of the 'appropriateness conditions' of the speech act, i.e. the motivation, sincerity and circumstantial authority of the speaker.

What are the 'appropriateness conditions' pertaining to the man's pseudo-dialogue with the raven? In order to be goal-directed an illocutionary act must presuppose the existence of an addressee. The raven exists but only to provide a verbal ricochet for the speaker's locutionary act. Moreover, any goal-directed utterance is by definition incomplete. A statement or a question can only qualify for illocutionary act status if it is assumed by the speaker that the addressee might be unaware of the former or be able to answer the latter. The textual properties of 'The Raven' are, as Jakobson demonstrates, an instance of regressive action: 'The subject knows beforehand the reply to the question he will put to himself' (*L in L*, p. 53). We know this not because of our contextual awareness of who the speaker is and of the conditions pertaining to his utterance, in Pratt's terms 'the particular disposition of speaker and audience', but because of 'the essence of literariness' or 'poeticality' which do, *contra* Pratt, 'reside . . . in the message'.

In her chapter on 'The Linguistics of Use' Pratt inadvertently discloses what is probably the principal flaw in the new paradigm assaults upon Jakobson's poetics. She cites Richard Ohmann, who concedes that,

> Since the quasi-speech-acts of literature are not carrying on the world's business – describing, urging, contracting etc. – the reader may well attend to them in a non-pragmatic way . . . the suspension of normal illocutionary forces tends to shift a reader's attention to the locutionary acts themselves.
>
> (Pratt, p. 90; Ohmann, p. 17)

She concedes Ohmann's general claim but points out that literary texts are not the only kind of locutionary acts that suspend normal illocutionary forces. What about the 'scenarios' in the Oval Office, or for that matter all kinds of imaginings, plannings, dreams, wishings, fantasisings? Why, she asks, should we treat these as merely 'similar' to literature? Such a distinction would be like describing apples in terms of oranges without reference to the category of 'fruit'.

> Does it not make more sense to say that our ability to conceive and manipulate hypothetical worlds and states of affairs, possible or impossible, real or unreal, and to mediate between those worlds and our own is part of our normal linguistic competence? And the capacity to use that faculty in aesthet-

ically and rhetorically effective ways is also part of our normal
linguistic competence.

(p. 92)

What both Ohmann and Pratt ignore, or perhaps fail to comprehend, is that in texts such as 'The Raven' normal illocutionary
forces are suspended not because of the unworldly contextual
positioning of addresser, addressee and speech act but because
the speech act itself effectively encodes and determines whatever
image of speaker, listener and situation we take away from the
text. Jakobson:

> The 'master' repeatedly exteriorized the elliptic one-word sen-
> tence of his inner speech, *nevermore*, the bird mimicked its
> sound sequence; the lover retained it in his memory and
> reported the Raven's part with reference to its probable prov-
> enance; the poet wrote and published the lover's story, actually
> inventing the lover's, Raven's, and master's roles; the actor
> read and recited for a recording the piece assigned by the
> poet to the lover with its *nevermore* attributed by the lover to
> the Raven; the radio station selected the record and put it
> on the air; the stranger listened, remembered, and quoted this
> message with reference to its sources, and the linguist noted
> his quotation reconstituting the whole sequence of transmitters
> and perhaps even making up the roles of the stranger, the
> broadcaster and the actor.
>
> (*L in L*, p. 51)

'Nevermore' is where the apex of the contextual gyre meets that
of its textual counterpart. It is the crystallisation of the complex
double pattern of the poem, and the double pattern encloses
and prefigures any outertextual conditions in which we might
attempt to situate the poem. Look again at the two diagrams.
Once the 'poetic' function fills the slot occupied in all other
situations by 'the message', then the five other positions are
caught in the web of the text.

Ohmann and Pratt might disagree on the means of classifying
literature and non-literature, but they share the premise that
locutionary acts of all types are functionally subservient to their
illocutionary context, and there are similarities between this
model and Husserl's belief in an interdependence between *Meinung* (that which is meant) and *Bedeutung* (the intentional force

which endows the statement with meaning). Jakobson's diver-
gence from conventional phenomenology and speech act theory
touches upon a more general and fundamental rift within late
twentieth-century theories of language and literature. This began
to open during the 1950s and it is principally responsible for the
contemporary belief that Jakobson's work, while of great historical
interest, is beyond its use-by date.

The single most influential figure in post-war Anglo-American
linguistics is without question Noam Chomsky. In 1957 Chomsky
published a short book called *Syntactic Structures*, which intro-
duced to linguistics the concept of transformational and generative grammar. Chomsky's original thesis has itself been
transformed, extended and revised, but it endures, and it underpins the new paradigm.

To offer a very crude definition, transformational–generative
grammar is employed to establish what is universal to all linguistic
statements, not just in relation to the abstract structure of the
linguistic system but also to explain how the system is transformed
by the individual into the event – Saussure's langue–parole model
adapted to the practicalities of human communication. Every
linguistic construction is seen as 'consisting of' other component
constructions. For instance, the sentence

The men were playing the game

would be represented as a sequence of NP (Noun Phrase – the
men) and a VP (Verb Phrase – were playing the game). At a
localised level the VP consists of V + NP, and the NP consists of
Art (article 'the') + N. The same sentence could be 'transformed'
from its active to its passive form, 'the game was played by the
men', and the elements of 'phrase structure grammar' described
above would be employed to show how the transformation takes
place. This mechanism allows the linguist to specify the ways in
which individual units of meaning are 'generated' from the rules
and conventions that underlie linguistic usage.

Chomsky's use of phrase structure grammar is thus a sophisticated version of the traditional practice of 'parsing' sentences,
and it is consistent with Jakobson's model of the syntagmatic and
paradigmatic axes as the fundamental elements of linguistic construction. Indeed, Chomsky and Jakobson have proceeded with
their respective studies and investigations without any real disagreement on the fundamentals of linguistic analysis, but one

element of Chomsky's model has, in a variety of ways, provided
the foundations for anti-Jakobson theory. Chomsky's system of
'phrase structure grammar' begs a number of questions: most
significantly, how and why do individual speakers choose an active
rather than a passive version of the above sentence, or vice versa?
Chomsky answered with the thesis that 'linguistic competence' is
what makes 'linguistic performance' possible. Linguistic competence is the internalised blueprint, the 'deep structure' that
enables the speaker to produce the statement, 'the surface structure'. Obviously, most speakers do not acquire linguistic competence by learning the rules of phrase structure grammar; rather
we become competent by communicating with other human
beings. This concept of intrapersonal competence acquisition
also explains the means by which individuals choose one type of
surface structure as opposed to others which might serve a similar
prelinguistic purpose: our process of competence acquisition also
involves the perceptual encoding of the circumstances in which
language is used. Hence the context in which a specific utterance
is used (its illocutionary force) becomes a significant feature in
its process of construction (the locutionary act). Chomsky himself
has not given much emphasis to the theoretical implications of
his context–speech act paradigm (though it features as an important element of his political writings of the 1980s and 1990s), but
it has become the gathering point for various branches of literary
theory and literary linguistics. Its relationship with speech act
theory is clear enough (see Labov, 1972, and Fillmore, 1973),
and its ramifications are elaborate and insidious. For example,
in the introduction to another theory-guide bestseller, *Literary
Theory. An Introduction* (1983), Terry Eagleton draws upon the
groundwork of speech act theory in his typically nimble-footed
attack on Formalist assumptions (pp. 6–9). A sign often encountered on the London underground reads: 'Dogs must be carried
on the escalator.' Eagleton argues that if we accept the Formalist
doctrine that poetry involves a form of 'estrangement' from
normal usage, then the nature of this statement (does it mean
that you must always carry a dog to be admitted to the escalator?)
makes it a literary text. Eagleton goes on to compare the late-
night drunk, who might prise this statement from its pragmatic
purpose and read some element of cosmic significance into it,
with the literary critic who similarly dislocates Burns's 'my love is
like a red red rose' from any pragmatic, contextual discourse

between ordinary men and women. For Eagleton, 'the fact that [Burns] puts this statement in metre' does not alter its intrinsic signifying function: rather it activates a shift from a pragmatic (non-literary) to a non-pragmatic (literary) response. Eagleton's general point is that 'literary competence', like linguistic competence, is founded upon our familiarity with a vast network of events and circumstances which are as much responsible for endowing a text with meaning as are its intrinsic linguistic features. It is but a short step from this assumption to Stanley Fish's argument that all interpretive strategies and their results are constructs of an interpretive community.

> . . . line endings exist by virtue of perceptual strategies rather than the other way around. Historically the strategy that we know as 'reading (or hearing) poetry' has included paying attention to the line as a unit, but it is precisely that attention which has made the line as a unit (either of print or of aural duration) available. . . . In short, what is noticed is what has been made noticeable, not by a clear and undistorting glass, but by an interpretive strategy.
>
> (Fish, pp. 165–6)

This is nonsense but the fact that Fish's proposition remains largely unchallenged testifies to the power of the context-dependent paradigm.

As Jakobson states, the line, or 'measure of sequences', is 'a device that, outside of poetic function, finds no application in language'. For 'application' we might substitute 'illocutionary force'. In speech act theory the verb is the axis between the abstract constituents of the locutionary act and representative, expressive, verdictive, directive, commissive and declarative functions performed by the illocutionary act. In short, any purposive statement can be comprehensively explained in terms of this context–text formula. But how do we explain Milton's use of the verb phrase 'what must be' in his description of Satan's condition in *Paradise Lost*?

> Now conscience wakes the bitter memory
> Of what he was, what is, and what must be
> Worse; of worse deeds worse sufferings must ensue.
>
> (IV, 24–6)

On the one hand the terminated phrase at the line ending

echoes the stoical resignation of the prayer-book formula; on the other the syntax continues into a more elaborate, speculative consideration of 'what must be worse'. We cannot follow Eagleton's example and explain the ambiguity simply in terms of the contextual/perceptual conditions of reading because the disjunction between the two patterns of meaning originates in the text: the cognitive framework of syntax is patently and verifiably interrupted by the conventional element of the iambic pentameter. Nor can we assume that the line ending replicates the hesitations and paratactic slippages of ordinary spoken discourse. If we did, we would have to treat each of the line breaks of the poem that does not coincide with a syntactic pause in the same way as this one. In any event this illocutionary act is Milton's, not Satan's; it is a representative (third-person account) of Satan's condition, not an expressive (first-person) account by Satan himself. Transformational–generative grammar deals with ambiguity first by specifying the relations between the uncertain meaning of the surface structure and its alternative deep structural counterparts and then by selecting the likeliest intended meaning by referring to the context in which the statement is made. But this sentence, as a complete syntactic unit, is unambiguous; there is no slide between surface and deep structure. The ambiguity is caused by a device that cannot be accounted for by the mechanisms of phrase structure grammar. Whether or not the reader chooses to acknowledge the hesitation or pause of the line ending is up to the reader, but the fact that such a choice is made available by a deliberate and purposive strategy on the part of the poet and not by a 'perceptual strategy' of the reader cannot be questioned.

Fish's discussion of such stylistic nuances as line endings might seem to exist in a somewhat specialised world of metrical data and taxonomy, but the premise upon which his context model is founded also underpins practically every literary-theoretical subelement of the new paradigm. Deconstruction, psychoanalytic theory, new historicism, post-Bakhtin Marxian theory: each of these is in some way dependent upon a shift in interpretive focus away from the text as an autonomous totality and towards the text as an amorphous, unstable entity whose structure and function is determined by a particular interpretive caucus of ideology, gender, scholarly expectation, etc. Fish:

What I am suggesting is that formal units are always a function of the interpretive model one brings to bear; they are not 'in' the text, and I would make the same argument for intentions. That is intention is no more embodied 'in' the text than are formal units.

(p. 164)

Fish's proposition represents the extremity of the context-based paradigm. Roger Fowler (1981) offers a more accurate summary of the new critical consensus.

I have tried to demonstrate the value of analysing texts in a way which differs from the emphasis upon objective, formal structure[s]. . . . This is not to deny the applicability of such concepts in the analysis of literature, of course; only to demand that they should not be invoked as compositional principles setting literature aloof from other communicative transactions.

(p. 94)

PHONOLOGY, POETICS AND SEMIOTICS

The relationship between Jakobson's text-centred model of the poetic function and the emphasis on context of the new paradigm raises a number of questions regarding the broader history of US–European semiotics and literary theory. Jakobson, throughout his life and writings, maintained and re-emphasised what were to become the most discredited principles of pre-Prague Formalism. Transformational–generative linguistics, speech act theory, the reader/interpretive method theses of Culler, Fish, Fowler *et al.*, are but folds in the much broader texture of the multi-genre multicultural garment of socio-semiotics that has, since the 1920s, come to envelop the expanding body of structuralist thinking. Why did Jakobson cling so tenaciously to a model of the poetic that by the late 1960s seemed to represent little more than an intriguing episode in the history of modern criticism? Was there an element of Jakobsonian Formalism that rendered it safely immune from the encroachments of the broader socio-ideological concept of the sign? Even if Jakobson's model of the poetic function can be defended against the likes of Culler and Fish is it really of much benefit to an age in which poetry study is at best a tactical playground for the poststructuralists, postfeminists, new historicists and the rest, and at worst the irrelevant and the most recently dead language of the academic establishment? In Part III I shall attempt to demonstrate the relevance of Jakobsonian poetics, but first we will consider the question of why Jakobson resisted the shifting of the paradigm.

The disintegration of the Formalism of the Moscow and St Petersburg schools was precipitated by the extension of Soviet politics and economics into the realms of education and organised culture; Victor Erlich (1955) has provided us with the accepted account of these events. But these external factors only accelerated the decline of a set of principles that effectively created their own counter-theoretical nemesis. Shklovsky's key concepts of 'device' (*priem*), 'deviation/defamiliarisation' (*ostranenie*) and 'literariness' (*literaturnost*) were at once original and dangerously unstable elements. On the one hand they offered an apparently clear and scientific basis for the identification of literary art; on the other they drew upon the same programme of discovery procedures that underpinned the increasingly influential Saussurean model of the linguistic sign and the linguistic system. If, as Saussure argued, all language is composed of material units legitimised as signs by an arbitrary network of relations and conventions, then surely the study of language must be an ancillary element of a much broader social, political and cross-disciplinary study of the relation between behaviour, events and their semiotic registers. As a consequence, literature or literariness would become a subelement of an overarching semiological network; in comparative terms it might be signs-made-strange but its strangeness could, like all other branches of human activity and expression, be codified and, more significantly, demystified. The complete recategorisation of literature would have to wait for post-war critics such as Barthes and Eco, but the process had begun in the 1920s. The most celebrated post-Formalist text is Bakhtin and Medvedev's *The Formal Method in Literary Scholarship* (1928), which pre-empted the speech act theorists' assumption that literary speech acts can only be understood in terms of, rather than as aloof from, 'ordinary' non-literary exchange. But doubts about the validity of pure-art Formalism were also emerging in the work of Jakobson's Prague associate Mukarovsky, who in his 1934 essay 'Art as a Semiotic Fact' argued that literature 'requires' an understanding of its social and historical context (see Galan, 1985). To understand why Jakobson did not join this early drift towards the new paradigm we must appreciate the connection between his pure linguistic work on phonetics and distinctive features and his concept of poetry as a uniquely independent sign system.

Jakobson's most important work on phonology appears in *Preliminaries to Speech Analysis* (with Fant and Halle, 1952). This publication was the culmination of work already done in Prague alongside Trubetzkoy. A full consideration of the relationship between Jakobson's findings and traditional (i.e. nineteenth-century) phonology, and their influence upon post-1950s generative phonology would require another book (see Sangster, 1982, Waugh, 1976, and Halle (in Armstrong and Van Schoonveld, 1987), for reasonably accessible accounts). I shall attempt to summarise those elements of his thesis that are most significant for our understanding of his definition of the poetic function.

The three most important concepts are: distinctive features; binary oppositions; markedness. The theory of distinctive features is based on the premise that the phonemes of a language can be analysed or broken down into a small number of components or features. These are the linguistic equivalent of 'atoms' from which the 'molecular' phoneme is composed. The binary principle gives each feature two 'values', symbolised '+' and '−'. Many phonetic features are 'naturally' binary; for example nasal (+) vs oral (−), voiced (+) vs voiceless (−). The concept of markedness is the most important of the three since it functions as a bridge between the traditional perception of speech sounds as inert phenomena and their function as meaning-differentiating elements within the applied linguistic system. Trubetzkoy (1931, p. 97) was the first to apply the terms 'marked' and 'unmarked' to the binary opposition of distinctive features.

> The two terms of a correlative opposition (e.g. voiced/ unvoiced) are not equivalent; the one term possesses the mark in question (or possesses it in its positive form), the other does not (or possesses it in its negative form). We designate the first as marked, the second as unmarked.

Jakobson (1932, *SW II*, pp. 3 ff.; 1939, *SW II*, pp. 211 ff.) adapted the phonological principles of markedness and applied these to the meaning-differentiating structures of morphology and syntax. The unmarked sign can have two distinct meanings − a general meaning and a restricted 'specific' one. The general meaning of the unmarked sign reveals nothing about the presence or absence of a particular property (P), but its specific meaning signals the absence of a property. The marked sign reveals its presence.

marked term   statement of P

unmarked term   (1) general meaning: non-statement of P
                     (2) specific meaning: statement of non-P

In comparison to the unmarked term, the marked term provides more information. For example, the statement 'Michael is as big as John' is less informative than the statement 'Michael is as small as John'. Someone unfamiliar with the sizes of Michael and John knows a lot more about their dimensions from the second statement than from the first. 'Small' is the marked term; 'big' is the unmarked term.

This example allows us only a slight insight into the function of the markedness model in linguistic exchanges, but it is clear the marked/unmarked relationship is at once an element of the linguistic system while being dependent upon the contextual circumstances of usage: if we already knew Michael and John, the information-supplying elements of the marked/unmarked terms would be irrelevant. Jakobson was fully aware of this context-dependent factor, but he was much more concerned with the identification of some specific, causal relationship between phonological markedness and its meaning-differentiating counterpart. In his 1965 essay 'Quest For the Essence of Language' he is very specific about this objective. He is engaged in a search for a specific relational model of the signans and the signatum.

There are languages where the plural forms are distinguished from the singular by an additional morpheme, whereas . . . there is no language in which this relation would be the reverse and, in contradistinction to the singular forms, the plural ones would be totally devoid of such an extra morpheme. . . . [T]hese and many similar facts of linguistic experience prove to be at variance with the Saussurean averment that 'in the sound structure of the signans there is nothing which would bear any resemblance to the value or meaning of the sign'.

(*SW II*, p. 352)

Here, the Jakobson programme is anti-Saussurean. His conception of language rests upon the premise that the distinctive
elements, the binary divisions of the material signans, are of
as much significance to the meaning-generating signatum as
Saussure's notion of the arbitrary relationship between signs. In
a broader sense, the post-Saussurean extension of relational semiotics into the sphere of non-linguistic sign systems is a development of which Jakobson approved (his working relationship with
Lévi-Strauss testifies to this), while he maintained that language
is both the principal, governing sign system and intrinsically different from its non-linguistic counterparts. We will consider
Jakobson's conception of the linguistic sign in more detail in Part
III, but there are two elements of his model which effectively
distance it from the socio-semiotic model. First, the linguistic sign
is an acoustic phenomenon which is divorced from the broader
continuum of 'gross acoustic sound matter' (1960, *SW II*, p. 395).
The distinctive features of speech sounds are reducible to an
inventory of fifteen universal 'atoms'; these are drawn upon by
all languages and, although their distribution within different
lexical, syntactic and morphophonemic frameworks will often
differ, their function as the primal link between signans and
signatum is universal. Second, the linguistic sign is unique in its
relationship with the mental and motor functions of the human
presence. There are non-speech sounds that can generate culturally or socially determined meanings (bird song, the wind, the
sea, etc.); there are visual and tactile signs (including written
language) whose signifying functions are purely arbitrary and
relational. But only the acoustic-linguistic sign combines the
necessary, physical participation of human speakers and hearers
with a complex network of relations and transformations. 'Phonemes draw on the sound matter but readjust this extrinsic
matter, selecting, classifying it along their own lines. These items
of sound matter are transformed into semiotic elements' (1949,
pp. 36–7). In short, language is the bridge between presence,
consciousness and everything else. Every event or impression
can be translated into a linguistic or non-linguistic sign, and
consequently it could be argued that reality, as we perceive it, is
enabled and constituted only by virtue of this transferability
between sign and referent. However, acoustic, linguistic signs are
capable of integrating sign, referent, and presence. On the one
hand we decode linguistic messages in terms of our competent

awareness of the system of language and of the relation between speech act and context. On the other, the principal enabling factor of this process of encoding and decoding consists of our ability to produce and recognise a correlation between sound and meaning. And speech sounds are unique to auditory and articulatory functions of human communication.

Jakobson did not deny that the sign–referent relationship of language could be adapted to the analysis of non-linguistic systems of representation – indeed, in his early essays on 'Futurism' and 'Dada' he employed the metonymy–metaphor polarity to classify different types and forms of modernist visual art. But he maintained that the art form which draws exclusively upon the material and the referential nature of the linguistic sign, poetry, involves formal and signifying capabilities which are denied to all other aesthetic or non-aesthetic, linguistic or non-linguistic sign systems. Poetry both centres upon the materiality of the linguistic sign (its phonemic and intrinsically human dimension) and combines this with an ability to effect transformational correspondence between linguistic signs, non-linguistic signs and their integrated referents. Poetry is uniquely 'about' the process by which the governing sign system operates (the relation between sound and meaning in language) and a medium through which language interfaces with signs and referents beyond its reflexive operational structure.

Let us return to the question of why Jakobson did not join the drift towards the context-based paradigm. The question invites all manner of complex speculations on Jakobson's personal, ideological and mental affiliations, but the answer is straightforward: poetry. It was not that Jakobson wished to protect the sanctified uniqueness of poetry because, like Arnold, he believed it might serve as a substitute for the decay of more conventional social and moral preservatives, or, like many of the British Leavisites or US New Critics, that it maintained a particular type of intellectual and artistic meritocracy against the incursions of low culture. Rather, he was certain that the writing and reading of poetry involved a nexus, a centralisation of potentially diffuse elements of our broader perceptions of language and existence. Poetry as art and poetry study as aesthetics versus language as phenomena and language study as science, was for Jakobson an outdated and inaccurate polarity: poetry could tell us as much about the nature of linguistic mediation as linguistics could tell us about the formal dimensions of the poem. In the *Dialogues* (pp. 20–1) he gives an account of the various prompters and influences that determined the direction of his early work in Russia and Prague, and one is struck by the way in which the traditional analyst–analysed relation between linguistics and poetry is replaced by equality and catalytic interaction.

> The phonic analysis of Khlebnikov's poetic texture prompted use of linguistic data about the sounds of speech. On the other hand, the new light that the original work of the poet shed on the sounds of language led me to question willy-nilly the habitual conception of phonic material in linguistics and to subject it to a fundamental revision. . . . Moreover the application of this concept [the phoneme featuring an indissoluble link between sound and meaning] in poetic analysis led me inevitably to revise closely and develop the theory of phonemes in their reciprocal relations, because, as one must not overlook, any linguistic concept applied to poetics automatically and inevitably puts into the foreground the idea of reciprocal relations.
>
> (p. 21)

In brief, poetry foregrounds and motivates an interactive relationship between the two elements that must be central to any understanding of the mechanism and function of language: the material substance of the sign and its signifying potential. I have already commented on the similarity between Jakobson's model of the poetic and the eighteenth-century Romantic thesis that the poetic determinants of rhythm and sound pattern predate prose and ordinary speech as the originary linguistic function (see Part I, pp. 21–2). Supplement this Enlightenment polarity of poetry and prose with the twentieth-century relation between the linguistic sign and the non-linguistic spectrum of codes, ideologies, behavioural instincts, contextual pressures and mental activities, and you have an accurate perception of Jakobson's position within the unfolding panorama of structuralism and poststructuralism. Poetry, for Jakobson, is not an engaging subgalaxy of the semiologic cosmos; it is, to extend the cosmic metaphor, the Big Bang.

In 'Linguistics and Poetics' Jakobson takes issue with Seymour Chatman's claim that 'meter exists as a system outside the language'. Jakobson concedes that in other non-linguistic art forms (principally dance and music) measure of time sequence, irrespective of signifying content, is a definitive element of the artefact or the performance. Similarly, 'there are other linguistic problems [*sic*] – for instance syntax – which likewise overstep the limit of language and are common to different semiotic systems'. He offers the widely used example of the 'grammar' of traffic lights. However, poetic metre can only be described from 'a purely linguistic point of view'. Jakobson claims that, although individual components of the poetic function are transferable to other semiotic systems and codes, only in poetry are these elements combined in a purposive interactive continuum – the double pattern.

To test the validity of his claim we need to be aware of an extremely diverse network of semiotic and linguistic programmes, all of which relate in some way to Jakobson's work.

First of all, his reference to Chatman must be understood within the context of the ongoing development of what has come to be known as linguistic metrics. Seymour Chatman was a contributor to a groundbreaking collection of articles that appeared in the *Kenyon Review* in 1956, and which involved attempts to apply the findings of G. L. Trager and H. L. Smith to the analysis of poetic form. Trager and Smith (1951) had identified in English four discrete levels of stress (primary, secondary, tertiary, weak), of pitch (highest, high, normal, low) and of juncture (internal, word, phrase, and clause-terminal). Their monograph did not refer specifically to metrical patterns in poetry but the implications of their discoveries for traditional methods of scansion were immense. The governing assumption of traditional prosodic study was that the units by which poetic structure was measured, the syllable, the foot and the line, were identifiable in terms of the ictic relation between alternating unstress and stress values – the classic structure of the iambic pentameter consisting of five unstressed syllables in the odd positions and five stressed syllables in the even. Trager and Smith had demonstrated that stress and pitch are much more complex and variable phenomena than could be accounted for by the binary unstress–stress relation of traditional prosody. For example, it might be possible to locate a syllable in an even-stressed position in an iambic line which was of equal or even of lower stress–pitch value than a syllable in an odd-unstressed position in a different part of the line. Chatman, in his *Kenyon Review* essay on Robert Frost's 'Mowing', proposed an analytic technique founded upon the identification of two systems: the abstract, usually iambic, metrical pattern and the more contingent stress, pitch and pause variations of spoken language (he charted eight different readings of Frost's poem). His chief point was that the study and indeed the performance of such a poem incorporate both. A succinct description of this thesis is provided by Roger Fowler in 'Structural Metrics' (1966).

> Structural metrics could be said to be concerned with the reconciliation (through phonemics) of two extremes of analysis. On the one hand is the old belief in two fixed degrees of stress alternating with perfect regularity and uniformly disposed in time. At the other extreme is the instrumental revelation that each of the syllables in a line is realised differently by various complexes of intensity, pitch and length.
>
> (p. 156)

The relationship between this model of structural metrics and Chomsky's concept of transformational–generative grammar should be clear enough. Indeed, Paul Kiparsky in two seminal essays (1975 and 1977) has adapted the so-called 'tree structure' of syntax analysis, which charts the relation between the deep and surface structures of a given sentence, to the strong–weak stress patterns generated by the relation between the deep and surface structures of a metrical line. Since the 1956 *Kenyon Review* symposium, linguistic or structural metrics has established itself as a literary-linguistic subdiscipline, and the emergence of each new discovery procedure and technique presents us with a mirror image of the post-Chomskyan revolution in pure linguistics (the history of linguistic metrics through the 1960s and 1970s is comprehensively charted in Brogan, 1981). Jakobson's relationship with these developments is at once intriguing and paradoxical.

Prior to the 1958 Indiana conference Jakobson's reputation in the USA was founded primarily upon his work on aphasia and on the non-literary study of phonology. One can only speculate on how Jakobson felt when he was composing his 'Linguistics and Poetics' paper but the facts are as follows. He includes a lengthy section on issues relating to the *Kenyon Review* proposals (*L in L*, p. 74–81) and renames deep and surface structure as verse design and verse instance. He deserves a good deal of praise for his modesty because, although his account might seem to draw upon the recent work of his American peers, their 'discovery' of a relationship between an abstract and a performative pattern in metrical language had been a keystone of his own work on poetry since 'New Russian Poetry' (1921) (see for example, '*O cesskom stixe*', 1923, *SW V*, pp. 3–130; 'Uber den Versbau der serbokroatishen Volksepen', 1932, *SW IV*, pp. 51–60; 'Slavic Epic Verse: Studies in Comparative Metrics', 1952, *SW IV*, pp. 414–63). It would be wrong to assume that during the 1940s and 1950s Jakobson's work had remained entirely unnoticed by the US literary-critical establishment, but the connection was, to say the least, oblique. For example, Trager and Smith's monograph, which provided the impetus for linguistic metrics, was closely related to Jakobson's spectrogram measurements of amplitude, pitch and duration conducted at Harvard and published in *Preliminaries to Speech Analysis* (1952). More significantly, although the founders of linguistic metrics (US branch) appeared to have reached conclusions similar to Jakobson's, there was a crucial difference, to which Jakobson alluded in his reference to Chatman.

Chomsky's model of deep and surface structure and linguistic competence and performance is largely consistent with Saussure's distinction between langue and parole. Both are founded upon a discrimination between an abstract network of choices, alternatives and conventions and the realisation of these in concrete manifestations. Jakobson objects to the imposition of this broad structural model upon verse form.

> Far from being an abstract, theoretical scheme, meter – or in more explicit terms, *verse design* – underlies the structure of any single line – or in logical terminology, any single *verse instance*. Design and instance are correlative concepts. . . . The verse design is embodied in verse instances.
>
> (*L in L*, pp. 78–9)

Poetry is the only sign system in which langue and parole, system and event, deep structure and surface structure are co-present and 'embodied' in the given text. This difference between Jakobson and the linguistic metrists is by no means limited to the particular field of prosodic analysis; it marks an episode in the effective marginalisation of his theories by the monolith of the new paradigm. It was the apparent colonisation of prosodic studies by the context-based structural paradigm of Chomskyan linguistics that would enable Stanley Fish, two decades later, to declare that the formal units of a text 'exist by virtue of perceptual strategies'. Once the 'intrinsic' nature of poetic form is compromised by its apparent dependence upon the deep–surface structure model of non-poetic language, then the edifice of poetic-aesthetic separateness begins to crumble.

LÉVI-STRAUSS, BARTHES AND LACAN

I began this part by noting the ironic downfall of the paradigm theorist at the hands of the new paradigm, and the irony runs very deep. The three figures whose work has been most clearly influenced by Jakobsonian linguistics have each, unwittingly, played their part in the unseating of his most vital and fundamental premise – the uniqueness of the poetic sign system. Jakobson and Lévi-Strauss, both refugees from Nazism, met in New York in 1941 and the former's current concern with phonology provided the basis for the latter's seminal work in structural anthropology. Jakobson's concept of the phoneme was extended by Lévi-Strauss into a functional matrix for the analysis of human social behaviour. Jakobson pointed out that the discernment of a binary opposition in the material structure of language was the child's first encounter with distinction and separateness in his/her engagements with an otherwise diffuse phenomenal continuum (see *Fundamentals of Language*, pp. 60–1). The acquisition of distinctive features was the first step towards the more complex ratiocinative structuring of events, behavioural characteristics and moral and ethical determinants in the individual's perceptual familiarisation with 'the world'. Lévi-Strauss extended this thesis into his model of human social groupings: just as Jakobson's isolation of fifteen universal phonemic features provides the common basis for different morphological and syntactic patterns, so a similar opposition of primary distinctions underpins the various types of social, familial, sexual, political and ritualistic conventions that constitute each human society or ethnic group. Hence, 'like phonemes, kinship terms are elements of meaning; like phonemes they acquire meaning only if they are integrated into systems' (1972, p. 34), 'like language ... the cuisine of a society may be analysed into constitutent elements, which in this case we might call "gustemes", and which may be organised according to certain structures of opposition and correlations' (1972, p. 85). Lévi-Strauss's most specific adaptation of Jakobsonian phonology to anthropological gustemology involves the use of Jakobson's triangular representation of a child's first encounter with the compact–diffuse/vowel–consonant relation and the grave–acute consonantal split between oral and nasal phonemes (*SW I*, p. 493). Lévi-Strauss transferred this to a similar triangular relation between processed/unprocessed, cooked/rotten, smoked/boiled and culture/nature as stages and classifications in food preparation and consumption.

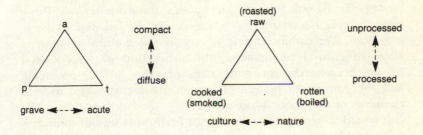

(Jakobson, 1956, *SW I*, p. 493)   (Lévi-Strauss, 1968, pp. 390 ff.)

Once it is accepted that objects, processes and behavioural conventions can be analysed as sign systems, then no form of human activity can remain immune from semiotic classification. For example, we might adapt Lévi-Strauss's gustemological triangle to the generic and functional relation between sound, speech and poetry.

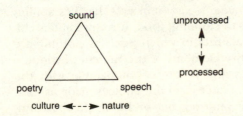

The assumption upon which such a classification is based is very similar to that which underpins the work of Culler, Fish and Pratt. Poetry, like smoked herrings, involves the imposition of an established cultural convention upon the amorphous raw material of existence. It would therefore be logical to assume that poetry is granted its superior status in the communicative hierarchy in the same way that smoked herrings are regarded, in Northern European societies, as gustemologically superior to their boiled or raw counterparts. Such hierarchies are arbitrarily imposed. The Japanese regard raw fish as superior to cooked, so why should we accept that the aesthetic deification of the poem is anything other than the product of a particular network of socio-cultural conventions? But, as Jakobson has pointed out, such an analogy is flawed because the poem incorporates all three elements of the triangle – 'verse design is *embodied* in verse instances'. We cannot classify poetry as the cultural transform-ation of natural phenomena, the processing of unprocessed matter, because the unregenerated substance of the phoneme and the contingent pattern of speech are incorporated as vital elements of the poetic function.

It would be wrong to assume that Lévi-Strauss set out to under-mine Jakobson's concept of the poetic function – indeed, their collaboration in the analysis of the Baudelaire sonnet suggests that the anthropologist was in agreement with the notion of poeticity as an intrinsic feature of the text rather than an imposed pattern of external expectations and conventions. But his brilli-antly logical adaptation of the study of linguistic signs to every type of human activity was a vital stage in the demolition of Jakobsonian poetics. A more influential and decisive blow was struck by Roland Barthes.

In *Elements of Semiology* (1967, first published 1964) Barthes extended Lévi-Strauss's concept of the gusteme into another Jakobsonian sphere, the syntagm–paradigm axis. Barthes applies the syntagm–paradigm axis to clothing, food, furniture and archi-tecture. For example, the manner in which items of clothing are associated with the distinctive elements of the human physique – primarily head, trunk, legs and feet – is comparable with the syntagmatic chain of the sentence, and the choices made at each stage in dressing – shirt or pullover, hat or hood, shoes or trai-ners, etc. – are comparable to the selective possibilities offered by each paradigmatic bag of nouns, adjectives, connectives, etc. Similarly, the convention of a 'menu' consisting of four or five different courses is the syntagmatic counterpart to the paradig-matic alternatives of, say, fruit or soup, lamb chops or chicken, spring vegetables or baked potatoes.

Deconstruction, that once-fashionable accessory of the post-structuralist, had not been heard of in 1964, but in sections IV. 2 to IV. 4 on connotation, denotation and metalanguage, Barthes attempts to deconstruct Jakobson's thesis that language and literature are intrinsically different from other sign systems. Barthes proposes a structural bifurcation between two apparently co-dependent sign systems, the connotative and the denotative. 'The signifiers of connotation, which we shall call *connotators* are made up of *signs* (signifiers and signifieds united) of the denoted system.' Denotation involves the process of decoding, classifying and, in basic terms, understanding the activity of connotation. The connotative systems of dress and eating are self-generating mechanisms, the motivating forces of the existing world:

> As for the signified of connotation, its character is at once general, global and diffuse; it is, if you like, a fragment of ideology: the sum of the messages in French refers, for instance, to the signified 'French'; a book can refer to the signified 'Literature'.

The denotative system is the means by which Barthes is able to decode and distinguish between such connotative subcategories as language ('French') and 'Literature'. The deconstructive unseating of this comfortable relationship comes with the introduction of a third element: metalanguage. Metalanguage, Jakobson would argue, is virtually identical to denotation since it involves the translation of the content of one statement into the structurally different, and often explanatory, form of another. Barthes at first seems to agree: 'semiology for instance, is a metalanguage, since as a second order system it takes over a first language (or language-object) which is the system under scrutiny; and this system-object is *signified* through the metalanguage of semiology'. However, such functional discriminations are not quite as straightforward as they might seem. For example, the fashion magazine which ' "speaks" the significations of garments' might appear to be 'denoting' the connotative system-object of clothes and fashion, but: 'we deal here with a complex ensemble, where language, at its denoted level, is a metalanguage, but where this metalanguage is in its turn caught up in a process of connotation'. In short, the connotative language of clothes and fashion cannot signify independently of the denotative metalanguage of the fashion magazine. This disclosure of a necessary interdependence of connotative, denotative and metalinguistic systems has serious implications for the idea of semiology as the ultimate denotative system, the science of signs, because 'Nothing in principle prevents a metalanguage from becoming in turn the language-object of a new metalanguage; this would, for example, be the case with semiology if it were to be "spoken" by another science'. Or, as he might have put it, 'Welcome to poststructuralism.'

This image of a self-renewing diachrony of metalanguages opens upon a whole variety of iconoclastic theses that we have come to regard as Barthesian and which chip away incessantly at Jakobson's linguistic–poetic model.

Barthes's concept of literary 'Writing' would seem to borrow quite freely from the Formalist distinction between ordinary language and poetic defamiliarisation,

> *writing* can no longer designate an operation of recording, notation, representation, 'depiction' (as the Classics would say); rather, it designates exactly what linguists ... call a performative ... in which the enunciation has no other content (contains no other proposition) than the act by which it is uttered.

('The Death of the Author', 1968, reprinted in Lodge, 1988)

But Barthes departs from the Formalistic model in his realignment of the relationship between writing, the author and the reader:

> a text is made of multiple writings, drawn from many cultures and entering into mutual relations of dialogue, parody, contestation, but there is one place where this multiplicity is focused and that place is the reader, not, as was hitherto said, the author.

(ibid., p. 171)

This would seem to be consistent with Jakobson's notion of poetic addresser and addressee as shifting, ambiguous figures, 'whose multiplicity is focused' upon the stabilising presence of the reader. But, as Barthes claims in the *Elements*, while the reader might well be the possessor of the metalinguistic counterpart to the object language of literature, he/she is also 'a semiologist overconfident in the face of connotation', a position of 'objectivity', 'made provisional by the very history which renews metalanguages'. Hence the assumption of semiological stability which underpins Jakobson's programme is itself a potential 'object language'. The notion of the reader as at once the focus of the text's multiplicity and him/herself a synthesis of codes and expectations is fully elaborated in Barthes's *S/Z* (1970), a classic text in the shift from structuralism to poststructuralism. His filleting of Balzac's *Sarrasine* into 561 lexies and his classification of the text–reader relationship into five interpretive codes has been widely discussed (see Scholes, pp. 148–60 and Merquior, pp. 128–47), but it is best summarised in his earlier *Elements*: 'a complex ensemble, where language, as its denoted level, is a metalanguage, but where this metalanguage is in its turn caught up in a process of connotation'. We are never certain of whether the hermeneutic, semic, symbolic, proairetic or cultural codes are elements of the text or constructs of the metalanguage which Barthes imposes upon this unstable phenomenon. Moreover, we begin to doubt the stability of these metalinguistic operations themselves: perhaps they, as much as *Sarrasine*, are the object language of Barthes's disorientating exegetical twists and turns.

The most significant body-blow to the Jakobsonian programme comes from Barthes's governing premise that object language and metalanguage are contingent functions, constantly at the mercy of shifting historical, cultural and ideological elements. Jakobson's interconnected analyses of linguistics and poetics are founded upon his belief in language as the ultimate, originary object language, and, more significantly, in poetry as a kind of object language laboratory in which the irreducible substance of the linguistic sign, the molecular phoneme, is seen to combine with its signifying (in Barthes's terms, connotative) function. The year 1970 provides us with an intriguing point of comparison and departure. *S/Z* and Jakobson and Jones's analysis of Shakespeare's sonnet were published in that year and they represent two very different directions taken by the late twentieth-century inheritors of Formalism, linguistics and semiology. There are similarities. Each involves a text that can be regarded as an intense concentration of the structures and functions of its generic family. The sonnet is, as we have seen, the archetype of interaction between the two elements of the double pattern; and Balzac's *Sarrasine* is at once a novella bordering on a short story and the synthesis of a vast network of cultural, sexual and formal codes. And the metalinguistic commentary upon each text reflects and releases this concentrated panorama of devices and effects (we find a correspondent relation between an 18-page commentary on a 14-line sonnet and a 200-page commentary on a 30-page story). Even Jakobson and Jones's division of the formal and signifying structures of the sonnet into distinct modules seems to be mirrored in Barthes's use of the lexies and the five codes. But the similarities are false. Barthes's method in *S/Z* could easily be mistaken for parody. The ninety-three numbered 'digressions' of the commentary function rather like Jonathan Swift's footnotes in *A Tale of A Tub*; the apparent motivating force of a search for some immanent pattern or truth is constantly disrupted and deferred and the reader begins to suspect that the commentary is more concerned with its own reflexive mechanisms than with its apparent objective. For example, digression number LXXI focuses upon lexie 414 where Sarrasine, thinking Zaminella is a woman and not a castrato, embraces this deceptive unit of signification. Barthes's digression begins with the relation between two different types of reader: one who, like Sarrasine, is caught in the mysterious unfolding of the narrative and one who, having read the story, is granted a more knowledgeable position. He then reflects upon the various financial, circumstantial and intellectual conditions that might cause such a distinction within the readerly perspective, and proceeds to compare the activity of double reading with the sexual appetite of the putative reader(s) – the finished text is like the deflowered virgin, squandered and thrown away. This is all good fun, but it has a more serious intention, again anticipated in the *Elements*:

> the history of the social sciences [including literary studies] would thus be, in a sense, a diachrony of metalanguages, and each science, including of course semiology, would contain the seeds of its own death, in the shape of the language destined to speak it.

S/Z, at least for Barthes, sounds the death knell for the type of literary-linguistic metalanguage currently being practised by Jakobson and Jones. As his digressions demonstrate, Barthes's text is an example of literary semiology distancing itself from the text-analysis, object language–metalanguage relation embodied in such schools as Formalism. Its subject is as much the cultural, sexual and ideological formation of the reader of *Sarrasine* as the means by which these elements function in a text which might occupy that reader's attention. And, as Culler's post-Barthesian summary of *Structuralist Poetics* (1975) shows, the literary-critical world was adapting well to Barthes's contribution to the changing diachrony of metalanguages: the object language was now the numerous and variously inadequate types of critical method. Barthes's thesis might have been fashionable, but was it valid?

Compare Barthes's invention of the concept of the lexie as a means of charting the textual object–metalanguage encounters with Jakobson's method of dividing the sonnet into units of form and signification. Again there would seem to be similarities. The lexie is, in Barthes's view, the minimal distinctive unit of meaning – and here we find echoes of Jakobson's concept of the configuration of phoneme and morpheme as the fundamental point of contact between the material and signifying nature of the linguistic sign. But the 561 lexies of *S/Z* can comprise anything from a single word to a series of sentences. Their identity is determined by their apparent function in organising the reader's metalinguistic encounters with the text: each lexie, irrespective of its size or duration, becomes an isolated unit because of its foregrounding of a particular stylistic, narrative, cultural, sexual, symbolic issue which will correspond with one or more of the five codes. Hence, Barthes implies that the apparently objective concept of formal structure is effectively a product of the particular metalinguistic inclinations of the reader. His tongue-in-cheek manner of numerical and formal precision virtually invites the reader to detect alternative patterns of single-word or multiple-sentence lexies which seem just as consistent with the object of identifying the true relation between form and signification.

Jakobson's equivalent of the lexie corresponds with his concept of linguistic choices as becoming more freely available as we move from distinctive feature to phoneme, to morpheme, to phrase, to sentence (see 'Two Types of Language', *SW II*, pp. 239–59). The lexie of sonnet 129 is the point at which the material element of this hierarchy of the sign is brought into productive contact with its signifying counterpart: rhyme words and semantic distinctions, metrical foregroundings and grammatical cruces, etc. Critics such as Riffaterre have pointed out that very few readers will be continuously aware of these numerous and disorientating collisions between the two elements of the double pattern, but only extremists such as Fish have claimed that they exist only by virtue of the reader's interpretive strategies. No one with any valid claim to common sense would assert that the interactions of the phonemic, metrical, lexical and grammatical structures that constitute the formal design of sonnet 129 are the products of readerly inclination or metalinguistic expectation.

Barthes deliberately and self-consciously unsettles any stable relationship between metalanguage and object language, critical method and text, but his means of doing so, paradoxically, lends credence to Jakobson's model of the poetic function. *Sarrasine* is a piece of prose fiction, and I would argue that Barthes would not have been able to perform an *S/Z*-style, poststructuralist *tour de force* with a regular poem, particularly a sonnet. As Culler demonstrated, it is easy enough to impose a pattern of lexies or meaning units upon any sequence of prose sentences, but with a regular poem it is impossible to ignore the pattern of metrical–grammatical lexies that are verifiably present within the structure of the artefact. The relationship between these meaning-generating units and the complex socio-historical circumstances of the reading of the poem is, as Barthes would argue, a shifting and contingent question; and perhaps Jakobson's refusal to move beyond the self-contained signifying function of the artefact to the broader questions of socio-semiotic 'meaning' signals his partial agreement with Barthes. But Jakobson's thesis that poetry is the working laboratory for the fundamental object language is not overturned by Barthes's poststructuralist exercises.

Let us return for a moment to the phenomenon of the shifting paradigm and its effective marginalisation of Jakobson's theory of poetry. The anti-Jakobson theorists considered so far have one important thing in common: each promotes the system above the event. It is almost as though the very nature of the individual object, be this the speech act, the literary text, the meal, the poetic line or the item of clothing, has become a tainted and valueless concept, perhaps dangerously reminiscent of some milieu or condition of iconicity, in which now discredited values, beliefs and practices were protected by their manifestation in concrete symbols. This would seem to be the only possible explanation for, on the one hand, the broad acceptance of Jakobson's general theories of structural linguistics and, on the other, the deliberate or unwitting blindness to his theory of poetry as a vital element of this broader linguistic programme. For example, J. C. Merquior published in 1986 an excellent historical account of the different directions taken by the post-Formalist schools of linguistics and structuralism (*From Prague to Paris. A Critique of Structuralist and Poststructuralist Thought*). Merquior's discussions of the interactions between the experiences, affiliations and theories of Lévi-Strauss, Barthes, Lacan, Foucault, Derrida, the stars in the European structuralist/poststructuralist galaxy, are impressively detailed and perceptive. But he misrepresents Jakobson's theory of the poetic function:

> From the fact that literature is made of language it does not follow that literary meaning (let alone value) is something reducible to language. My car is made of metal, glass and rubber; but it would never cross my mind to say that it is in any sense 'about' transportation. Matthew Arnold... was surely closer to the point when he said that literature was a criticism of life. It is a matter of not mistaking the functions of a product, or goal of an activity, for what one needs in order to produce the former or perform the latter.
>
> (p. 31)

This is an exemplary instance of the type of context-emphasis which has infected everyone from Barthes to the speech-act theorists, and it foregrounds two common misreadings of Jakobson. First, Jakobson does not argue that 'literature' is definable as something composed of, and therefore 'about', language. He states, in 'On Realism in Art' (1921), that 'the object of study in literary science is not literature but "literariness", that is, what makes a given work a literary work'. The opposition of the term 'literariness' (*literarturnost*) to the broader generic category of literature has been isolated by a number of sceptical post-Formalists as an instance of the fundamental ambiguities and self-contradictions of the Formalist art–science collaboration (see Pratt, pp. 26–7). But what Jakobson means is this: Literariness involves the foregrounding of the signifying function of language at the expense, but without the complete disappearance, of its referential objective, and as such it can be identified in all types of linguistic usage – political slogans, jokes, advertisements, fictional and non-fictional prose, etc. This raises the question to which Jakobson addressed 'Linguistics and Poetics': 'What makes a verbal message a work of art?' If literariness migrates through different levels and functions of linguistic usage, how can we isolate its container-text either as a work of art or a functional non-aesthetic object? Jakobson finds that the novel is primarily, though not exclusively, a literary work/work of art. In a 1956 paper on aphasia he gives an example of how grammatical parallelism can be found in conversation, in novels, in folktales, and the bible (*SW II*, pp. 256–7). In the novel its use is much closer to the general tension between 'syuzhet' (the plot, or the constructed narrative design) and the 'fabula' (the necessary relation between the text and the ordering of the non-fictional world). For example, the comic parallelistic device, 'Thomas is a bachelor; Jeremiah is unmarried', consists of two parallel clauses but creates a tension between the unmarked term (bachelor is a general condition) and its marked counterpart (unmarried implies the specific situation or motivation of Jeremiah). In conversation this parallelistic construction would defer to the actual contextual-referential continuum of known and unknown people and events inhabited by the addresser and addressee. In the novel it would relate more closely to the broader textual pattern of what the text allows the reader to infer from its constructed continuum (*syuzhet*). But in both instances priority is given to the syntagmatic-metonymic relation between language and circumstance. In poetry, however, grammatical parallelism will always be interconnected with the phonemic-metrical pattern of the text. Whatever deictic counterpart to the parallelistic device is identified can never be fully isolated from the purely internal network of sound patterns into which the device is tied. Hence the paradigmatic-metaphoric dimension is guaranteed as an internalised textual counterpart to any contextual frame of reference. And Merquior is correct to state that not all literature is exclusively reducible to being about language. Jakobson would agree, with the crucial qualification that it depends on what type of literature, or to be more accurate what degree of literariness, we are talking about. Poetry is indeed both about language and, in Arnold's terms, a 'criticism of life', and this leads us to Merquior's second misreading. True, we should not mistake the function, goal or activity of all products with the means and substance of their production: cars are not intended as statements about transportation. But Jakobson did not make such a claim. Poetry is the only object–sign system in which function and substance are causally related. On the one hand the poem cannot help making a statement: all objects consisting of language, however oblique and chaotic they might happen to be, must create some relation between sign and meaning. On the other hand, only the poem creates a constant interaction between its substance and means of production (in basic terms its metrical-sound pattern) and its signifying function. There will always be some immanent connection between what a poem says and what it is made of – literariness. The poem is the only type of linguistic object that involves the exclusive and comprehensive enactment of literariness, and as such it is the only purely literary work of art.

With this sweeping but verifiable proposition in mind let us move from Lévi-Strauss and Barthes to the third member of the structuralist *dramatis personae* whose work bears the Jakobsonian imprint: Jacques Lacan.

Lacan is widely credited as the most influential and revolutionary of all post-Freudian theorists of psychoanalysis, and to appreciate Lacan's relationship with Jakobson we had better begin with Jakobson's relationship with Freud. The following is from Freud's 'The Interpretation of Dreams' (1900).

> Suppose I have a picture-puzzle, a rebus [Freud described the dream as a rebus], in front of me. It depicts a house with a boat on its roof, a single letter of the alphabet, the figure of a running man whose head has been conjured away, and so on. Now I might be misled into raising objections and declaring that the picture as a whole and its component parts are nonsensical. A boat has no business to be on the roof of a house, and a headless man cannot run [etc.]. . . . But obviously we can only form a proper judgement of the rebus if we put aside such criticisms as these of the whole composition and its parts and if, instead, we try to replace each separate element by a syllable or word that can be represented by that element in some way or other. The words which are put together in this way are no longer nonsensical but may form a poetical phrase of the greatest beauty and significance. A dream is a picture-puzzle of this sort.
>
> (pp. 277–8)

There seems here to be a close connection between Freud's notion of transference of images from the latent dream to its manifest counterpart in language and Jakobson's distinction between ordinary language and poetic deformation. Freud's pictorial dream image of the headless running man is nonsensical but it acquires a degree of 'beauty and significance' when realised in language. This recalls Jakobson's reference to Dostoevskij's 'semantic' image of the decapitated saint kissing his own head ('New Russian Poetry'): what is inconceivable in any real, pre-linguistic situation can be translated into a 'fixed' semantic unit. But the relationship between Freud's model of transference from dream images to language and Jakobson's concept of the linguistic sign is uneasy and potentially contradictory. Jakobson's most significant reference to Freud occurs in his essay on 'Two Aspects of Language'.

> A competition between both devices, metonymic and metaphoric, is manifest in any symbolic process, be it intrapersonal or social. Thus in an inquiry into the structure of dreams, the decisive question is whether the symbols and the temporal sequences used are based on contiguity (Freud's metonymic 'displacement' and synecdochic 'condensation') or on similarity (Freud's 'identification' and 'symbolism').
>
> (*SW II*, p. 258)

Jakobson does not provide an answer to this 'decisive question' because Freud's distinction between condensation, displacement and symbol is inconsistent with his own model of the relation between linguistic and prelinguistic continua. In 'The Interpretation of Dreams' (p. 160), Freud classified the dream as the '(disguised) fulfilment of a (suppressed or repressed) wish'. The two primary processes of transference from latent dreams to manifest or 'permitted' stories are condensation and displacement. The former involves 'overdetermination', in which several latent images converge on one manifest item, and the latter involves a chain of associations whereby key images of the latent dream are disguised within a pattern of obliquely related substitutes. Freud's concept of the symbol, later to be referred to as an element of 'vulgar' Freudianism, applies to both processes; indeed, all elements of the latent dream are symbolic and can be explained in terms of their manifest counterparts: all things vertical are the male sexual organ and all things horizontal are the mother's body.

The problem for Jakobson is that Freud's model involves a finally indecisive mixture of prelinguistic and linguistic analogues. Condensation and displacement are metonymic-synecdochic, which means that the process of latent–manifest transference makes use of the syntagmatic pole of contiguity, but each item in the latent dream is immanently symbolic and thus invokes the paradigmatic, selective pole. So if we encounter a manifest dream story (and apart from our own latent dreams, this is the only type that we can encounter), we can fit it into the universal model of the syntagm–paradigm and metonymy–metaphor axes. We can note foregroundings of metonymic devices and the use of metaphoric selections, but how do we make this linguistic phonomenon correspond with Freud's theory of transference? In Freud's view all linguistic elements are manifest symbols of their dream counterparts, so even if the manifest pattern is primarily metonymic the units in this syntagmatic chain are symbolically (metaphorically) related to the visual, prelinguistic images of the dream. Jakobson, in his post-1940s work, often adapted C. S. Peirce's three-part model of symbol, index and icon to his own post-Saussurean distinction between signans and signatum. All morphophonemic units (usually individual words) are symbolic in that they enable us to distinguish one prelinguistic concept or image from another, and the principal problem for the Jakobson–Freud relationship exists in the former's premise that the speaker's use of linguistic symbols is motivated primarily by his/her conscious balancing of the syntagm–paradigm axes against the prelinguistic intention of the message. Freud's concept of the symbolic relation between word and image as being motivated by some disguised fulfilment of a repressed or suppressed wish is at odds with Jakobson's notion of signans and signatum, material sign and concept, as necessarily co-present and available to the consciousness of the user. It was not that Jakobson did not believe in Freud's model of conscious and unconscious activities; rather that Freud's consistent argument that creative writing, literature, is analogous to and sometimes an example of dream manifestation undermines Jakobson's conception of poetry as the originary object-language laboratory. Obviously there is some connection between the dream stories of Freud's patients and the more respectable cultural activity of literary writing, but there is a conflict between Freud's all-embracing classification of creative writers and Jakobson's distinction between ordinary and literary language and, most significantly, between poetry and prose. In 'Creative Writers and Day Dreaming' Freud gave particular emphasis to the type of 'egocentric' novel in which the activities, the psychological condition and the speech patterns of 'His Majesty the Ego, the hero' betray some symbolic relationship with the unconscious drives and conflicts of the author. Of secondary interest was the 'eccentric' novel in which the central character plays a less active part in the events of the story (Zola is cited as an example). Indeed, Culler (1980) has suggested a connection between the Formalist concepts of syuzhet and fabula and Freud's psychoanalytic model of the centralised and decentralised author-hero. This would seem to correspond with Jakobson's formulaic connection between 'metonymy as the leading trope in epic poetry' (and, by implication, in the novel) and 'metaphor as the inherent trope in lyric poetry'. 'In this connection, the lyric poet, we note, endeavours to present himself as the speaker, whereas the epic poet takes on the role of a listener who is supposed to recount deeds learned by hearsay' (*SW II*, p. 297). However, these two classifications of literary genre are diametrically opposed. Jakobson's apparent extension of the 'egocentric' author-hero of the novel to the commanding presence of the poetic lyric voice is anti-Freudian. The Freudian author-hero is a figure for whom the syuzhet is a double-edged deployment of literariness: on the one hand, it corresponds with the real world fabula of sequences and events, and on the other it mediates the unconscious, repressed fabula of drives and conflicts. Jakobson's lyric poet similarly creates two patterns of signification. The poem is referential, in the sense that it is bound to refer to something, but it also creates an internalised, reflexive pattern of significations from its network of interactions between sound and meaning. The difference between these two figures is that while the former exerts partial control over unconscious and conscious determinants of the syuzhet, the latter consciously and deliberately controls the relation between the metonymic and metaphoric axes and the pattern of metre and sound with which these are interwoven. One could cite as an example Donne's 'The Flea', in which the addresser at once submits to an egocentric fantasy of phallocentric metaphors while the poet deploys the metrical scheme as a reminder that the entire text is a contrived, self-mocking exercise (see pp. 91–6). Freud often uses the terms 'poetic language' and 'poetical effects', but we must assume that he means any type of extravagant verbal invention. His patients resemble novelists in the sense that both create self-evident stories in which there is a tension between syuzhet and fabula, but none of them, as far as we know, enclosed their dream-stories within a persistent metrical or sound pattern.

Lacan inserted himself into this fissure between Freudian and Jakobsonian theories of the sign by reinterpreting the Freudian model of language and the unconscious. In his 1953 paper 'Discourse at Rome' (later reprinted under the title 'The Function and Field of Speech and Language in Psychoanalysis', 1977, in *Ecrits. A Selection* trans. A. Sheridan) Lacan followed the route of Lévi-Strauss. He argued that the irreducible distinctive features of the phoneme are the points at which the gross materiality of perception and experience, in this instance the acoustic material of the linguistic sign, becomes a formative element in the human being's ability to distinguish between concepts of identity, culture, society, indeed the entire discriminatory framework of human interaction. In this essay Lacan returned to Freud's famous passage in 'Beyond the Pleasure Principle' (1920) where he describes how his grandson dealt with separation from his mother by throwing a spool tied to a string over the edge of his curtained crib, while crying 'Oooo' – 'Da', 'Fort!' – 'Da!' ('Oooo' – 'Here', 'Gone!' – 'Here!'). For Freud the linguistic separation between presence and absence was a symbolic manifestation of the child's renunciation of 'instinctual satisfaction': 'It was related to the child's great cultural achievement . . . he had made his mother go away without protesting' (p. 15). For Lacan, however, the unconscious residue of instinctual satisfaction does not precede its linguistic enactment. The two continua, the linguistic and the unconscious or instinctual, demand the presence of each other; the moment 'in which desire becomes human is also that in which the child is born into language' (1953, p. 103). Lacan's debt to Jakobson's theory of distinctive features and the molecular phoneme becomes evident in his claim that the child's action is

> immediately embodied in the symbolic dyad of two elementary exclamations, announces in the subject the . . . integration of the dichotomy of the phonemes, whose structure existing language offers to his assimilation; moreover the child begins to become engaged in the system of the concrete discourse of the environment, by reproducing more or less approximately in his *Fort!* and in his *Da!* the vocables that he receives from it.
>
> (1953, p. 103)

Lacan's prose has been credited, even by his most devoted followers, with a remarkable and consistent level of impenetrability, and without some awareness of Jakobson's theory of the phoneme the above passage is somewhat confused and confusing. When Lacan refers to the symbolic dyad of the two exclamations, the integrated dichotomy of the phonemes, the engagement of the child in the concrete discourse of the environment, he is liberally adapting Jakobson's notion of the ascending scale of linguistic freedom.

> In the combination of distinctive features into phonemes, the freedom of the individual speaker is zero: the code has already established all the possibilities which may be utilized in the given language. Freedom to combine phonemes into words is circumscribed. In forming sentences with words the speaker is less constrained.
>
> (*SW II*, p. 242)

The principal difference between Jakobson's and Lacan's theses exists in the latter's insistence that the zero condition of freedom extends far beyond the individual's first encounter with the integrated dichotomy of the phoneme. In his essay on 'The Mirror Stage' (1949, in *Ecrits*, 1977) Lacan lays the groundwork for the 'Discourse at Rome' and maps out his post-Freudian concept of language and the unconscious. Lacan sees the unconscious as coming into being simultaneously with language. Desire, the driving force, in Freud's view, towards prelinguistic instinctual satisfaction, can only be properly understood in terms of the tension between the subject and 'that condition which is imposed upon him by the existence of the discourse to cause his need to pass through the defiles of the signifier' (p. 264). In brief, desire, far from being an element of our prelinguistic unconscious condition, is actually the result of our being 'born into language'. In the Freudian scheme the unconscious exists in a mass of instinctual representatives; in Lacan's scheme the unconscious is the product of the structuring of desire by language. The signifier invests desire with meaning. As a consequence the material signifier becomes the focus of subjectively felt needs and is in a constantly 'sliding' state above the continuum of the signified.

If an inability to accept fully, let alone comprehend, Lacan's model is an extreme instance of being, as he puts it, 'a slave of language', then I gladly accept my state of serfdom. My problem is this: I accept that the phenomena apprehended by human consciousness (and I include the remembered images from the latent dream in this category) can never be fully disconnected from their counterparts in linguistic signs. Even if we are not certain of how to name or describe something our manifest sense of unease is a token of the desired triangular equation between signifier, signified and referent. However, I am equally convinced that the material phenomenon of language (at its most basic the distinctive features of the phoneme) is something that enables us to deal with (classify, interrogate, or whatever) the material phenomenon of mental and physical existence and not something that effectively creates consciousness, unconsciousness and its various bodily manifestations. I descend to the personal in order to take on the role of the Jakobsonian advocate. Jakobson (*SW II*, p. 672) acknowledges that the psychoanalytic endeavour to 'disclose the *privata privatissima* of language [the fundamental level of inner speech] may find stimulation in Lacan's attempts to revise and reinterpret the correlation between *signans* and *signatum* in the mental and verbal experience of the patient', but his use of the conditional term and his implication that mental *and* verbal experiences are not the same thing signals a degree of tension between Jakobson and Lacan. In Lacan's 1957 essay 'The Insistence of the Letter in the Unconscious' (all references from the reprint in Lodge, 1988) this tension becomes strikingly evident. In one of his footnotes Lacan refers to Jakobson's 'purely linguistic' analysis of aphasia and directs the reader to the *Fundamentals of Language*, published the previous year. Lacan's essay draws extensively upon the *Fundamentals* and, in a number of instances, grossly distorts Jakobson's arguments. These distortions are most significant in Lacan's treatment of metaphor and metonymy. Jakobson acknowledges that in using these two terms he invokes the linguistic subdisciplines of stylistics and rhetoric, but his broader purpose is to establish a binary distinction within all linguistic usages in which metaphor is a function of the paradigmatic, selective axis and metonymy a function of its syntagmatic, combinatory counterpart. Lacan is far more concerned with validating his thesis that the unconscious is structured *by* and not, as Freud argued, *like* language. As a consequence we find that metonymy is classified as a device in which one word is substituted for another in the same semantic-contextual field ('thirty sails' instead of 'fleet' is cited by Lacan) and linked with displacement, 'that veering off of meaning that we see in metonymy, and which from its first appearance in Freud is described as the main method by which the unconscious gets around censorship' (p. 92). Metaphor is described as the 'superimposition of signifiers' and is linked with the substitution of surface meaning for repressed meaning (p. 92). In short, metonymy-displacement involves disclosure, and metaphor-condensation involves disguise. A large number of critics and commentators have noted how Lacan's distinction between metonymy-displacement and meta-phor-condensation differs from Freud's classification of both pro-cesses of transference as metonymic, but none has pointed out that Lacan's is not really a distinction at all. It is, in fact, a farrago of self-contradictions. Consider the following:

> The creative spark of the metaphor does not spring from the conjunction of two images, that is of two signifiers equally actualised. It springs from two signifiers one of which has taken the place of the other in the signifying chain, the hidden signifier then remaining present through its (metonymic) relation to the rest of the chain.

> (p. 89)

Lacan is attempting to reverse the traditional hierarchy of the signified preceding the signifier, and he stresses that it is not the 'images' of the metaphoric transference that create a particu-lar effect, rather the sense of the substituted signifier as inconsist-ent with the remainder of the syntagmatic chain. However, as Jakobson states, the syntagmatic chain, the axis of contiguity, is primarily related to the association between meaning and pre-linguistic context. A discourse that foregrounds the syntagmatic-metonymic chain (such as Tolstoy's obsessive listing of the objects in Anna Karenina's room) is mimetic in the sense that the con-tiguous relation between the signifiers mirrors the way in which the addresser defers to the spatio-temporal ordering of objects and experience. A discourse that foregrounds the paradigmatic-metaphoric axis shifts the emphasis towards the relation between the addresser and the linguistic code – an unusual choice of signifier from the paradigmatic bag involves the addresser's attempt to use language as a means of directing the addressee's attention from the 'objective' perceptual experience to objects, experiences, feelings, memories with which the addresser associ-ates it. Lacan's argument: (a) that the 'creative spark' of meta-phor is generated not by the signifier–signified relation but by the relation between signifiers, and (b) that the 'hidden signifier' of the metaphor becomes evident in its relation to the rest of the metonymic chain is at best contradictory and at worst absolute nonsense. If metaphor is focused upon the non-actualised signifier, then how can it also be dependent upon the function of the metonymic chain which, as Lacan has already conceded, demands an awareness of the actualised signifier? How would we know that 'thirty sails' is a metonymic substitute for 'fleet' if we did not 'actualise' these signifiers?

The essay bristles with similarly ungrateful 'borrowings' from Jakobsonian theory, but of more importance is the element of the *Fundamentals* that Lacan fails to comprehend: 'the principle of similarity underlies poetry; the metrical parallelism of lines, or the phonic equivalence of rhyming words prompts the question of semantic similarity or contrast' (p. 95). At one point Lacan refers to the 'law of the parallelism of the signifier' in verse, but his intended meaning is selective and one-dimensional (p. 88). For Lacan the parallelism of the phonic and metrical patterns of the signifier is what enables verse to foreground and disclose the more general 'notion of an incessant sliding of the signified under the signifier' (p. 87), and again we encounter a distortion of Jakobson's theory. Jakobson's point is that verse projects the material signifier into a second level of organisation which supplements but does not displace the balance between signifier and signified in non-poetic discourse. So in verse the relation between signifier and signified is not one of 'incessant sliding' but of a productive, multidimensional tension between what language is and what language does. Lacan shares with Jakobson the belief in poetry as a medium which isolates and foregrounds general elements in the nature and function of language, but for the latter this process requires a conscious and intensive manipulation of the agreed relation between signifier, signified and referent, while for the former it discloses the uncontrollable structuration of signified and referent by the signifier in both the conscious and the unconscious continua. Lacan's notion of literature, and poetry in particular, as a condition or a symptom, rather than a deliberate, self-aware practice, is an extension of Freudianism, and it leads us into a territory of literary theory where the validity, let alone the relevance, of Jakobson's theories has become a distant memory. I speak of deconstruction.

Lacan's 'Seminar on the Purloined Letter' appeared in the original French edition of *Ecrits* (1966) and J. Mehlman's English translation was published in *Yale French Studies* (1972). It has since become a kind of *cause célèbre* in the deconstructive and, it could be argued, the post-deconstructive world. A proper analysis of the subsequent rereadings of Lacan's reading of Poe's story by Derrida (1975), Felman (1977) and Johnson (1979) would require another chapter, and I shall limit my summary to the relevance of this episode to Jakobsonian theory.

Poe's story of 'The Purloined Letter' involves the transference, the theft and the hiding of the eponymous missive by a bizarre assembly of aristocrats and retainers: the king, the queen (Lacan's term), the minister and the prefect of police. The 'mystery' of why and where the letter is hidden is solved by Dupin, an amateur detective, but the actual, and it is presumed incriminatory, substance of the letter remains undisclosed. Lacan could hardly have hoped for a more lucid and symptomatic demonstration of his model of desire as structured by the incessantly sliding signifier. The term 'letter' is metonymic in that it transposes the original meaning of written or printed character with a particular and, most significantly, a sealed collection of these. It is metaphorically related to the treatment of the signifier in the world, in that its 'meaning' (whatever that happens to be) is displaced by its operational effect upon the anxieties, desires and behaviour of those who hide it, seek it, fear it and exploit it. Dupin, at least for Lacan, is a perfect example of the analyst. He is no more aware of the content of the letter-signifier than his patients-employers, but by returning it to the queen he diffuses its uneasy symptomatic effects, and, by exploiting its effects, he too becomes a participant in this deterministic circuit of unknowing – rather than, in the more traditional Freudian sense, exerting his superior position as the expert who discloses the true meaning of the symbol. Derrida deconstructs Lacan's reading by pointing out that he has contradicted his own premise by investing the signifier with a particular function – that of 'phallogocentric' desire. Johnson deconstructs the deconstructor, and accuses Derrida of being over-subjectivist, of privileging his own particular belief in différance, dissemination and, necessarily, equivocation over Lacan's specific association of the letter-signifier with phallic desire.

All of this, assuming a 'translator' could be found, might provide the basis for an academic farce, but beneath the slapstick we encounter a more serious correspondence with Jakobsonian theory. First of all there is some connection between Poe's short story and his poem 'The Raven' – the latter being the subject of Jakobson's 'Language in Operation'. In each text thematic and structural precedence is given to a particular signifier, respectively 'the letter' and 'nevermore', whose relation to a particular signified or context-grounded referent is diffuse and uncertain. Moreover, Jakobson's ingenious tracing of the word's journey between bird and speaker to actor, radio listener, conversationalists on a train and curious linguist bears an intriguing resemblance to the textual journey of the letter, first between king, queen and minister, next between policeman, minister and Dupin and its outertextual journey from Lacan to Derrida to Johnson. But there is a crucial difference between these two textual-interpretive episodes. What Lacan, Derrida and Johnson ignore is that their opportunity for psychoanalytic–deconstructive game-playing has been created first by Poe's choice of a particular genre, prose fiction, and second by his deliberate and purposive use of the devices and effects made available by that genre. It is Poe the fiction writer who decides that the letter will never be opened and that its content-signified will remain undisclosed. This does not mean that in the general, universal continuum of signs and events all signifiers or their non-linguistic counterparts will incessantly refuse to come to rest upon a particular signified. Neither Derrida nor Johnson questions Lacan's premise that literary gestures are intensified instances of the broader psychological condition of the ever-sliding signifier, but it could be argued that Poe's decision to leave the letter unopened is motivated more by a deliberate strategy to prolong the reader's engagement with the self-consciously unreal mystery of his Gothic tale than by his entrapment in some kind of signifier fetish. Lacan's insistence that the letter is a metaphoric enactment of the universal treatment of the signifier becomes less valid if we recognise that the reader's sense of curiosity is generated entirely by its metonymic function. Without our knowledge that the letter must have a specific content (incriminatory, innocuous or whatever) we would lose interest in its passage along the syntagmatic chain of thieves, conspirators and detectives. In short, its function as a signifier is governed by the relationship between its signified content and the contiguous structuring of objects, events and activities in the real world. It is this dependency of the prose text upon imagined context that allows Lacan to make his paradoxical, or as Derrida might argue self-deconstructive, move of positioning Dupin as the analyst-surrogate. Any attempt to shift the addresser of 'The Raven' from text to context would be blocked by what Jakobson refers to as the 'double sensed message [finding] correspondence in a split addresser, in a split addressee, as well as a split reference' (*L in L*, p. 85). Any attempt, either objectively or via the self-focused discourse of the addresser, to determine the elusive, referential meaning of 'nevermore' is complicated by its function as a focal catylist for the dense refractory sound patterns of the text. The deictic circumstances of the text, the chamber, the door, the lost love Lenore, even the addresser himself, are bound into its pattern of material signifiers and are at the same time the signifieds of its imagined context. As Jakobson puts it, 'similarity superimposed upon contiguity imparts to poetry its thoroughgoing symbolic, multiplex, polysemantic essence . . . where similarity is superinduced upon contiguity, any metonymy is slightly metaphorical and any metaphor has a metonymical tint' (*L in L*, p. 85). Jakobson's model of the poetic function is radically antithetical to Lacan's thesis that the signifier governs and determines the signified. For poetry to register at all we need to be aware that language can relate specifically to a prelinguistic continuum (the syntagmatic-metonymic axis) *and* by its own means distort and reorder this continuum (the paradigmatic-metaphoric axis). By foregrounding the sometimes perverse and arbitrary relationship between signifier, signified and referent, poetry reminds us that, to understand each element properly, we should not allow one of them to displace the others. Lacan, by privileging the signifier, and the speech act theorists, by privileging the context of the signifier's use, stand at opposing ends of the linguistic-philosophic spectrum; Jakobson and his language laboratory of the poetic function stand at the centre – the point at which the poetic function of the textual circuit becomes perversely and productively intermingled with the message of its contextual counterpart.

Jakobson's closest involvement with the relation between conscious and unconscious states was inspired by his interest and participation in the *Zaum* transrational school of poetic writing, and we have already considered his belief that 'any significant poetic composition . . . implies a goal directed choice of verbal material' (*L in L*, p. 250). The antithetical relation between Jakobson's model and those of Freud and Lacan becomes most evident in his short essay on 'Supraconscious Turgenev'. In this Jakobson examines Turgenev's account (via the memoirs of Count V. A. Sollagub) of a gloomy dinner with his expatriate acquaintance N. M. Zemcuznikov at 'one of [London's] grandest clubs'. Turgenev tells of how the mechanical formality of the club and the automaton-like behaviour of a 'trinity' of serving butlers 'began to exasperate me to the extreme. . . . I was suddenly seized by some sort of frenzy. With all my might I banged my fist on the table and started screaming like a madman: *Réd'ka! Týkva! Kobýla! Répa! Bába! Kásǎ! Kásǎ!* (Radish! Pumpkin! Mare! Turnip! Peasant woman! Kasha! Kasha!) (*L in L*, pp. 262–3). This catalogue would no doubt be interpreted by Lacan as an instance of the desire-invested signifier disrupting the meaning-referent conventions of normal discourse: we find a metonymic relation between rural images, a metaphoric transposition of sexuality with food and, crucially, an assonantal-alliterative pattern of vowels and consonants which, at least in Lacan's schema, promotes the 'enigmatic signifier of a sexual trauma' (Lodge, p. 97) above any conscious or controlled relation between signifier and signified. Jakobson's analysis, though founded upon the same empirical observations, is quite different. To appreciate fully the lucid subtlety of Jakobson's account you would need to read his essay, but I'll attempt a brief summary. Jakobson's point is this: Language is an element of both our environment and our consciousness. Turgenev's response to the stifling and exasperating conditions of the dinner is not to seek consolation in an ordered, discursive reminiscence of Old Russia. To have done so would have involved a submission to circumstances, to the dominance of the contiguity axis. He could have told a story which drew attention to the difference between rural Russia and the stultifying environment of the London club, but rather than displace his sense of anger and frustration into the counter-pattern of two narratives – the ongoing immediacy of the club and the story of somewhere else – he foregrounds the concrete signifier as a means of projecting the principle of equivalence from the axis of selection (his memories, his command of the linguistic code) into the axis of combination (the stranglehold of the context upon expression). Jakobson recounts the way in which the butler's announcements of 'First cutlet! Second cutlet! Third cutlet!' reinforced Turgenev's sense of being trapped within parallel contiguity axes of words and events. He escaped into that realm of language where the addresser assumes command of a less predictable relation between signifier and signified, the poetic.

> Watching the ritualistic appearance of the invariable viands served on a silver plate covered by a silver bellglass, he experienced something, as it were, beyond words: the five velar consonants of his fevish tirade – concluding with the hypnotic catchword 'Kasha! Kasha!' – alliteratively echo the overwhelmingly crushing, thrice repeated announcement: 'Cutlet!'
>
> (*L in L,* p. 265)

Jakobson locates in Turgenev's account the originary essence of the poetic function. The referential-contextual element of language is interposed with the addresser's perverse and unpredictable command of the signans–signatum relationship. However, the implied assumption that every instance of the poetic function involves the patterned foregrounding of linguistic materiality might be regarded as a somewhat partial and selective conception of literary history; and the most obvious challenge to this model comes from the Anglo-American tradition of unrhymed, unmetrical free verse. This part has been concerned with the uncomfortable interface between Jakobsonian poetics and the broader context of twentieth-century linguistics, semiotics and interpretive theory; in the next part I shall test his thesis against two radically opposed models of the poetic function, a division caused by the originators of the poem rather than its interpreters.

Part III

Space and time

SPACE AND TIME

Jakobson's treatment of the concepts of space and time and the perceptual, existential and methodological issues that underpin them represents the most important element of his thesis that the poetic function is uniquely different from all other linguistic and non-linguistic systems of representation.

We will begin with Saussure. Twentieth-century linguistics and semiotics have inherited three pairs of binary oppositions from Saussure and each has played its part in establishing him as the father of structuralism: signifier and signified, langue and parole, and synchrony and diachrony. The third pair has proved to be the most problematic for the simple reason that, while we might understand that an emphasis upon language as a synchronic system in a given time and place is distinguishable from an emphasis upon the changes that occur diachronically within language through time, the practical implementation of this distinction means that we must not only freeze time but also regard its effect on language as existing independently of human activities. For example, Saussure (*Course*, pp. 83–4) identifies three crucial stages in the phonetic transformation of the Anglo-Saxon plural of 'foot' into its modern form. Stage 1 (*fōti*, pron. 'foati') becomes stage 2 when the 'o' is displaced by the 'e' (*fēti*, pron. 'feeti'), and stage 2 becomes stage 3 when the 'i' is dropped (*fēt*, pron. 'feet'). First, this raises the unanswerable question of the exact moment at which each stage had effectively displaced its predecessor (it is likely that for long periods people would pronounce the same word in different ways), and second, the more significant question of why such changes take place. Saussure argues that changes originate in linguistic performance (parole) and that the system (langue) responds to these, but as to why linguistic acts can have such broader systemic effects, he answers that accident motivates adaptation. '*Fōt*: *fēt* is no better suited to this purpose [distinguishing between singular and plural] than *fōt*: *fōti*. In each state, mind breathes life into a substance that is given' (*Course*, p. 85).

It would be wrong to regard the uneasy questions raised by Saussure's formula as inherent flaws. Neither Saussure nor anyone else can identify the precise moment and cause of linguistic change, but for the Prague Linguists, and for Jakobson in particular, Saussure seemed to be paying insufficient attention to the crucial concept of a causal relation between phonemic change and intention.

> The question of the goal of a phonetic event is gaining ascendence for the linguist over the traditional question of causes. One transcends the tradition of the 'neogrammarians', not by renouncing the concept of the 'phonetic law', but rather by interpreting this concept teleologically and abandoning the mechanistic concept. To the extent that phonetic changes are treated without consideration of the phonological system that undergoes them, the laws of general phonetics remain in the dark.
>
> ('Proposition au premier congrès international de linguistes', 1928, *SW I*, p. 6)

Jakobson's proposition here can only be properly understood in terms of his ongoing work on the hierarchical model of phonemic–semantic relations. The material substance of the molecular phoneme (its distinctive features) becomes an active, meaning-generating, unit when it enters the complex differential system of morphophonemes and syntax. This latter element is governed by the interactive addresser–addressee relations of the apperceptive 'set'. Therefore, although we may not be able to identify the precise moment at which phonemic alterations take place we should pay particular attention to how the teleological function of imposing specific meanings upon phonemic substance affects the progress of these alterations. In a 1953 paper Jakobson illustrates his argument with the example of how the /e/ and /i/ phonemes in Russian were distinguished by his grandparents' generation, while for his generation the two merged into one /i/. He offers what is, in effect, a teleological reinterpretation of Saussure's three-stage model. His generation used the /e/ /i/ distinction to link specific usage self-consciously with archaic or outdated discourse (stage 3). His parents' generation (stage 2) preserved the distinction in formal exchanges but in familiar conversation fused the two phonemes 'to produce the impression of being younger than one really was' (*SW II*, p. 562). So although the reason for the original /e/ /i/ fusion remains obscure its subsequent integration in the conventions of linguistic usage can be explained in terms of the specific intention of its users. In a 1940 paper Mukarovsky, working upon the same thesis, represented Saussure's use of the synchrony/diachrony distinction as a straightforward diagram of cross-hairs.

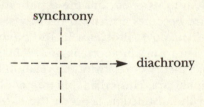

This interactive relation could, he argued, be more accurately represented by a prism. (This model was adapted by Jakobson in 'Der Stuctur des Phonems', 1939, *SW I*, pp. 280–310).

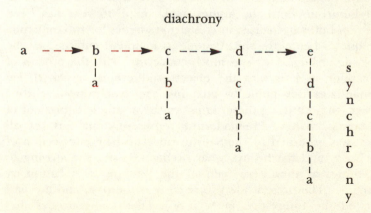

What this diagram seeks to demonstrate is that the clinical distinction between synchrony and diachrony is a necessary methodological fiction that must in turn be qualified by our awareness that at any putative point in time on the diachronic scale there is a continuous tension between elements of the linguistic past and the present, with the implication that our more extended and active awareness of the past will produce an increasingly complex present. Let us now turn from the purely linguistic issues raised by these models of synchrony and diachrony and consider their influence upon Formalist and Jakobsonian concepts of art and literature.

Jakobson's most innovative and, it could be argued, revolutionary disquisition on space, time and art was also his first. His 1919 essay on 'Futurism' pays more attention to the visual artists of the movement than to its poets, but the significance of his argument for literature becomes evident in his essays on 'The Dominant' and (with Tynjanov) 'Problems in the Study of Language and Literature'. 'Futurism', in approximately 2,500 words, brings together Einstein's theory of relativity, the relation between cubist and representational art, Husserlian phenomenology, aesthetics and politics, and the distinction between the substance and the signifying potential of the sign, and it might easily be mistaken for a typically chaotic farrago of intellectual fashions, *circa* 1919. However, a more informed reading discloses the manifesto for Jakobsonian poetics that would be elaborated and substantiated during the following six decades. Jakobson's principal point involves the aesthetic and compositional relation between cubism and Futurism. Both, he argues, make explicit what has been inherent but marginalised in Western aesthetics for two millennia (he quotes Leonardo and Aristotle as incipient cubists): art, be it plastic or linguistic, is as much concerned with the process of perception as it is with the objects and events perceived. He substantiates this point by adapting the synchrony–diachrony model (without using these terms) to the aesthetic equivalent of phonemic change. Pre-modernist representational art, of all types, was governed by the Saussurean cross-hair intersection of synchrony and diachrony: 'what is characteristic is a striving to see things as they were seen in the past, as it is customary to see. . . . The present was projected into the past, and the past dictated the future' (*L in L*, p. 30). Jakobson concedes that changes took place, but he regards these as merely adjustments to the overarching compositional and representational assumption that the pre-modernist aesthetic artefact was, in various ways, an attempt to mediate its pre-representational object. Cubism and the visual and poetic manifestations of Futurism foreground the substantive presence of the representational sign:

> the laying bare of the device . . . the realized texture no longer seeks any sort of justification for itself; it becomes autonomous, demands for itself new methods of formulation, new material. Pieces of paper begin to be pasted on the picture, sand is thrown on it. Finally, cardboard, wood, tin, and so on, are used.
>
> (*L in L*, p. 30)

The poetic counterpart to this baring of the plastic device involves the chaotic interpenetration of sound pattern and syntactic structure of Xlebnikov's and Jakobson's *Zaum* poems.

The part played in this signifying revolution by the synchronic–diachronic relation is complex. Saussure's model of phonemic change begs rather than engages with the question of its semantic counterpart. The signified of *fóti* and *fĕt* is an irreducible quantity, comparable to the notion of a stable pre-representational continuum which representational art seeks, in various ways, to mediate. Hence the Saussurean model of phonemic diachrony mirrors the history of pre-modernist art: the altered signifier is accommodated by an agreed, consensual notion of the signified. Jakobson's alternative model of time, space and representation is an attempt to validate both Formalist doctrine and his own belief in poetry as the originary, groundbreaking laboratory for all sign systems. His proposition is this: Futurist painting and poetry enacts, at an immediate, localised level, the true nature of our much broader, and previously misperceived, encounters with spatio-temporal phenomena. The *Zaum* poem and the cubist-Futurist painting focus upon 'the message for its own sake'; they expose the material and fragmentary nature of the objects, and by implication the signs, through which we measure the relation between stasis and temporal progress. The paintings oblige the perceiver to consider the contingent relation between geometrical absolutes – cubes, circles, angles, shapes of all types – and the dependency of these elements upon a specific perceptual situation: objects are presented in a way that is inconsistent with a 'normal' visual perspective. Similarly, the Futurist poem allows the material upon which the linguistic sign depends – the phonemic substance of language – to interface with the normal, orderly deployment of these same linguistic signs. These art forms compromise the stability of an absolute signified upon which different signifiers – be they the traditions of representational art or the mutant phoneme – allow us different perspectives; and the traditional notion of time as a measurable progressive continuum is dependent upon the stability of such absolute signifieds. The Formalist notion of 'making strange' is thus projected from the aesthetic sphere into the regions of philosophy and physics. The proposing of a causal relation between immediate, subjective encounters with time and space realised in art forms and our shared, consensual engagement with the extensive conditions of past, present and future brings to the surface a point of conflict between Saussure's model and the so-called Prague prism that Mukarovsky did not fully engage with. In the *Dialogues*, at the beginning of Chapter 7 on 'The Time Factor in Language and Literature', Krystyna Pomorska asks Jakobson to elaborate on his charge that Saussure had 'reduced the object of study of the system of language to only one of its aspects, namely the static synchrony' (p. 56). Jakobson begins his answer by citing the 'Futurism' essay and stressing that his intention was to challenge the Saussurean model with two alternative perceptions of the space–time relation, supplied by Einstein and the Futurists. In the essay he quotes extensively from the work of two Russian commentators on Einstein's physics, Xvol'son and Umov.

> The new doctrine rejects the absolute character of time, and therefore the existence of 'world' time as well. Every identical self moving system has its own time; the speed of time flow is not identical in each such system. . . . These pictures in the field of philosophical thought should produce a revolution greater than Copernicus' displacement of the earth from the center of the universe. . . . The newly discovered, offers a . . . new style, one which far outdistances in its free lines the borders not only of the old external world, but also of our basic forms of thinking.
> (*L in L*, pp. 31–2, quoted by Jakobson from Xvol'son's *The Principle of Relativity* and Umov's *The Characteristic Features of Contemporary Natural-Scientific Thought*)

It would be a gross understatement to claim that Jakobson simply approved of this concept of relativity. For him, and for a number of his contemporaries, relativity was something more than the next stage in post-Copernican, post-Newtonian science; relativity was part of the contemporary experience.

> The overcoming of *statics*, the discarding of the absolute, is the main thrust of modern times, the order of the day. A negative philosophy and tanks, scientific experiment and deputies of Soviets, the principle of relativity and the Futurist 'Down With!' are destroying the garden hedges of the old culture.
>
> (*L in L*, pp. 30–1)

For Jakobson cubism and Futurism were the aesthetic elements of a universal condition: relativity, political revolution, cubist art, the *Zaum* poem – all of these were involved in the exposure of the means by which conventional intellectual systems fabricated and perpetuated notions of the absolute.

Let us return to Saussure. Jakobson claims that Saussure effectively promoted synchrony (or 'statics') above diachrony because he believed that in order to discuss the history of language it is necessary for the linguist to assume a position within a stable, synchronic present. Jakobson counters this: 'Synchrony contains many a diachronic element, and it is necessary to take this into account when using a synchronic approach' (*Dialogues*, p. 57). Jakobson's counter-thesis of a continuous dynamic of synchronic–diachronic relations was inspired by his realisation that subjective time is a mutable concept, its apparent stability being a function of the arbitrary system of signs that enable us to isolate past, present and future within what would otherwise be a chaotic flux of experience and data. This notion of ordered temporal progress as essentially a linguistic fabrication underpins every element of Jakobson's science of language. 'As a result [of Saussure's privileging of synchrony] dynamism was excluded from the study of the system and the *signans* was reduced to pure linearity, thus precluding any possibility of viewing the phoneme as a bundle of distinctive characteristics' (*Dialogues*, p. 59). This realisation that temporality and simultaneity are co-present elements in our cognitive response to distinctive features extends to the sphere of morphology and syntax. In his essay on 'Shifters, Verbal Categories and the Russian Verb' (1957, *SW II*, pp. 130–47) and in *Dialogues* (pp. 76–7) Jakobson emphasises the enabling function of the primary deictic marker in any speech act, the pronoun, as a means of placing the addresser and addressee within a particular spatio-temporal continuum. The child's acquisition of the pronoun and, as a consequence, of the subject and predicate matrix of the sentence

> frees the child, liberating him from the immediate temporal and spatial circumstances. From this moment on he can speak of events that take place at a distance from him in time and space. The notion of time appears in the language of the child, as does that of spatial proximity and distance.
>
> (*Dialogues*, p. 77)

Indeed, the general model of language based upon the two axes of the syntagm and the paradigm involves the necessary separation of the present from the past and the future. The syntagm is an immediate enactment of diachronic progress: we move forward from one grammatical class to the next, remembering the structures that have preceded our arrival at a particular point and envisaging those that will follow it. But this progression is made possible by the static, synchronic axis of paradigm or selection: each choice from the paradigmatic bag involves the use of a fixed, atemporal continuum. Each speech pause, hesitation or paratactic slippage is caused primarily by our temporary inability to locate a word or phrase which accommodates the prelinguistic situation or intention we are attempting to mediate. This situation of choice is static; even if the speaker were to wander away to consult a dictionary or thesaurus, he/she would still be encountering a static, synchronic continuum of alternatives. Jakobson's point is that the dynamic interpenetration of synchrony and diachrony operates not just for the linguistic historian but for every user of language, irrespective of their knowledge of etymology or semantic origin. In our use of non-poetic language – a category which includes discourses from the non-literary speech act to prose fiction – the relation between the linguistic and the prelinguistic temporal continua is unproblematic. The contiguity axis presents addresser and addressee with a parallel progress of signans and signata. Certain prose forms (note Shklovsky's emphasis upon *Tristram Shandy* as the exemplary fictional text) can foreground distinctions between subjectively perceived time (syuzhet) and its objectified counterpart (fabula), but at both levels contiguity (progression and diachrony) is the dominant function (see *Dialogues*, pp. 71–2). With poetry, however, the dynamic relation between diachrony and synchrony is immediate and foregrounded. Jakobson states that 'in poetry where similarity is superinduced upon contiguity, any metonymy is slightly metaphorical and any metaphor has a metonymical tint' (*L in L*, p. 85). The distinction between this poetic effect and the metaphor–metonymy, paradigm–syntagm relation of non-poetic language is comparable to the distinction between the Prague–prism and the Saussurian cross-hairs diagram. In the prism diachrony-syntagm is never immune from the encroachments of synchrony-paradigm and vice versa, and the factor that maintains this dynamic, interactive condition in poetry is the double pattern: the universal linguistic feature of the syntagm–paradigm axes is supplemented by the arbitrary structures of metre and rhyme. And here we encounter the basis for Jakobson's theory of literary history proposed in 'The Dominant' and 'Problems in the Relation Between Language and Literature'.

In the specific poem the abstract structure of metre and sound pattern involves a localised synthesis of synchrony and diachrony. In ordinary speech,

> the listener becomes conscious of the words after the units of which they are composed have already been pronounced, and he understands the sentences after the words of which they are composed have already been uttered. In order for the utterance to be understood, attention to the flow of speech must be combined with the moments of 'simultaneous synthesis'. . . . This is the procedure that combines the elements that have escaped immediate perception with those that already belong to immediate memory. These elements are then combined into larger groupings: sounds into words, words into sentences, and sentences into utterances.
>
> (*Dialogues*, p. 70)

This is the Jakobsonian linguistic hierarchy of distinctive features – phoneme–morpheme–syntax adapted to the temporal immediacies of speech and cognition. The anchor, the point of stability for the listener's synthetic reconstitution of linguistic data, is sound. Consider what happens when sound pattern is not simply the founding register for the building of more complex phonemic, semantic and syntactic structures, but a recognisably ordered structure in its own right – metre and rhyme. The sound–word–sentence–utterance combination is complicated by a secondary pattern in which the signans of a particular signatum is also a constituent feature of a regular stress pattern and occasionally an echo of one or more signans–signatum confluences elsewhere in the text. At this localised textual level poetic form effectively organises the dynamic relation between synchrony and diachrony, and within the broader continuum of literary and linguistic history it serves a similar purpose as the factor which isolates the poetic function from the synchronic–diachronic shifts of other linguistic discourses – the dominant.

> Inquiry into the dominant had important consequences for Formalist views of literary evolution. In the evolution of poetic form it is not so much a question of the disappearance of certain elements and the emergence of others as it is a question of shifts in the mutual relationships among the diverse components of the system, in other words a question of the shifting dominant . . . the hierarchy of artistic devices changes within the framework of a given poetic genre; the change, moreover, affects the hierarchy or poetic genres, and, simultaneously, the distribution of artistic devices among the individual genres. Genres which were originally secondary paths, subsidiary variants, now come to the fore, whereas the canonical genres are pushed toward the rear.
>
> ('The Dominant', *L in L*, p. 44)

The dominant is the element of the poetic function which, at any particular synchronic point, preserves its essential difference from other linguistic discourses and which consequently ensures that the synchronic–diachronic shifts that occur within the history of poetry are governed as much by the definitive and inherent nature of the dominant as by external, contextual elements such as politics and socio-cultural change. The dominant is effectively Jakobson's definition of the poetic function as 'the focus upon the message for its own sake' viewed from the socio-historical perspective, and in immediate, textual terms it is the double pattern. Jakobson goes on to summarise the work of his Formalist colleagues Ejxenbaum, Gukovskij, Vinogradov and Tynjanov on how the dominant can clarify our perceptions of Russian poetic history. How would it affect our perceptions of the history of English poetry?

To engage properly with this question we should first re-examine Jakobson's six-part diagram (see Part II, p. 84). The diagram consists of two strata of interchangeable properties: context-referential, contact-phatic, code-metalingual, addresser-emotive, addressee-conative. The special case is the matching of message with poetic. It is possible to envisage context, contact, code, addresser and addressee as consisting of syntactic structures, objects, locations, events and individuals existing independently of the message but brought into action at the moment of the speech act. As such it is the message that is the active link between the abstract conception of the diagram and its specific enactment. Jakobson proposes that the poetic function of a given text serves the same purpose, both for the external elements described above (diagram 1) and for their textual counterparts – referential, phatic, etc. (diagram 2). The two diagrams could also be linked with the two continua of synchrony and diachrony. Diagram 1 consists of elements that are far more subject to historical and temporal change than those of diagram 2. For example, the notion of the telephone as the governing element of contact would be untenable in eighteenth-century discourse, while the linguistic subcategory of phatic utterances can be identified in one-to-one verbal exchanges in the eighteenth century and in telephone conversations of the 1990s. Similarly, the conventions of the specific linguistic code drawn upon by the speech act will be subject to historical change while any given speech act can be matched by a metalingual substitute. The sentence 'Today I saw a dodo' carries its referential object, irrespective of the time of the utterance; but, since the dodo is now extinct, the contextual effect of such an utterance in the late twentieth century differs radically from its early nineteenth-century counterpart. But just as the individual poem infects the metonymic axis with metaphoric parallels, and vice versa, so it causes an equally dynamic relation between the diachronic affiliation of diagram 2 and the synchronic affiliation of diagram 1. The short essay on 'Problems in the Study of Language and Literature' is essentially an extension of the historical issues raised in 'The Dominant'.

> The concept of a synchronic literary system does not coincide with the naively envisaged concept of a chronological epoch, since the former embraces not only works of art which are close to each other in time but also works which are drawn

into the orbit of the system from foreign literatures or previous epochs.

(L in L, p. 48)

For example, Wordsworth's use of the ballad form in *Lyrical Ballads* involves a disorientating confluence of the intertextual and historical axes, respectively distinguished by diagrams 2 and 1. At the end of the eighteenth century the ballad was an icon of subliterary popular culture and Wordsworth's deliberate juxtaposition of this with issues and themes more readily associated with the high cultural status of the lyric or even with the philosophical essay caused a disruption of expectation: matters such as natural justice and existential angst were being addressed in rustic circumstances by low-life personae. This uncomfortable disruption of context-reference, contact-phatic levels was caused and foregrounded by his use of the dominant, the element which ties the poetic to the message and involves the otherwise potentially independent elements of the two diagrams. In this instance the dominant is the ballad form, whose abstract double pattern remains identical through time but whose interaction with distinct cultural and historical contexts can transform them (Jakobson, in 'The Dominant', cites similar examples from the history of 'Czech verse', *L in L*, p. 42). The dominant is essentially the point of contact between the specific type of poetic form and the social, cultural or referential elements mediated by this form.

To summarise, Jakobson's model of literary history (in effect poetic history) involves the identification of two synchronic–diachronic systems. The first incorporates a variety of non-literary strata – politics, social and ideological convention, the visual arts, music, and non-literary language. The second involves the history of the poetic function. The poetic function, as a formal device, is itself subject to alterations – in English the unseating of the Augustan couplet poem by the lyric-centred eclecticism of the Romantics, the twentieth-century free verse revolution, etc. – but the cause of these alterations and their effect upon the relation between poetic and non-poetic discourses is by no means predictable or reducible to any specific socio-cultural formula.

A disclosure of the immanent laws of the history of literature ... allows us to determine the character of each specific change in literary ... systems. However these laws do not allow us to explain the tempo of evolution or the chosen path of evolution when several theoretically possible evolutionary paths are given. This is owing to the fact that the immanent laws of literary . . . evolution form an indeterminate equation: although they admit only a limited number of possible solutions, they do not necessarily specify a unique solution. The question of a specific choice of path, or at least of the dominant, can be solved only through the correlation between the literary series and other historical series.

('Problems in the Study of Language and Literature', *L in L*, p. 49)

The concluding sentence of this passage could well be cited as an unfulfilled promise. After 'Futurism', 'Problems in the Study of Language and Literature' and 'The Dominant' Jakobson never again devoted a single work to the problematic relation between literary and other historical series. And, as we have seen, the allegedly ahistorical, acontextual nature of Jakobson's studies of poetry has featured as a key element in anti-Jakobson criticism. However, by examining Jakobson's work on the nature of the linguistic sign and on the relation between poetic and non-poetic discourse, it is possible to disclose a Jakobsonian formula which does indeed 'explain the tempo of evolution or the chosen path of evolution when several theoretically possible evolutionary paths are given'.

JAKOBSON, AUDEN AND MAJAKOVSKIJ

Jakobson's essay 'On a Generation that Squandered its Poets' (1931) and W. H. Auden's poem 'In Memory of W. B. Yeats' (1939) are elegies on the life and work of, respectively, V. Majakovskij and W. B. Yeats. Leaving aside the intrinsic differences between the prose essay and the poem, these two pieces of work possess uncanny, eerie similarities. It could indeed be argued that Jakobson and Auden founded their work upon the same model of poetic individuality and literary history.

Jakobson returns to the aesthetics–relativity thesis of 'Futurism'; that the modernist/Futurist movement had replaced the conventional, progressive model of time and events with a dynamic, prismatic interpenetration of the diachronic and synchronic axes. Many of the Russian groundbreakers of this revolution – Gumilev,

Blok, Xlebnikov, Esenin and Majakovskij – are now dead, and for Jakobson personal grief is supplemented by a grim recognition that there will be 'no replacements not even any partial reinforcements' for this squandered generation. What he fears is that Majakovskij's songs will be 'no longer part of the dynamic of history [but be] transformed into historico-literary facts' (*L in L*, p. 300), that the vital ahistoric element of poetic writing which Majakovskij foregrounded and which preserves the poem from deterministic mechanics of present, past and future will be smothered by these same processes: 'When singers have been killed and their song has been dragged into a museum and pinned to a wall of the past, the generation they represent is even more desolate, orphaned and lost' (p. 300).

It is unlikely that in the 1930s W. H. Auden had heard of Roman Jakobson, but his elegy on Yeats is a magically precise answer to Jakobson's fears. Yeats, like Majakovskij, had borne witness in his work to a revolution, a series of events that had, both in Russia and in Ireland, gathered up the solemn progress of history into a single prismatic confluence of past, present and future. But, argues Auden, the poetic record can remain immune from the distortions and transformations that follow the event.

> Now Ireland has her madness and her weather still,
> For poetry makes nothing happen: it survives
> In the valley of its making where executives
> Would never want to tamper, flows on south
> From ranches of isolation and the busy griefs,
> Raw towns that we believe and die in; it survives,
> A way of happening, a mouth.

Jakobson's essay and Auden's poem reverberate with allusions and references to, in Jakobson's terms, the ambiguous relation between the real, context-bound presence of the poet and his counterpart within the transformed context of the poem. Jakobson: 'the words "Majakovskij's last poems" have suddenly taken on a tragic meaning. Sheer grief at his absence has overshadowed the absent one.' Auden:

> By mourning tongues
> The death of the poet was kept from his poems.

> The words of the dead man
> Are modified in the guts of the living.

Jakobson: 'our poet is a Majakomorphist, and he populates the squares, the streets and the fields of the Revolution only with himself' (p. 276).

> The provinces of his body revolted,
> The squares of his mind were empty,
> Silence invaded the suburbs,
> The current of his feeling failed; he became his admirers.

One could continue to list the verbal echoes, but the most striking correspondence is, in the Jakobsonian sense, non-verbal. Auden's poem embodies and brilliantly synthesises practically every element of Jakobsonian poetics upon which the Majakovskij prose elegy is founded. 'In Memory of W. B. Yeats' is as much about the stylistic revolutions of the previous half-century as it is about Yeats's life. It is effectively a distilled history of nineteenth- to twentieth-century (English) poetic form, played backwards. Section I is in free verse, and the fact that I feel confident enough to make such a statement raises a number of questions about the comprehensive validity of Jakobson's models of poetic form of literary history. But before addressing these, let us consider the details of Auden's text. The line divisions of section I are determined by the relation between the rhetorical emphases of the syntagmatic chain and their referential counterparts and not by any abstract metrical or sound pattern. Section II makes concessions to formal regularity: the rhyme scheme is irregular and consists of the type of off-rhyme made famous by Wilfred Owen. The rhythmic pattern is similarly unconventional: there is a slight iambic undertow and the rhyme scheme/line endings break into the syntagmatic chain in a random, apparently spontaneous, manner. Section III consists of dutifully regular aa bb stanzas, with 7-syllable, ballad-like trochaic lines. According to Jakobson's model of the poetic function there should be a causal relationship between these shifts in the metrical pattern and the meshing of the syntagmatic-metonymic with the paradigmatic-metaphoric poles.

Most of section I involves a kind of double metonym: the parts of a landscape, perhaps a nation ('forests', 'rivers', 'squares', 'cities', 'provinces'), are listed rather than juxtaposed and this discursive progress is paralleled by a similar part–whole synecdoche in which the physical and cultural elements of Yeats's presence ('his illness', 'his body', 'the mind', 'the words') are enumerated. The progressive, combinative nature of the syntagm seems to dominate both elements of the double pattern – the discourse is consecutive, prosaic, and syntax controls the duration and positioning of the unmetrical lines. In section II we find that the adventurous illogic of the selective, paradigmatic axis begins to replace the contiguous logic of the first section. The relation between poet, poetry, landscape and nation is maintained but now, as Jakobson put it, 'metaphor' [not] 'metonymy is the line of least resistance'. Poetry is actually part of 'the valley of its making' and like the river 'it flows' and 'survives', 'A way of happening, a mouth' (mouth of poet, mouth of river). The image complexes of section I are maintained, but in this section there is a much less certain distinction between metonymic and metaphoric usages. Jakobson: 'In poetry where similarity is superinduced on contiguity, any metonymy is slightly metaphorical and any metaphor has a metonymical tint.'

In Jakobson's model, prose tends to be organised according to some perceived relation between text, external events and circumstances while poetry gathers these into an enclosed field in which there is a constant interplay between the material elements of the double pattern and its referential function. Something similar happens between sections I and II. The speaking presence of II is effectively recuperating the details of I as elements of a self-determined artefact. By section III the uncertain patterns of metrical and phonic equivalence of II have become fully synchronised with the metaphoric excursions. Yeats is both an object (vessel) and a poet, time is a person, the night is a physical as well as a temporal dimension, verses are farmed, the heart is a desert, temporal existence is a prison. Again the relation between physical and symbolic conditions is maintained but they have now become fully interwoven with the text; no referential or ideational concept remains immune from the insistent parallelism of rhyme and metrical regularity.

One could argue that the three sections of this poem represent the same text at different stages of composition; as the poem proceeds the tentative, discursive pattern, in which the poetic function makes concessions to the specificities of detail and circumstance, is gradually enclosed within an autonomous, self-determined condition of textuality. As such it offers a creative enactment of Jakobson's thesis that there is a predictable, causal relationship between the metrical and phonic density of the text and poetic or non-poetic deployments of the syntagm–paradigm axes. In doing so, however, it implicates Jakobsonian poetics in a rather narrow, selective view of poetic history and aesthetics. Section I, in free verse, is by these standards largely unpoetic. Auden has inadvertently foregrounded what is, potentially, the most serious flaw in Jakobsonian poetics.

Let us return to the model of literary history presented in 'Futurism'. Jakobson implies that the aesthetic–scientific combination of cubism, Futurism and relativity theory has effectively brought (literary) history to a close. Indeed, in the Majakovskij essay Jakobson gives an account of how on a brief visit to Majakovskij in the blockaded Moscow of 1920 the latter had claimed that Einstein's theories offered a form of immortality. Jakobson did not disparage this somewhat optimistic interpretation because it was an, albeit extravagant, extension of his own model of time and space. He did not believe that these new theories would enable us to transcend the limitations of mortality but he was convinced that the traditional conception of time as an abstract continuum operating independently of spatial and substantial determinants was no longer valid. The scientific and philosophic validity of relativity cannot be questioned, but Jakobson's extension of this same thesis to the history of art and, more significantly, poetry is open to charges of partiality. Cubist art and Futurist poetry foreground the multidimensional nature of the aesthetic object. In the latter case these effects are achieved by causing a deliberate and intensive conflict between the materiality of the phoneme and its function within the linguistic system of sign differentiation. It is possible to understand why he would regard this as the terminus of conventional poetic history because if we regard the poetic function as dependent upon the double pattern then, after the Futurists, poetry had nowhere else to go. Conventional, regular verse involves a sometimes harmonious, sometimes uneasy tension between the materiality and the signifying function of the linguistic sign. In Xlebnikov's, and indeed in Jakobson's, Futurist poems interplay had become fusion, the ultimate double pattern. So although Auden's poem and Jakobson's distinction between poetic and non-poetic discourse possess clear correspondences, they also disclose two distinctly opposed models of the relation between modernist and traditional verse: for Jakobson poetic modernism (with Futurism as the archetype) was the next stage beyond the dense and regular patterns of section III; but for many poets and theorists, particularly those within the Anglo-American modernist tradition, experimentation and poetic innovation involved the untangling of the restrictive conventions of the double pattern, a practice not unlike that of Auden's section I.

TWO MODELS OF POETIC HISTORY

Jakobson is rather sparing in his remarks on the nature and provenance of free verse. In 'The Dominant' (*L in L*, p. 42) he argues that contemporary Czech free verse replaces the conventional constituents of the dominant (rhyme, metrical and syllabic pattern) with the 'mandatory component... of intonational integrity'. What he means is that grammatical parallelism is substituted for its metrical or phonemic counterpart as the organising feature of each line. He maintains a version of this thesis in 'Linguistics and Poetics'. 'Except the varieties of the so-called *vers libre* that are based on conjugate intonations and pauses only, any metre uses the syllable as a unit of measure at least in certain sections of the verse' (*L in L*, p. 73). Jakobson does not demonstrate how a pattern constituted of intonational conjugations and pauses can operate as a free verse substitute for metrical regularity but he offers an account of the use of 'grammetrics' in Mark Antony's blank verse challenge to Brutus in the crowd scene of *Julius Caesar* (*L in L*, pp. 90–2). His working principle is as follows: blank verse, consisting of metrically regular lines but lacking the regular phonic equivalences of rhyme or internal sound pattern occupies a grey area between the poetic function and its nonpoetic counterparts. The enjambed, unrhymed pentameter runs dangerously close to being dominated by the conventions of the syntagm and becoming a form of rhythmic prose. However, the parallelistic sound pattern of rhyme, the cement of the metrical blocks, is replaced by the binding structure of morphological, semantic and grammatical units. For example, the two lines,

> My heart is in the coffin there with Caesar,
> And I must pause till it come back to me,

involve an interpenetration of metonymy, metaphor and metrical form very similar to the defining characteristic of regular, rhymed verse. The first line is predominantly metaphoric, while carrying metonymic traces of the synecdochic notion of the heart as the essence of emotional and spiritual identity. In the second line this metonymic overlay is thickened: the immediate, literal connotation of 'must pause till' generates the mildly surreal image of Antony waiting for the return of the physical organ. Jakobson's point is that the disorientating shifts between the metonymic and the metaphoric, the literal and the figurative, are co-ordinated by the division of the extended trope between two pentameters: 'the trope becomes part of poetic reality' (p. 91) in the sense that the metrical symmetry or parallelism of the two lines serves to foreground and accentuate the bizarre interweaving of the metonymic–metaphoric elements of the grammatical figure.

Jakobson's discussion of blank verse is significant. He acknowledges that it is 'more difficult to analyse linguistically . . . such literary forms [in which] verbal devices are unostentatious and language seems a nearly transparent garment', and he quotes Peirce: 'this clothing can never be stripped off; it is only changed for something more diaphanous'. He continues:

> 'Verseless composition' as Hopkins calls the prosaic variety of verbal art – where parallelisms are not so strictly marked and strictly regular as 'continuous parallelism' and where there is no dominant figure of sound – present more entangled problems for poetics, as does any transitional linguistic area. In this case the transition is between strictly poetic and strictly referential language.
>
> (*L in L*, p. 89)

Jakobson here is restating the thesis of his 1930s essays: transitions in literary history will involve alterations in the structural function and status of the dominant. But his use of blank verse as a means of illustrating this thesis brings him, unwittingly, up against what is at once the most problematic and influential transition in the history of post-sixteenth-century English poetry: the transition of blank verse from its pre-*Paradise Lost* classification as a vehicle for drama to its post-Miltonic status as the least formal and unostentatious non-dramatic form, and, arguably, as the vital stage in the later transition from metrical regularity to free verse. Jakobson's phrase 'the transition . . . between strictly poetic and strictly referential language' runs like a refrain through English literary history from the publication of *Paradise Lost* in 1667 to the beginning of the modernist revolution. A full account would require another book, but consider the following series of transitions, extensions and divisions.

Milton's poem caused an interpretive controversy that anticipates key elements of the debate on the literary qualities of modernist poetry and the more recent discussion of the relation between the 'intrinsic' form of literature and the role of the reader. Dryden, in his *Essay of Dramatic Poesie* (1668), represented orthodox contemporary opinion: blank verse was suitable only for drama because it lacked a sufficient degree of formal integrity to qualify for the status of the non-dramatic poetic artform. Milton, in his note on 'The Verse', offered a somewhat enigmatic answer to this charge, claiming that the 'barbarous' invention of rhyme would be replaced by 'apt numbers, fit quantity of syllables, and the sense variously drawn out from one verse into another', a statement which bears a close resemblance to Jakobson's thesis that the formal structure of blank verse involves a combination of metrical and grammatical devices.

Through the eighteenth century non-dramatic blank verse became established as an acceptable vehicle for non-dramatic poetry (particularly for the type of descriptive nature poem which draws upon the conventions of 'strictly referential language'). But the debate on its true formal identity continued, the best known pronouncement being Johnson's classification of it as 'verse only to the eye' (1779). Johnson's dismissive judgment is the tip of widespread interpretive conflict which divided eighteenth-century critics, commentators and editors. Some believed that post-Miltonic blank verse possessed a delicate combination of intrinsic formal features and celebrated its emergence as the vital next stage in the development of an unrhymed post-classical form. Others, like Johnson, regarded its alleged formal qualities as an illusion: a combination of readerly expectation and unsubstantiated formal signals. It was 'verse only to the eye' in the sense that, since it looked like verse on the page, the reader's interpretive response would play an important part in imposing a formal design upon rhythmic prose (see Bradford's *Silence and Sound*, 1992, for a full account of this debate).

During the Romantic period this same conflict underpinned broader aesthetic and indeed existential divisions. Coleridge, in the *Biographia*, expressed doubts about the validity of blank verse as a formal structure, and, by implication, about its use in such texts as Wordsworth's 'Tintern Abbey' and *The Prelude.* A more serious dismissal occurs in Blake's prose Introduction to *Jerusalem.*

> When this Verse was first dictated to me I considered a Monotonous Cadence like that used by Milton and Shakespeare and all writers of English Blank Verse, derived from the modern Bondage of Rhyming, to be a necessary and indispensible part of Verse. But I soon found that in the mouth of a true Orator such monotony was not only awkward, but as much a bondage as rhyme itself. I therefore have produced a variety in every line, both of cadences and number of syllables. Every word and every letter is studied and put into its fit place; the terrific numbers are reserved for the terrific parts, the mild and gentle, for the mild and gentle parts, and the prosaic for inferior parts; all are necessary to each other. Poetry Fettered, Fetters the Human Race.
>
> (Blake, p. 434)

Blake could be conducting a dialogue with Jakobson. He claims that blank verse, at the time the least restrictive of conventional forms, imposes a degree of bondage upon the creative faculty. His alternative involves allowing the contingent and unpredictable conditions of mood and circumstance to override the abstract patterns of metrical parallelism. In Jakobson's terms this would prioritise the contiguous-contextual axis of language and loosen the grip of the double pattern upon the relation between code and message. The progress of Blake's poetic technique is rather like Auden's poem in reverse. The *Songs of Innocence and Experience* are self-consciously, sometimes uncomfortably, traditional – compressed, dutifully regular, stanzaic patterns. The *Poetical Sketches* (1783) include blank verse poems which involve Miltonic complexities of grammar and metre. In *The First Book of Urizen, The Book of Ahania* and *The Song of Los* we find unrhymed, irregular iambics of varied line lengths. In *Jerusalem* and in his other long, prophetic poems all concessions to regularity have been abandoned.

Blake's revolutionary gestures are significant for our understanding of Jakobson's model of the dominant and literary history. Prior to the late eighteenth to early nineteenth century there were very few English or European poets who questioned the validity of the regular double pattern. Doubts began to surface in the work of the late eighteenth-century pre-Romantic critics and linguists. Their premise, shared by Jakobson, is that the poem is intrinsically different from other linguistic discourses (see above, Part I, pp. 21–2), but they differ from Jakobson in their belief that the poetic function predates both prose and the conventions of regular poetry, that metre is a natural, originary element of the syntagm rather than a complex interpenetration of abstract form, paradigm and syntagm. Daniel Webb (1769):

> Let us imagine ourselves in a state not far removed from the origin of things. Let our voice follow freely the impulse of sentiment, and run uncontrolled into the natural variations of emphasis and accent. We have traced in these variations the origin of measure.
>
> (p. 84)

It could be argued that Blake and such pre-Romantic theorists as Webb represent a smouldering counter-tradition that would be fully ignited by the modernists, or more specifically the Imagists. Other pre-modernist manifestations of this trend would include Coleridge's preface to 'Christabel', which echoes Blake's Introduction to *Jerusalem* in its call for formal design to be governed by the referential fabula of the text, and Whitman's preface to *Leaves of Grass*, which celebrates the 'free growth of metrical laws', 'shapes as compact as the shapes of chestnuts and oranges and lemons and pears [which] shed the perfume impalpable to form'. To appreciate properly how this sub-tradition corresponds with Jakobson's model of the poetic function we should reconsider the two columns of oppositions that constitute the sliding scale (see above, pp. 70–1).

Internal	External
Textual	Referential
The line	The sentence
Paradigm	Syntagm
Metaphor	Metonymy
Centripetal	Centrifugal
Signans	Signatum
Versus	Proversa
Sound	Meaning

To qualify for inclusion on the sliding scale – in effect to qualify as a poem – a text must involve the deployment of the two most tangible oppositions, the line and the sentence. The relationship between these two phenomena will affect the tensions and balances between each of the other oppositions. For example, a dense framework of sound patterns (promoting the signans above the signatum) will be organised according to the structure of each line and the broader network of echoes and correspondences that constitute stanzaic structures. Jakobson argues that any increase in density will result in a more intricate meshing of the metonymic-syntagmatic and the metaphoric-paradigmatic poles – and his concentration upon arguably the most discrete and intimate collusion between line and sentence, the sonnet, implicitly testifies to this belief. In such texts what Jakobson refers to as the ambiguous relation between the textual presences of addresser and addressee becomes further detached from any imagined or projected notion of their 'real' counterparts: internal-textual features effectively blur our vision of an external referent.

The scale is sliding because in any given text a prominent shift towards one of the binary elements will not preclude allegiances to features in the opposing column. For example, in 'Christabel' Coleridge shifts the balance towards the right-hand column in the sense that the rhyme scheme, the metrical structure and the duration of each line are governed more by the apparent unpredictability of the narrative (the external-referential features) than by the abstract regulations of repetitive metrical form (internal-textual features). However, this shift towards the right-hand column is less extreme than in Blake's longer prophetic poems, where the line becomes virtually a function of syntagmatic-referential axis, with no concessions to the arbitrary structuration of the signans.

The sliding scale enables us to identify two opposed traditions in the history of post-Renaissance English poetry, which, borrowing from the above columns, we shall call versus and proversa. The proversa tradition, whose pre-modernist members include Blake and Whitman, rose to prominence during the first two decades of this century. Most of the spokespersons for the Imagist school of poetic writing state that their objective is to mediate the referent, usually the immediate multidimensional experience, in a way that is undiminished by the refractory conventions of language and conventional literary form.

Williams (1908): 'To paint the thing as I see it.'

F. S. Flint (1913): 'Direct treatment of the "thing" whether subjective or objective.'

Pound (1913): 'An "Image" is that which presents an intellectual and emotional complex in an instance of time.'

The Imagists, while maintaining a distinction between poetic and non-poetic discourse, attempted to free the text from what they regarded as the refractory limitations of the left-hand column. Amy Lowell (1920) stated that the 'cadence', 'a rhythmic curve ... corresponding roughly to the necessity of breathing', should replace the foot or the syllabic measure as the organising feature of the line: the external vocal source of the speech act should override concessions to abstract textual structure.

The versus tradition is the mainstay of conventional, regular poetry. Jakobson: 'on every level of language, the essence of poetic artifice consists in recurrent returns' (*L in L*, p. 146). When we consider the texts and the poets to which Jakobson most frequently returns – the sonneteers, Poe, Hopkins, Xlebnikov, Majakovskij, the Futurists – it is evident that his theoretical and no doubt his temperamental allegiances lie with the versus tradition. In each instance the material signans operates as the structural and functional nexus of textual operations; these poems and poets are to the versus tradition what free verse or Blake's and Whitman's unmetrical lines are to its proversa counterpart. The reason for his allegiance becomes evident when we re-examine Jakobson's perception of the nature of the linguistic sign, and this is most clearly expressed in his dealings with the theories of C. S. Peirce.

Jakobson began to study Peirce after his move to the USA in 1941, and he is far less critical of Peirce's system of sign classification than he is of Saussure's. There are similarities: Peirce's differentiation between representamen (or vehicle), interpretant and object is roughly equivalent to Saussure's signifier, signified and referent. The principal difference exists in Peirce's attempt to codify all types of sign, linguistic and non-linguistic, as functions of three representational continua: symbolic, indexical and iconic. The iconic sign carries a direct physical resemblance to its referent or object and consequently minimalises the function of the signified or interpretant: most pre-modernist pictures and sculptures of human beings do not need to be decoded. The indexical sign is of particular interest for Jakobson in that he regards it as an extended version of the contiguity axis. The index draws upon the iconic notion of natural resemblance, in that a footprint in the sand infers a human presence and smoke infers fire, but in its non-accidental representational function ('male' or 'female' silhouettes on lavatory doors, the picture of a pointing finger indicating direction, etc.) it also borders upon the symbolic act. Symbolic signs, like linguistic signifiers, bear no physical and situational resemblance to signified or referent and consequently depend upon an arbitrary differential system. In 'Quest for the Essence of Language' Jakobson interprets, or more accurately reinterprets, Peirce's system in a number of ways. He accepts that language constitutes the principal system of symbolic signs, but he questions the exclusion from this system of the indexical and, he infers, the iconic function. He claims (citing Jesperson and others, *L in L*, p. 417) that 'the role of arbitrariness in language was excessively overstated', and his essentially anti-Saussurean thesis is as follows.

The belief that our familiarity with the signans–signatum–referent relation of linguistic signs is simply an acquired habit involves an inaccurate distinction between language and all other means by which we negotiate the existential continuum of consciousness, expression and behaviour. Language acquisition, argues Jakobson (and here we should note the attraction of his theory for Lacan), cannot be fully detached from a hypothetical notion of prelinguistic consciousness. True, we are aware that there is no natural resemblance between linguistic sounds and, say, the colours represented by specific signifiers, but at the antecedent stage of linguistic cognition where sound is decoded as meaning we cannot help but automatically associate the linguistic sign with its phenomenal counterpart. This process, irrespective of its origins in language acquisition, becomes as immediate and automatic as our ability to associate a picture of a tree with a real tree. In 'Linguistics and Poetics' (*L in L*, p. 87) Jakobson claims that poetic sound symbolism (primarily rhyme) is

> often confusingly labeled 'arbitrariness of the verbal sign'. . . . Sound symbolism is an undeniably objective relation founded on a phenomenal connection between different sensory modes, in particular between the visual and the auditory experience. . . . (W)hen on testing, for example, such phonemic oppositions as grave versus acute we ask whether /i/

or /u/ is darker, some of the subjects may respond that this question makes no sense to them, but hardly one will state that /i/ is the darker of the two.

Jakobson's point is that Peirce's distinction between symbolic, iconic and indexical signs should not be regarded as a means of separating the arbitrary symbolic nature of a language from other sign systems; rather that the three levels of representation should be seen to operate within language as much as they do within the networks of visual signs. In 'Quest for the Essence of Language' and in 'Shifters, Verbal Categories and the Russian Verb' he offers examples of how this method of classification would work. In the latter he pays specific attention to the function of the pronoun as an indexical symbol (*SW II*, p. 132–3). The personal pronoun 'I' is at once a symbol and in that it 'cannot represent its object without "being in existential relation" with this object', an index. In 'Quest for the Essence of Language' he notes that 'veni, vidi, vici' is mimetic (and potentially iconic) in the sense that it both reproduces 'the succession of reported occurrences' and indicates their similarity–dissimilarity in its use of slight assonantal-alliterative shifts.

In terms of a broader theory of semiotics Jakobson is arguing for the recognition of methodological ties between linguistic and non-linguistic systems – he points out, for instance ('Quest', *L in L*, p. 417), that iconicity in painting is often as much due to 'imputed, habitual connections as is its linguistic counterpart' – but, as usual, poetry proves to be an exception to the general formula. Clearly the indexical sign in language is closely associated with the metonymy-contiguity axis (the synecdoche of 'hands' for workers depends upon a part-for-whole contextual relation very similar to the pointing forefinger on the signpost), and the symbolic sign, in which there is no physical or circumstantial relation between signans and signatum, offers itself as a broader manifestation of the metaphoric-paradigmatic axis. The closest that language can come to the iconic sign is in the relation between sound and meaning – this is obviously not a natural or unitary resemblance, but a governing principle by which objects and events can never be detached fully from the interpenetration of phonetic, morphological and semantic elements. In poetry, 'the relevance of the sound–meaning nexus is a simple corollary of the superimposition of similarity upon contiguity' (*L in L*,

p. 87). In effect the poetic double pattern, the promotion of sound pattern to the status of an organising feature in syntagm–paradigm relation, not only distinguishes poetry from other linguistic usages, but it also grants poetry a special prominence within the broader network of linguistic and non-linguistic sign systems. What other representational act involves such a perplexing yet purposive integration of symbolic, iconic and indexical signs? Pictures can, of course, involve all three but they cannot draw upon, let alone foreground, the raw material of our primary communicative medium – speech sounds. We will return to Jakobson's treatment of poetry and the visual arts in due course, but for the moment let us return to the question of why he maintains an allegiance to the versus tradition of poetic history. The answer should by now be clear enough: the poems of the versus tradition, and particularly those of Xlebnikov, Hopkins and Poe which give special prominence to the signans, are the true explorers of that shifting territory between sign and referent.

JAKOBSON AND BAKHTIN

To understand properly Jakobson's somewhat enigmatic views on the relation between literature and history we need to consult his binary 'other half', a role which could be filled by a number of theorists and critics but none so intriguingly as Mikhail Bakhtin. Bakhtin's life and work is shrouded in the half-truths and mystifications of the history of the Soviet Union. Clark and Holquist's study (1984) provides the most respected account of who he was and what he did, but some doubt still surrounds the true relation between the two major works, *The Formal Method in Literary Scholarship* (1928) and *Marxism and the Philosophy of Language* (1929), and the names of Bakhtin, Medvedev and Vološinov – collaborators, pseudonyms, actual authors? The progressive continuity of the arguments developed in these works carries at the very least the Bakhtinian imprint and for the sake of convenience I shall append his name to each.

Bakhtin can claim to be the most prominent and influential of the post-Formalist thinkers, though his influence in the West has only begun to register over the past two decades. In brief, it could be argued that Bakhtin extended and revised the founding principles of Formalism in a way that bears a close resemblance to the thinking of the theorists of the new paradigm – his allegiances, like theirs, are context-bound and, at least on the surface, anti-Jakobsonian. In *The Formal Method* Bakhtin summarises the thesis of Jakobson's 'New Russian Poetry' and identifies in this the primary flaw in Formalist doctrine.

> The Formalists presuppose tacitly . . . an entirely predetermined and fixed communication, and an equally fixed transmission. . . . [But] in reality the relations between A and B [author and reader] are in a state of permanent formation and transformation; they continue to alter in the very process of communication. Nor is there a ready-made message X. It takes form in the process of communication between A and B. Nor is it transmitted from the first to the second, but constructed between them, like an ideological bridge; it is constructed in the process of their interaction.
> (*The Formal Method in Literary Scholarship*, p. 203)

Here we find the origins of Bakhtin's widely celebrated dialogic principle, or, as he called it, metalinguistics. The relationship between Bakhtin's concept of dialogism-metalinguistics and Jakobson's model of the set is at once intimate and uneasy. They agree that addresser, message and addressee are functionally and structurally interdependent, but while Jakobson maintains that certain messages, particularly the poetic, are immutable immanent structures, Bakhtin shifts the emphasis towards the situational conditions occupied by addresser and addressee. Bakhtin:

> Every word gives off the scent of a profession, a genre, a current, a party, a particular work, a particular man, a generation, an era, a day and an hour. Every word smells of the context and contexts in which it has lived its intense social life; all words and all forms are inhabited by intentions. In a word, contextual harmonies (of the genre, of the current, the individual) are unavoidable.
> (Written in 1934–5, extract from *Voprosy Literatury i éstetiki*, Moscow, 1975, p. 106)

It is easy to see why the recently discovered Bakhtin struck such an attractive chord in the unfolding poststructuralist ethos of the 1970s and 1980s. The speech act theorists and their literary-critical cousins were operating from the same principle of contextualism: 'all forms are inhabited by intentions'. Culler and Fish base their models of the relation between literature and criticism upon a contingent, dialogic process: inherent structures and processes of signification are seen to be dependent upon the 'contextual harmonies of the genre, of the current, of the individual'. Julia Kristeva (1980) calls for a Bakhtinian revision of Jakobsonian poetics (see below, p. 203). Even the Derridean concept of linguistic différance promotes a very similar notion of meaning as incessantly transferable and ungrounded in any final signifier–signified union. But before we categorise Bakhtin as the natural ally of the anti-Jakobson camp we should examine how his literary application of the dialogic principle relates to Jakobson's model of the poetic function.

Bakhtin does not ignore poetry but his perspective on literary history is founded upon the development of the novel.

> Herein lies the profound distinction between prose style and poetic style . . . for the prose artist the world is full of other people's words, among which he must orient himself and whose speech characteristics he must be able to perceive with a very keen ear. He must introduce them into the plane of his own discourse, but in such a way that this plane is not destroyed. He works with a very rich palette.
>
> (*Problems of Dostoyevsky's Poetics*, pp. 200–1)

This view of the novel is largely consistent with Jakobson's perception of prose fiction as more closely allied to the axis of contiguity than the axis of selection. Bakhtin supplements Jakobson's model of the contextual orientation of the syntagm with his complex formulation of dialogism. At one level the novelist must necessarily speak to his context (the most obvious instance being the use of the apparently contingent and formless mode of spoken exchange within the text); at another, the novel itself occupies the message function within a dialogic interchange between addresser-author and addressee-reader. It is the combination of these two levels of dialogic process that enables Bakhtin to propose a formula for the typology of literary history – in effect a (prose) alternative to Jakobson's concept of the dominant. For example, Bakhtin regarded Dostoyevsky's style as essentially polyphonic, in that the dialogic relation between the inferred authorial voice and those of his characters is uncertain and potentially chaotic: authorial control over the character's voices as literary devices is surrendered to a carnivalesque style of apparently free exchange. He contrasts this with Tolstoy's monologic authoritarian voice. The dialogue between novelist and reader operates, in the case of the former, as a perception of the uneasy relation between linguistic exchange and social-ideological conditions, and in the case of the latter as an organised register of these mediations. The reader's 'reply' is of course silent, but it constitutes an active comparison of the text with a perception of the atextual conditions upon which it is based. Again, this model is not inconsistent with Jakobson's example of the epic writer-cum-novelist as the listener (the person who shares the contiguity axis with the reader), and Bakhtin's distinction between the very different dialogic functions of poetry and the novel is an almost exact copy of the Jakobsonian formula. The difference emerges in the role which Bakhtin assigns to the novel as an index to broader patterns of society, language and ideology.

> The category of common language is the theoretical expression of historical processes of linguistic unification and centralisation, the expression of the centripetal forces of the language. The common language is never given but in fact always ordained, and at every moment of the life of the language it is opposed to genuine heterology. But at the same time, it is perfectly real as a force that overcomes this heterology.
>
> (*Voprosy Literatury i éstetiki*, pp. 83–4)

What Bakhtin claims is that 'common language', or the type of daily, 'ordinary' speech generated by external circumstances, is capable both of reflecting the centripetal forces of language and ideology, and, by virtue of its unpredictable nature, undermining them. And since the novel is generically focused upon such exchanges, it too becomes a vital element in any understanding of the relation between perceived reality and the structuration of such perceptions in language. But with poetry:

> The principal species of poetic genres arise in the current of unifying and centralising centripetal forces of verbal and ideological life, [whereas] the novel and the genres of literary prose that are bound to it have historically taken form in the current of decentralizing, centrifugal forces.
>
> (*Voprosy Literatury i éstetiki*, p. 86)

Bakhtin and Jakobson are in perfect unity on the subject of what literary genres are and how they come into being, but they are diametrically opposed on the question of how and why the two principal genres, poetry and prose, reflect or reconstitute their linguistic and non-linguistic conditions. Bakhtin argues that the overtly semiotic features of poetry (the left-hand column of the sliding scale) are allied to the 'unifying and centralising centripetal forces of verbal and ideological life' and that the 'decentralising' rift between the verbal-ideological norm and literary history is motivated by the constitutive features of the novel (drawing upon the right-hand column). Jakobson reverses this equation and argues that poetry, through its ability to interrogate and unsettle the relation between the concrete sign and its differential-contextual function, represents the point at which literature shifts towards an oblique, perverse and potentially subversive relation to the verbal-ideological norm.

In a number of essays published in Prague in the 1930s Jakobson developed, ironically enough, a dialogic counter-pattern to Bakhtin's developing theories of literary history. Bakhtin, Medvedev and Vološinov are never mentioned but throughout this period Jakobson maintained contacts with friends and ex-colleagues in the then post-Formalist Soviet Union and he would have been familiar with the activities of the so-called Bakhtin group in St Petersburg/Leningrad. In 'What is Poetry?' (1933), 'Marginal Notes on the Prose of the Poet Pasternak' (1935) and 'The Statue in Puškin's Poetic Mythology' (1937) Jakobson offers what is without doubt a response to the theories propounded in *The Formal Method of Literary Scholarship* (1928, Bakhtin and Medvedev), *Marxism and the Philosophy of Language* (1929, Vološinov/Bakhtin) and *Problems of Dostoyevsky's Poetics* (1929, Bakhtin).

The Pasternak essay (first published in German) contains the original version of the prose-metonymy, poetry-metaphor formula that would resurface in Jakobson's writing, in English, in the 1950s and 1960s. Here we also find echoes of his association of metonymy with the Freudian concepts of displacement and condensation and of metaphor with identification and symbolism. Jakobson compares Pasternak as poet and novelist with the poets Majakovskij and Xlebnikov. He begins with the proposition that there are 'striking' differences between the poet's and the prose writer's prose and between the prose writer's and the poet's poetry.

A mountaineer walking in the plains can find no foothold and stumbles over the level ground. He moves either with touching awkwardness or with overemphatic artistry; in either case it is not his natural gait, but involves obvious effort and looks too much like the steps of a dancer. It is easy to distinguish a language that has been learnt, however perfect its command, from one that has been naturally acquired.

(*L in L*, p. 301)

Jakobson does not argue that Pasternak the poet is a bad stylist or a generic overreacher; rather that his temperamental affiliations to the metonymic foregrounding of prose becomes evident in his poetic writing. He notes that Pasternak's poetry and prose 'is imbued with metonymy; in other words, it is association by contiguity that predominates' (*L in L*, p. 307). Jakobson concedes that Pasternak's prose is deservedly celebrated as lyrical, but he shows that his overtly figurative style is grounded upon the figure of displacement: 'two characteristic features – the mutual penetration of objects (the realisation of metonymy in the strict sense of the word) and their decomposition (the realisation of synecdoche) – bring Pasternak's work close to the endeavours of Cubist painters' (*L in L*, p. 311). He gives an example from the short story 'Safe Conduct', where the items which occupy the referential scene effectively govern and enclose the figurative excursions.

The lamps only accentuated the emptiness of the evening air. They did not give light, but swelled from within, like sick fruits, from the turbid and bright dropsy that puffed up their bloated shades.... The lamps came much less in contact with the rooms than with the spring sky which they seemed to be pushed straight up to.

(*L in L*, p. 311)

And he shows how Pasternak adapts this metonymic-contiguous affiliation to the 'dominant' features of poetic discourse. In effect, he argues that Pasternak's poetry exhibits a tension between the metonymic-contextual affiliations of its creator and the intrinsic demands of poetic structure, where the concrete nature of the sign pulls against its referential function. Majakovskij and Xlebnikov, however, are happy to submit to the dominance of the sign.

Xlebnikov's symbolic world is so fully realised that for him every symbol, every created word, is endowed with a complete independent reality, and the question of its relations to any external object, indeed the very question of the existence of such an object, becomes entirely superfluous.

(*L in L,* p. 305)

The tensions between Jakobson's model of the poetic and of literary history and those of the Bakhtin group are already evident – Jakobson argues that a foregrounding of the concrete sign is just as relevant to perceived 'reality' as the discursive submission to the 'external object' – and at the end of the essay it is clear to whom his argument is addressed.

> We have tried to deduce the themes of Pasternak's and Majakovskij's work from the basic structural features of their poetics. Does that mean that the former are determined by the latter? Mechanistic formalists would answer in the affirmative, supporting their case with Pasternak's claim that in his youth he had formed affinities with Majakovskij which threatened to get out of hand, thus causing him radically to alter his poetic manner and, with it, the sense of life that lay at the base of it. The position of the master of metaphor was filled, so the poet became master of metonymy and drew the appropriate ideological conclusions.

(*L in L,* p. 315)

In short, Pasternak's allegiances to the contiguity axis cannot be explained simply in terms of an ideological commitment to, in Bakhtin's view, the centrifugal decentralising forces of prose; rather:

> despite the ideological confusion of the period. . . Pasternak's debt to his age comes out very strongly in his poetry. It is revealed both in his persistent creative annulment of the object and in his reconstruction of the grammar of art. This latter used to consist of past and present; in contrast to the simple past the present was seen as a featureless 'nonpast'. It was, in fact, Futurism that wished to introduce the future into the poetic system by rubric, theory, and practice, and to introduce it as a decisive category.

(*L in L,* p. 317)

Bakhtin would argue that Pasternak's rejection of the sign-centred techniques of Xlebnikov, Majakovskij and the Futurists indicates a direct causal relationship between the heterology of prose and the turbulent social and political conditions of the period (we are talking about Russia before and during the revolution), but Jakobson claims that literary history, particularly poetic history, is involved as much with its own past, present and future as it is with operating as a register or symptom of non-literary events and conditions. He does not claim that literary history proceeds independently of history, but that, *contra* Bakhtin, the literary artist's treatment of the relation between sign and referent should be regarded as an independent activity and not as an event in which the referent controls the sign. Bakhtin refers to the necessity of the novelist 'orienting himself' to the non-literary conditions of language and introducing these 'characteristics' 'into the plane of his own discourse'. Jakobson, using the same terminology, disagrees.

> It is legitimate to strive to find a correspondence between the different planes of reality, as it is also to try to infer facts about one of its planes from the corresponding facts about another – the method is one of projecting a multidimensional reality onto one surface. It would be a mistake, however, to confuse this projection with reality itself and to disregard both the characteristic structure and the autonomous movement of the individual planes.
>
> (*L in L*, p. 316)

Jakobson's argument shares the same structuralist premise as the work of the Bakhtin school, but differs from it in one important degree. Both agree that reality is a friable, relativistic concept; more a construction of perspective, ideology and sign system than an immutable entity. But whereas the Bakhtin school regards the literary artist, primarily the novelist, as someone who reconstitutes the social, ideological and linguistic spectrum of a particular milieu, Jakobson maintains that poetry is a milieu in itself, at once an independent, ahistoric langue and a system which can absorb and reflect the individuality of the poet and the poet's perspective on his world.

> If many individual characteristics of Pasternak's poetry are in accord with the characteristic features of his personality and his social environment, so, inevitably there are also phenomena in his work which the contemporary poetic idiom forces upon every one of its poets, even if they contradict his own

individual and social personality. . . . The poet's artistic mission never penetrates his biography without a struggle, just as his biography is never entirely absorbed into his artistic mission.

(*L in L*, p. 316)

One has to admire the thoroughgoing unity and consistency of Jakobson's lifelong treatment of the poetic function. The above model of the relation between individuality, context and the poem anticipates his six-part diagram of the communicative circuit (p. 84): the marriage of the poetic function with the message performs the paradoxical role of attaching the five other parts of diagram 2 (text) to those of 1 (context), while ensuring that each is 'never entirely absorbed' by the other.

It is in 'The Statue in Puškin's Poetic Mythology' (1937) – by Jakobson's usual economic standards, a monograph – that we encounter the most complex and original application of this model to the life and work of a particular poet. By 'mythology' Jakobson means: 'certain constant organising, cementing elements which are the vehicle of unity in the multiplicity of the poet's works and which stamp these works with the poet's individuality' (*L in L*, p. 318). This specification is deliberately and purposively ambiguous. He goes on to identify the conspicuous 'constant organising, cementing elements' as in effect the dominant, those 'invariant' features of each text – rhyme scheme, metrical pattern, etc. – which both govern the structural and functional mechanisms of specific texts and ensure a relationship between these texts and the general langue of poetic form. But these elements can also consist of 'scattered symbols' which 'can be understood fully only in their relation to a whole symbolic system' – in this instance Puškin's interest in, perhaps obsession with, the statue is the organising, cementing element. Here we encounter the crucial and decisive point at which the literary theories of Jakobson and those of the Bakhtin school (and those based on similar context-dependent models) meet and diverge. It is possible to identify a recurrent theme which migrates through the work of writers whose stylistic and generic affiliations are quite different – childhood in Wordsworth and Dickens, social mores in the novels of Amis and the poems of Larkin, for instance – but problems arise when we then attempt to specify whether the transformational nature of the particular medium or genre, or the extra-textual condition of the poet's life and circumstances is the more important motivating force in the relation between text and context. Jakobson's choice of Puškin and the statue is cunning and illuminating. On the one hand, the statue operates as a symbolic and iconic axis between the writer's life and work – its function as a memorial to political and military action and its capacity to capture life as at once active and immobile is related by Jakobson to, respectively, Pŭskin's experience of the political turmoil of early nineteenth-century Russia and his uneasy relationship with women. On the other hand, the statue, as a sign, possesses features which, Jakobson implies, demand its linguistic treatment in poetry rather than in prose. Reading this essay, one begins to understand why Jakobson's later encounter with the work of Peirce registers like the discovery of letters from a long-lost friend. The statue is the perfect example of icon, index and symbol combined. It is primarily, multidimensionally iconic; its posture and situation is an indexical pointer to a particular situation; and its function within the socio-cultural langue of Western art (pillars, horsemen, nakedness, dress and uniform, etc.) gives it a symbolic role within a predetermined differential system. As Jakobson was later to point out, the linguistic sign also embodies this tripartite signifying complex, with the hierarchy of icon, index and symbol reversed (see above, pp. 166–8). Puškin's treatment of statues is important, argues Jakobson, because it foregrounds the interdependency of the two dimensions of the poet's mythological world, text and context:

> it concerns the transposition of a work belonging to one kind of art into another artistic mode – into poetry. A statue, a poem – in brief, every artistic work – is a particular sign. Verse about a statue is accordingly a sign of a sign or an image of an image. In a poem about a statue a sign (signum) becomes a theme or a signified object (signatum).
>
> (*L in L*, p. 352)

In poems there will always be a tension between the referential continuum mediated by the sign and the internal pattern of concrete signs, but in poems about statues this tension is doubled by the fact that the principal continuum of referents consists itself of signs. Jakobson does not argue, as might Bakhtin, that this is an instance of poetry foregrounding its role as 'a centralising centripetal force of verbal and ideological life' (also known as 'art for art's sake'); rather that Puškin's poetry–statue syntheses

actually incorporate a more vivid and exploratory plane of
'realism' than could be provided by the novel. Jakobson's essay
is intensely argued and meticulously detailed in its tracing of
connections between Puškin's life, circumstances and work; and
although it is difficult and probably unjust to attempt a summary
of what in my opinion is his best literary critical work, consider
the following. The statue is a discomforting combination of actuality and untruth; like its observers and its subject, it will occupy
a three-dimensional space that is eerily familiar and ordinary; it
will tell a brief story of an act, a movement or a situation; but
it must continue to announce its status as a sign. It is, in effect,
the closest non-verbal signum to the word. Statues, like our native
language, are easily mistaken for pure signata; familiarity breeds
transparency. For Puškin the ideal continuum of referents – freedom, political tolerance, emotional and sexual contentment –
continually seemed to slide beneath the unbearable weight of
discordant fact, and where did he turn for an expressionistic,
possibly cathartic, enactment of this fissure? To the combination
of the statue and the poem. Both occupy an uneasy position
between ordered signans and disorderly signatum. Jakobson gives
dozens of examples of how the poetisation of the linguistic sign,
its creation of semantic bundles which can bear no relation to
any logical conception of a referent, is paralleled by the statue's
disjunctive relation between signification and meaning.

> The cancellation of the internal dualism of the sign obliterates
> the boundary between the world of the sign and the world
> of the objects. The equation between the 'eternal sleep' of the
> deceased Peter and the eternal repose of his bronze double
> and the simultaneous contradiction between the ephemerality
> of his mortal remains and the steadfastness of his statue pro-
> duce the notion of the life of the represented being continued
> in its sculptural image, in the monument.
>
> (*L in L*, p. 358)

Jakobson concludes his essay with the claim that 'Puškin's symbolism of the statue continues to affect Russian poetry to the present
day, and it constantly points to its creator' (*L in L*, p. 363) and
he cites the work of 'the three outstanding Russian poets of
this century', Blok, Xlebnikov and Majakovskij. His point, more
implied than dogmatically stated, is that there is a correlation
between periods of social, political and ideological uncertainty

and the proliferation of poets and texts which foreground the sign as a concrete refractory phenomenon. And again we encounter the emergence of Jakobson's affiliation to the versus tradition of literary history.

CLOSING SECTION: JAKOBSON AND MODERNISM

Jakobson died in 1982, and as each new paradigm of literary-critical awareness and affiliation replaces the last his name and his work become more and more like carefully preserved exhibits in the museum of semiology and literary studies. During the 1970s, and less so in the 1980s, journals such as *Poetics, Language and Style* and *Linguistics* contained essays which acknowledged, sometimes productively, sometimes dismissively, the Jakobsonian method. By the 1990s the critic who acknowledges his/her debt to the working methods of Jakobson is as rare as the reborn New Critic.

My objective, in this closing section, is to show that Jakobson's theory of the poetic function, along with its attendant linguistic and semiological premises, is unjustly ignored.

We have already noted that Jakobson's allegiance to the versus tradition places him in an uneasy position with regard to modernism – particularly its Anglo-American manifestation. It is not that versus modernism was confined to Xlebnikov and the Futurists: Hopkins, T. S. Eliot, e. e. cummings, Dylan Thomas, the sound poets and the concretists, all in varying degrees pay allegiance to the materiality of the linguistic sign as a prominent organisational feature of the text. But it is the practitioners of the proversa tradition – those who appear to be more brutally indifferent to the icon of the regular sound poem – who are most enthusiastically celebrated as the true aesthetic revolutionaries: the Imagists, William Carlos Williams, the ideogram tradition of Zukofsky, Olson, Duncan, Creeley, Levertov and others. One reason for this unequal grading could be that the readers, the addressees, of proversa modernist texts are able to consider the relation between text and addresser or poet in a way that bears a close resemblance to the empowering models of speech act theory and context-based structuralism and poststructuralism. Proversa poems are rarely transparent, but they are sufficiently unencumbered by the double pattern to enable the reader to treat them more as functions of an interpretive context than as autonomous signifying structures. The proversa addressee can shed the mystique of ambiguity and speak to the issues raised by the poetic function. The addressee's reply has become a trademark of such new-paradigmists as Fish, Culler, Forrest-Thomson and Eagleton. Each illustrates their shared premise that literariness is non-intrinsic, an element of the periodic shifts in ideological/cultural norms, by breaking a prose sequence into 'lines' (in Fish's case a random list of surnames on a blackboard) and demonstrating how specifically 'poetic' qualities can be imposed upon any putative text. Modernism, at least in its proversa affiliation, offers itself as the perfect object language for the theorists of the new paradigm. Consider again Pound's 'In a Station of the Metro', a text that I earlier used to illustrate the poetic counterpart of 'contexture deficient' aphasia. In his 1964 book on modernist poetry Harvey Gross naturalises the poem.

> Here 'ideogrammatic method' means poetry without complete sentences. The absence of verb and preposition enhances both rhythm and significance; a certain mystery evaporates if we supply the implied cupola and relational word:
>
> The apparition of these faces in the crowd
> (Are like) Petals on a wet black bough.
>
> No harm comes if we want to see this as vaguely analogous to Chinese writings; the two images have spatial and emotional relationships. Grammar, however, is not missing; it is automatically supplied by the reader.
>
> (p. 162)

Gross's method tells us a lot about the relationship between modernist poetry and modern criticism. 'Ideogrammatic method', inspired by Pound's enthusiasm for Fenollosa's remarks on the relation between the Chinese character and Western language, was an attractive proposition for the early modernists because it engaged with the tantalising possibility that poets might do with language what language by its very nature forbade them from doing. The ideogram could juxtapose images, signs, without submitting to the arbitrary codes and regulations that normally attend the construction of a trope. Indeed, the Chinese character seemed at last to offer a new perspective upon an interaesthetic problem that had troubled Horace, Leonardo and Lessing: how might the poem free itself from the fetters of the consecutive sequential sign and, like the painting, mediate the multi-dimensional simultaneity of prelinguistic experience? Leaving aside his specific influence, the issues raised by Fenollosa's essay went to the heart of the unrealised and unrealisable ideal of modernist poetics. Free verse, at least the type practised by the Imagists, involved a rejection of the consecutive nature of the linguistic sign. Its rejection of metrical regularity and repetitive sound pattern was a revolt against the aesthetic of the signifier. As Jakobson continually states, the phoneme involves an immutable interdependency of sound and meaning, and regular poetry at once celebrates and intricates this relationship by its promotion of sound from the status of the ephemeral signal for decoding to that of the central unit of textual organisation. Free verse, the terminus of the proversa tradition, dispensed with the auditory double pattern of regular poetry, and it also effectively forbade the use of formal effects that would establish the poem as a self-referential artefact, an icon, that would stand between addresser and addressee. By removing the physical barriers of auditory form in order to realise the long-sought objective of simultaneity and transparency, the free versifiers created a degree of textual discontinuity which encourages the reader to impose an ordered framework of understanding – Barthes's 'scriptible' text which invites readers such as Gross to supply 'automatically' the missing relational word. It is the proversa tradition of modernism that enables Culler (1975, p. 163) to typographically break up the opening sentence of a philosophical essay by Quine and read it as a piece of modernist verse: 'We are dealing less with a property of language (intrinsic irony or paradox) than with a strategy of reading.' In an important sense proversa free verse represents the ultimate challenge to Jakobsonian poetics. If we share Culler's belief that once the appropriate socio-cultural signals are in place (in this case line divisions) the 'intrinsic' qualities of the text can be supplied by a 'strategy of reading', then we would have to concede that elements such as the dominant are also conventions of reading rather than, as Jakobson argues, the defining, if variable, features of an exclusive sign system known as poetry. How else could we explain the admission of formless examples of free verse to the respected poetic canon? Many poems, Pound's 'In a Station of the Metro' included, fail to satisfy the formal criteria of the poetic function and the projection principle, but they now share the same bookshelves and poetry reading lists as other 'classics' of the genre, such as Shakespeare's sonnet 129. To address this issue properly we must first consider the teleological premise upon which Culler's, and other critics', model of the imposed 'strategy of reading' is based.

They are, in effect, extending a critical practice established in the eighteenth century (Johnson's '[blank] verse only to the eye') and resurgent in many of the earliest responses to free verse: the unmetrical and/or unrhymed line is not in itself a formal device; rather it is a signal which enables the reader to impose (in Levin's terms) a conventional pattern upon a cognitive framework and then to naturalise the alleged, but in fact illusory, relation between the two – the 'poetic' element of the double pattern becomes like the smile on the Cheshire Cat. There are many examples of accredited 'poems' which could be used to justify this thesis. Culler, for example, cites William Carlos Williams's 'This Is Just To Say' (1934):

This Is Just To Say

I have eaten
the plums
that were in
the icebox

and which
you were probably
saving
for breakfast

Forgive me
they were delicious
so sweet
and so cold

Culler points out, with tongue firmly in cheek, that the text is a 'mediating force'; it engages the reader in the semantics of 'forgiveness', 'the sensuous experience' of eating fruit, and it foregrounds a situation of domestic intimacy ('I', 'you', 'me') (1975, p. 175). His point, of course, is that a similar strategy of reading could be applied to any note left on any kitchen table, provided that the appropriate contextual-interpretive signals were in place to motivate such a strategy. The implied conclusion is that all poems which dispense with the metrical parallelisms of the versus tradition involve merely an alteration in modes of attention; that line division (in Jakobson's model the crucial determinant of the poetic function) is no more than a fore-grounding of structures and patterns already present within the dominant structure of the contiguity-syntagm axis. The 'principle of equivalence' is not 'projected from the axis of selection into the axis of combination' by any innate textual figuration; the projection principle is in the hands of the reader. In a curious way – which from Jakobson's point of view might smack of fatalistic conspiracy – proversa poems such as Williams's operate as one half of a dialogic exchange between text and reader. Bakhtin:

> [The message] takes form in the process of communication between A and B. Nor is it transmitted from the first to the second, but constructed between them, like an ideological bridge; it is constructed in the process of their interaction.
>
> (*The Formal Method in Literary Scholarship* p. 204)

It seems that the monologic identity of the poem has finally, through modernism, submitted to the heterology of the novel, and in doing so it has provided ample ammunition for those new-paradigmists who argue that, in any event, its pristine exclusi-vity from the shifting contours of discourse and the real world was an illusion. In an even more curious way it is to another, seemingly more hostile, theorist of the new paradigm that we might turn to begin a defence of Jakobsonian poetics – Jacques Derrida.

In *Of Grammatology*, that seminal deconstructive text, Derrida engages in a typically enigmatic unseating of the phonocentric hierarchy manifested in the work of Saussure and in Jakobson's emphasis upon phonology (see particularly pp. 68–73). But, per-haps unwittingly, he also provides us with a bridge between Jakob-son's model of the poetic function and the formal fragmentations of modernism. He quotes Hegel: 'the visible language is related only as a sign to the audible language; intelligence expresses itself immediately and unconditionally through speech', and com-ments, 'What writing itself in its non-phonetic moment, betrays, is life. It menaces at once the breath, the spirit, and history as the spirit's relationship with itself' (p. 25). Later, Derrida postulates a 'necessary decentring', a 'dislocation of the founding categories of language, through access to another system linking speech and writing'. This system is not philosophical or linguistic, but poetic. 'This is the meaning of the work of Fenellosa [*sic*] whose influence upon Ezra Pound and his poetics is well known: this irreducibly graphic poetics was, with that of Mallarmé, the first break in the most entrenched western tradition' (p. 92). Derrida exaggerates the influence of Fenollosa's notion of 'irreducibly graphic poetics': this would account for the subtradition of concrete poetry, but there are very few texts which employ the visual sign without making some concessions to the consecutive, phonocentric element of language. However, his notion of 'writing' as a 'menace to the breath, the spirit, and history as the spirit's relationship with itself' bears an intriguing resemblance to Jakobson's model of the poetic function. Jakobson's projection principle consists of three interwoven elements: the syntagmatic and paradigmatic axes and the parallelism of the poetic line. Anyone who has attempted to compose a regular or irregular poem will have recognised the co-presence of these three elements. The first two affect all linguistic engagements, but the composition of a poem must also involve the third. Crudely translated from the Italian, stanza means room, a physical space within which movement, along the syntagm or across the paradigmatic field, is confined. Poetry, even that which is governed by abstract phonemic patterns, is self-evidently a form of writing – the regular line and the rhyme scheme is a 'measure', a spatial determinant of the phoneme. The question posed by texts such as Williams's and critics such as Culler is whether it is necessary or even possible for this third element of the projection principle to operate in verse (i.e. writing in lines) which makes no concessions to the abstract regulations of traditional form. It is. In fact, the presence of this effect within a wide variety of modernist poetry is, I believe, a final validation of Jakobson's model of the poetic function.

Consider the following widely praised Imagist poem, T. E. Hulme's 'Autumn'.

A touch of cold in the Autumn night –
I walked abroad,
And saw the ruddy moon lean over a hedge
Like a red-faced farmer.
I did not stop to speak, but nodded,
And round about were the wistful stars
With white faces like town children.

On the surface the interlineal pattern of active and perceptual verb phrases seems far more significant than the line divisions, but in fact the line structure operates as a kind of metasyntax, as much controlling as reflecting the shifts between impression and self-conscious metaphor. For example, in line 3 the interposing of human attributes and activities (ruddy and lean) with non-human referents (the moon and the hedge) is transformed in line 4 into a more controlled self-conscious trope (*Like* a red faced farmer). In lines 5–7 we experience a continuation of what Jakobson describes as 'similarity superinduced upon contiguity, [where] any metonymy is slightly metaphorical and any metaphor has a metonymical tint'. The metonymy–metaphor interaction is not enclosed within a traditional metrical or sound pattern, but the line as a unit is used by Hulme as a means of at once recording and foregrounding the subtle shifts in balance between the referential, ratiocinative and linguistic registers of impression. As Jakobson comments on Antony's 'daring' metonymic–metaphoric use of 'heart', 'the trope becomes part of poetic reality' (see above, pp. 160–1). Hulme's lines are not metrical units, but nor can they simply be dismissed as signs without substance, indicators for interpretive strategies.

A similar effect is achieved in the title poem of Williams's *Spring and All* (1923), from which the following is an extract:

> All along the road the reddish
> purplish, forked, upstanding, twiggy
> stuff of bushes and small trees
> with dead, brown leaves under them
> leafless vines –

This is a perfect synthesis of Poundian technique and unreflecting slang. As part of the following continuous sequence,

> with dead brown leaves under them leafless vines[,]

'them leafless vines' echoes the colloquial and ambiguous title of 'Spring and All' (all what?). The line division at once preserves the improvisational informality and complements it with a stark figurative juxtaposition, recalling 'In a Station of the Metro'.

> with dead, brown leaves under them
> leafless vines.

There is no sense in which the poet has simply reshaped a

syntagmatic progression, but nor can each line be fully isolated from the broader progressive pattern. We, as readers, are not the arbiters of the relation between form and signification, but we are thrown into a constant state of uncertainty by the shifts between the poetic function (the line) and its referential counterpart (syntax). And one could argue that Williams and Hulme create effects from their use of the unmetrical line that are very similar to those disclosed by Jakobson in his readings of parallelism. Often, particularly in Williams's text, it is the graphemic as much as the phonemic substance of the sign which interacts with, interferes with, its differential signifying function, and perhaps this is what Derrida meant in his remarks on 'a dislocation of the founding categories of language through access to another system linking speech and writing'. Jakobson, in his essay on Puškin and statues deals tentatively with the productive co-presence of auditory and visual signs, and in 'On the Relation Between Visual and Auditory Signs' (1970) he examines in more detail the history and aesthetics of the literature–visual arts relationship. Here he reconsiders the seminal work of Lessing and Herder.

> When the observer arrives at the simultaneous synthesis of a contemplated painting, the painting as a whole remains before his eyes, it is still present; but when the listener reaches a synthesis of what he has heard, the phonemes have in fact already vanished. They survive as afterimages, somewhat abridged reminiscences, and this creates an essential difference between the two types of perception and percepts.
>
> (*L in L*, pp. 472–3)

The difference is essential but not absolute. For example, synthesis is a vital element of linguistic cognition and decoding, 'a transposition of a sequential event into a synchronous structure' (*L in L*, p. 471). Regular poetry complicates this process by interposing a second level of intonational and phonemic patterns with the normal sequential–synchronous relationship. More significantly, and this point is dealt with more specifically in the *Dialogues*, the poem on the page offers itself as a phenomenon that is subtly different both from prose and from its auditory poetic counterpart.

[Spoken language] has a purely temporal character, whereas

[written language] connects time and space. While the sounds that we hear disappear, when we read we usually have immobile letters before us and the time of the written flow of words is reversible: we can read and reread, and, what is more, we can be ahead of an event. Anticipation, which is subjective in the listener, becomes objective in the reader.

(*Dialogues*, p. 71)

This, in effect, is a description of Jakobson's interpretive perspective. The term 'parallelism' is not entirely figurative since it becomes clear, particularly from his readings of sonnets, that spatial segmentation, both in terms of the text on the page and of the mental synthesis of the progressive syntagm with the spatial configurations of sound pattern, projects the poem into a multidimensional realm of time and space that is somewhere between ordinary language, spoken and written, and the visual arts.

As the etymology of the Latin term *versus* itself suggests, verse contains the idea of regular recurrence, in contradistinction to prose, which is represented through its etymological composition (Latin *prosa-proversa*) as a movement directed forward. Verse involves the immediate sensation of the present, as well as the return of the gaze to the impulse of preceding verses and the lively anticipation of the verses to follow. These three conjoined impressions form the active play of the invariant and the variations.

(*Dialogues*, pp. 75–6)

In one sense this model of poetic cognition and comprehension provides a new and intriguing perspective upon the New Critics' notion of close reading. The poem on the page, and in the ear, enables the critic to assume a command of the art object which is denied to readers or hearers of non-poetic language; and for an impressive demonstration of how a combination of these New Critical and Jakobsonian methods can operate read John Hollander's *Vision and Resonance*.

To return to the subject in hand, Jakobson's model of the poetic function as involving a multidimensional flux of visual and auditory patterns finds a creative counterpart in a variety of modernist texts.

William Carlos Williams and T. S. Eliot are often regarded as the principal spokesmen for modernist manifestations of, respectively, the proversa and the versus traditions. Indeed, Eliot's early critical essays contain propositions on modernism, literary history and poetic form that are virtually identical with Jakobson's arguments of the 1920s and 1930s (see, for example, 'Tradition and the Individual Talent', 1919, p. 84, for an English version of Jakobson's notion of the poet's 'mythology', and 'Reflections on *Vers Libre*', 1917, p. 101, for Eliot's idea of 'the dominant'). From our distant perspective of the late twentieth century it is easy to classify Eliot as the founder of the anti-modernist brand of postmodernism, a trend which reached its apex in the – very British – movement poetry of the 1950s, and Williams as the vital link between the early years of pure innovation and the later, mostly US, subtraditions of objectivism, projectivism, beat poetry, etc. Their poetry is indeed very different, with Eliot constantly invoking, adapting and revivifying pre-modernist elements of parallelism and the dominant and Williams constantly seeking new configurations of the line–syntax relationship. However, in certain instances their methods are remarkably similar.

In 'On Measure: Statement for Cid Corman' (1948) Williams laments the failure of modernists to evolve a new 'measure' of the line.

> Certainly an art which implies a discipline as the poem does, a rule, a measure, will not tolerate it [formlessness]. . . . Measure an ancient word in poetry, something we have almost forgotten in its literal significance as something measured, becomes related again to the poetic. We have today to do with the poetic, as always, but a *relatively* stable foot, not a rigid one. That is all the difference. It is that which must become the object of our search.

What Williams actually means by the 'relatively stable foot' (also known as the 'variable foot') is still open to question, but it is certain that he borrows the term from Einstein (see Weaver, 1971, and Bradford, 1993a), and in his own work formal relativity can be regarded as a creative manifestation of Jakobson's discussions of Einstein, cubism and Futurism. In effect, the linguistic sign, as a spatio-temporal axis, becomes as much the subject as the medium of representation, and this effect is achieved by drawing upon the innate tension between the line (writing, stasis, graphic) and the syntagm (speech, kinesis, auditory). Consider the following, from 'To a Poor Old Woman':

> munching a plum on
> the street a paper bag
> of them in her hand
>
> They taste good to her
> They taste good
> to her. They taste
> good to her.
>
> You can see it by
> the way she gives herself
> to the one half
> sucked out in her hand.

In the second stanza we encounter a device that would later be used by Chomsky and Hollander to illustrate what might be regarded as the relative nature of the speech act: the same sequence of signs can, when interpreted, or indeed looked at, differently create different patterns of signification. But Williams takes the device a stage further by conflating the static materiality of the signans with the signatum of movement. You can 'see' the referential, ideational image of the woman eating the plum and you can also 'see it' in the visual restructuring of the signans. It is, I would argue, impossible fully to dissociate the referential image of

> the way she gives herself
> to the one half

from the signans – bound image on the page of the same syntactic unit being halved or eaten into by the visual spaces.

A very similar signans–signatum conflation is achieved in section II of 'Perpetuum Mobile' (1949), where a group of girls are 'described' as

> putting
>
> their feet down
> one before the other
> one two
>
> one two they
> pause sometimes before
> a store window and

reform the line
from here
to China everywhere

back and
forth and back and forth
and back and forth.

As Jakobson puts it, 'verse involves the immediate sensation of
the present, as well as the return of the gaze to the impulse
of preceding verses and the lively anticipation of the verses to
follow', and he could have been referring to Williams's poem.
'They', 'the girls', the referential image, 'pause sometimes before
a store window', but we also 'hear' the word 'pause' five syllables
'before' the break in the line (the 'pause'). The 'line' (line of
girls or line of poetry?) is 'reform(ed)' but not quite 'from here'
because the phrase follows, by two syllables, the physical reform-
ing of 'the line'. And we might be prompted to ask if 'their feet'
refers only to the girls or whether 'their feet' are also those
(variable) feet of the poet, put down on the page 'one before
the other', and, in their stillness, able to evoke movement,

back and
forth and back and forth
and back and forth.

We should not dismiss these as instances of formal trivia. The
following is from Book II of *Paterson*.

Without invention nothing is well spaced,
unless the mind change, unless
the stars are new measured, according
to their relative positions, the
line will not change, the necessity
will not matriculate: unless there is
a new mind there cannot be a new
line, the old will go on
repeating itself with recurring
deadliness: without invention
nothing lies under the witch-hazel
bush

Jakobson's argument that the signifier can involve a combination
of the iconic, indexical and symbolic functions of the sign is

based mainly, but not exclusively, on the auditory sign and its deployment in verse. Williams demonstrates that the graphemic sign can operate on a similar three-dimensional plane. It is impossible when reading this sequence fully to disconnect the referential from the purely poetic levels of structuration and signification. The 'relative positions' of the words, like those of the stars, persistently resist co-ordinate stability. In Jakobsonian linguistics 'nothing' is the semantically 'unmarked' term: its signifying function is secondary to the 'somethings' (invention, spacing, relative positions, the witch-hazel bush) to which it relates. Through its graphemic-iconic function, it shifts to the role of the 'marked' unit, 'without invention / nothing lies under the witch-hazel / bush', but on the page and with 'invention', the 'bush' literally lies under 'nothing'. What we naturalise or decode is not quite what we see: the ideational images generated by 'the new mind', 'the new / line', the 'old' that 'will go on / repeating itself' are tantalisingly separate from the effects of watching the graphic signifiers. While Williams tell us, conditionally, that 'there cannot be a new line', we watch

> a new

line

begin. And as he invokes the ability of the 'old' (regular, metrical) line to 'go on repeating itself with recurring deadliness', we watch its new unmetrical counterpart create poetic effects without repetition or regularity.

Jakobson's most detailed investigation of the poetry–painting relationship is 'On the Verbal Art of William Blake and Other Poet-Painters' (1970). His thesis and his disclosures provide a theoretical model for the modernist reworking of the double pattern: it is, in effect, a semiotic exegesis of Williams's mysterious graphemic prosody. Jakobson begins by comparing Blake's 'Infant Sorrow' with its accompanying engraving (*Songs of Experience*, 1794) and his method differs from conventional interaesthetic discussions in one important respect. Instead of marginalising the poetic function of the language and comparing its ideational, metalinguistic product with the signifying function of the picture he works from the premise that the linguistic and the visual signs achieve a textual interface at a level which precedes naturalisation. He analyses the poem in his usual manner – phonemic, metrical and grammatical interlacings are comprehensively documented – and he then reconstructs this textual mechanism in the form of a diagram.

In the diagram below, numerals followed by a dot show the order of the eight lines; the subsequent vertical indicates the beginning, and the oblong vertical at the right of the table, the end of the line. The syllables of the line from its end toward its beginning are designated by the upper horizontal row of numerals. The vertical between the two limits of each line renders its inner pause, while the secondary, optional inner pause is represented by a dotted vertical. A slant marks the increasingly regressive tendency displayed by the disposition of the interlinear and then, in the last couplet, prelinear pauses.

(*L in L*, p. 487)

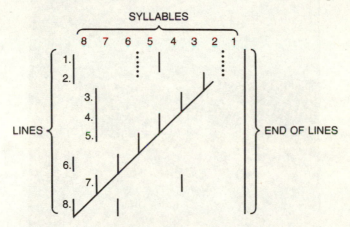

Jakobson rarely uses diagrams in his critical essays and rather than offer a direct explanation of his reason for doing so here he allows what is the principal point of his essay to surface gradually, through subtle suggestion and a trust in readerly acumen. The diagram is an accurate specification of the texture of the poem, on the page and in the ear, and, more significantly, its foregrounding of formal nuances follows the format of the engraving. The mother, on the right, is bent over in a way that replicates the shape of the right vertical (lower body) and the upper horizontal (upper body) of the diagram. Her arms form a diagonal link between these two axes and the body of the infant,

Infant Sorrow

My mother groand! my father wept.
Into the dangerous world I leapt:
Helpless, naked, piping loud:
Like a fiend hid in a cloud.

Struggling in my fathers hands:
Striving against my swadling bands:
Bound and weary I thought best
To sulk upon my mothers breast.

who is half-lying, half-sitting in an almost symmetrical vertical–
horizontal posture.

Jakobson goes on to disclose similar poetic–visual correspondences in the poems and paintings of Henri Rousseau and Paul
Klee, and (in the case of Rousseau) he becomes more explicit
on how the spatio-temporal relation between text and picture
functions as a semiotic interface (again represented by diagrams).
'This distribution of the four grammatical subjects proves to correspond to the *relative* disposition of the pictorial referents on
Rousseau's canvas' (*L in L*, p. 492).

Anyone who suspects a merely coincidental relation between
Jakobson's thesis and Williams's formal techniques should consider the latter's *Pictures from Brueghel* (1949). A detailed discussion
of this volume will be found in Bradford (1993a), but consider
the following from 'The Corn Harvest'. A young reaper is

> sleeping
> unbuttoned
> on his back
>
> the women
> have brought him his lunch
> perhaps
>
> a spot of wine

The unpunctuated syntax has become detached from any certain
referential function. Does the visually detached 'perhaps' refer
back to the preceding syntactic unit or does it initiate the clause
that succeeds it? In the painting *The Harvesters* (1565) this same
sequential–static point of ambiguity is achieved by Brueghel's
placing of the sleeping reaper to the left of a tree, while on the
right a group of women sit, eating, drinking and talking. Has he
shared their food and drink or has he been excluded from it? Is
his unconscious condition the result of a 'spot of wine'? Theirs
or his? 'Perhaps.'

Neither Jakobson nor Williams would claim that the creation
of a new interface between literature and the visual arts is the
single innovative achievement or objective of modernist poetics.
However, the poetry–painting experiments point to a more general trend in modernist poetry, one that is shared by Eliot and
Williams. As the dependency of modern poetic form upon the
abstract criteria of metrical regularity declined, so it became less

strictly determined by the conventions and regulations shared by all other linguistic discourses. As Jakobson has demonstrated, the relation between the two elements of the double pattern – at their most basic the line and syntax – is unpredictable, but at least metrical regularity provided the reader-critic with a stable counterpoint to that other deterministic structure, the sentence. Once the line had become a unit of any length, pattern or structure, so its formal and signifying function began to focus upon the pure materiality of language. If syntax represents the primary organisational element in the displacement of the sign in favour of the signified referent, then its opposing force, no longer constrained by any abstract code, could claim closer allegiance to the material sign, either as an auditory or a visual phenomenon. And here we should recall Jakobson's apparently perverse association of cubism and Dadaism with modernist poetry – both focus upon the materiality and the contingent spatio-temporal function of the sign.

Consider the following from Eliot's *Ash Wednesday*,

If the lost word is lost; if the spent word is spent
If the unheard, unspoken
Word is unspoken unheard;
Still is the unspoken word, the Word unheard,
The Word without a word, the Word within
The world and for the world;
And the light shone in darkness and
Against the World the unstilled world still whirled
About the centre of the silent Word.

O my people, what have I done unto thee.

Where shall the word be found, where will the word
Resound? Not here, there is not enough silence . . . .

The parallels and intertextual correspondences evoked by this passage are legion. Like Xlebnikov and the Futurists, Eliot forces parallelism to its limits; the sound pattern does not merely organise or interfere with signification, it becomes the dominant signifying element. Like Williams, Eliot turns formal self-reference, 'the message for its own sake', into a condition that is inhabited and not simply endured. The texts of Xlebnikov, Williams and Eliot all involve a kind of neo-cubist implosion of the opposing features of the sliding scale. Eliot's referential subject is the word

– its physical properties, its difference from the world, its function as a chord between addresser and addressee – but as we follow his hand and his mind across the page we share his experience of never finally being able to detach signans from signatum. We can 'see' the distinction between the 'unstilled world' and the 'still whirled', but the acoustic–semantic distinction is delayed until the verb connects with its object in the following line. The unspoken Word is literally 'Still' (static, frozen in print), and the printed characters of 'w-o-r-d' are indeed literally 'within' the graphemes of 'w-o-r-l-d'. The spatial question of 'where' the word might 'be found' is granted a mimetic, ironic edge by the visual separation of 'Resound' from its auditory partner. 'Not here' he writes, and we are reminded of Williams's 'spacing' of 'nothing' – 'here' on the page, within the text, or 'here' in the mind and the circumstances of the poet-addresser? Some might argue that this passage is an aberration from Eliot's more orderly practices, but from *Prufrock* to the *Four Quartets* he is continuously aware of the function of the dominant as at once part of the poet's mythology and his method. In 'Tradition and the Individual Talent' he echoes Jakobson: 'the poet has not a "personality" to express, but a particular medium, which is only a medium and not a personality, in which impressions and experiences combine in peculiar and unexpected ways' (p. 84).

Jakobson's theoretical and aesthetic affiliations were born out of the modernist revolution. As he tells us, the inspiration for his work on phonology and the structures of regular poetry was Xlebnikov and the Futurist movement. His analytical devices – parallelism, the projection principle, the six-part diagrams, the interfusion of time and space – are admirably, often irritatingly, comprehensive: they might focus upon the poetic function but they continually remind us that the poetic function is finally about language. Jakobson the linguist shares the questions and the paradigms of the modernist poet. The double pattern, line and syntax, at once defines poetry and foregrounds the uneasy paradoxes of all linguistic usage. It involves limitless tensions and co-operations between the referential function of language – what it does – and its material identity as sounds and shapes – what it is. The rules and conventions that govern this relationship were challenged, extended, amended, foregrounded and celebrated by the modernists, but the relationship endures. Why? This question confronted the teenage Formalist poet and has motivated his lifetime thesis that poetics cannot be understood without linguistics and, more significantly, that language cannot be understood without poetry. Poetry is, and always has been, the form that consciously and deliberately obscures the distinction between language and whatever exists beyond language. The possibility that linguistic and prelinguistic experience are inseparable and mutually dependent dimensions of the human condition has held centre ground in recent poststructuralist–deconstructionist controversies, but the tenacious attraction of the double pattern for writers and readers of poetry provides us with a much more engaging perspective on this question. Language is not simply a means of mediating our condition; it is part of our condition and poetry allows us to experience rather than just ponder this relationship. If all communicative acts and functions were primarily governed and motivated by the contiguity-syntagm axis then we would, in Lacan's terms, be prisoners of the sign. In a broader context the Chomsky tradition of transformational–generative syntax testifies to this. Rules and conventions change; the deep structure is not an invariable commodity. But the necessary interdependency – one might say determinism – of the surface–deep structure relationship is invariable. There is only one way to assume a personal, commanding position over this deterministic pairing, and this is provided by the poetic line. For any combination of words, even the most ungrammatical or nonsensical, a deep structure can be located as either a normative, correctional undertow or as the basis for speculation on what the surface structure might mean. But the poetic line, in either its regular or irregular manifestation, enables addresser and addressee to project the text beyond the governance of deep and surface structure. The echo of rhyme, the repetition of metrical sequences, the foregrounding of iconic and indexical relations in graphemic prosody: all of these devices affect the signifying properties of the non-poetic syntagm. There is no abstract formula that can fully predict or codify the effects discharged when a particular auditory or visual unit of language creates a pattern of form and meaning as a supplement to normal syntax. As Jakobson demonstrates, in specific textual instances these effects can be laboriously documented by employing the abstract continua of the two elements of the double pattern, the structure of the sentence and the structure of the line. But what we cannot do is to specify how, why and to exactly what effect these two elements might be brought together in other texts. Jakobson, in his short discussion of Chomsky's theory (*SW II*, pp. 494f.), argues that the latter's system is flawed because of its objective: to construct 'a completely non-semantic theory of grammatical structure'. He justifies his objection by citing the poetic function in which any semantic entity can be divided in its allegiance both to the proversa (syntactic) and the versus element of the text. To return to one of the above examples, how might we interpret Williams's

> nothing lies under the witch-hazel
> bush

purely in terms of transformational–generative grammar? The model of deep and surface structure would not enable us to deal with the peculiar tension between visual and auditory cognition or explain why the signifier 'nothing' recurs in the text as a nuance of iconic/semantic forces.

The proversa modernists might have rejected the schema of metrical regularity, but by retaining the mysterious phenomenon of the line they maintained a crucial element of the versus tradition: the tension between the materiality and the signifying properties of the sign. Their reason for not abandoning the line is the same one that has motivated Jakobson's belief in the poem as the ultimate object language: the poem is the laboratory in which our experiments with the relation between what language is and what it does can never entirely be reduced to the abstract formulae of the linguist.

Suggestions for further reading on context and influence

The correspondences between the objectives and practices of the Formalists and the Anglo-American New Critics are dealt with, in a clear and non-judgemental manner, by Ewa M. Thompson (*Russian Formalism and Anglo-American New Criticism. A Comparative Study*, 1971, The Hague: Mouton). Two points should be made regarding Jakobson's relation to the New Critics. First, his theory of literary (principally poetic) history and that of T. S. Eliot resonate with similarities, and these have been noted in the closing part (see above pp. 189). Second, there is a fundamental difference between Jakobsonian and New Critical approaches to the poetic function. Cleanth Brooks (*The Well Wrought Urn*, 1947, New York: Harcourt & Brace) and William Empson (*Seven Types of Ambiguity*, 1961, London: Penguin – first published in 1930) are often cited as the achetypes of New Critical positivism in that they both sought to identify ahistorical common denominators in English poetry – respectively the functions of paradox and ambiguity. There are clear similarities between their methods and Jakobson's general model of the metonymy–metaphor projection principle, but neither Brooks nor Empson propose a general formula which explains the integration of the syntactic–semantic dimension of language with stress and sound patterns (in Jakobsonian poetics, 'parallelism'). This sense of prosody, metre, or versification as a specialised subdiscipline to be drawn upon only when the sensitive critical intelligence feels it necessary to do so is a common feature of much Anglo-American poetry criticism. For example, F. R. Leavis, in his dismissive reading of Shelley (*Revaluation: Tradition and Development in English Poetry*, 1949, London: Chatto & Windus), judges the 'Ode on the West Wind' as symptomatic of Shelley's 'weak grasp upon the actual'. Leavis does not consider (or properly evaluate) the possibility that Shelley's dense patternings of metre, alliteration, assonance and rhyme might specifically be intended to shift our attention from the 'actual' (in Jakobson's terms the foregrounding of the versus-selective axis above its proversa-contiguity counterpart). For a similar reading of Shelley's 'The Cloud' see Donald Davie's *Purity of Diction in English Verse* (1967, London: Routledge & Kegan Paul). Among the New Critics, W. K. Wimsatt's programme of formal and critical emphases bears the closest resemblance to Jakobson's methods (see *The Verbal Icon*, 1954, Lexington: University of Kentucky Press). I. A. Richards was perhaps the most prominent Anglo-American critic to recognise the analytical power of Jakobsonian poetics. At the Indiana conference Richards praised 'Linguistics and Poetics' and in the *TLS* (28 May 1970, pp. 589–90) he enthusiastically reviewed Jakobson and Jones's reading of Shakespeare's sonnet 129. Jakobson's influence becomes evident in Richard's essays 'Factors and Functions in Linguistics' and 'Powers and Limits of Signs' (in his *Poetries: Their Media and Ends*, 1974, ed. T. Eaton, The Hague: Mouton). See also Helen Vendler's 'Jakobson, Richards and Shakespeare's Sonnet CXXIX' (in *I. A. Richards: Essays in His Honour*, 1973, ed. R. Brower, Oxford: Oxford University Press).

As I have argued, Jakobson's literary theories have been less readily accepted and more easily misinterpreted than his work in linguistics, but there are a few exceptions to this. Jerzy Strzetelski in *The English Sonnet: Syntax and Style* (1970, Cracow: Jagiell University Press) analyses 278 sonnets by 55 authors and employs a dutifully detailed version of Jakobson's centrifugal–centripetal formula. For a context–reader-based alternative to Jakobson's model of the sonnet see Roger Fowler's 'Language and the Reader: Shakespeare's Sonnet 73' (in *Style and Structure in Literature: Essays in the New Stylistics*, 1975, ed. R. Fowler, Oxford: Basil Blackwell).

In the general field of poetry and poetics there are a number of intriguing works which adapt and extend Jakobsonian concepts. Jerzy Kurylowicz, in 'The Linguistic Foundations of Metre' (*Biuletin Polskiego towarzystwa jazyko nawczego*, 34, 1976, pp. 63–72), re-examines the paradigm–syntagm projection principle and builds on Jakobson's premise that poetry involves a system of organisation and signification that is intrinsically different from that of non-poetic discourses. Jiri Levy in 'The Meanings of Form and the Forms of Meaning' (in *Paralipomena*, 1971, Brunn: J. E. Purkyne University Philosophical Faculty – first published in 1964) offers a complex typology of the 'acoustic' and 'semantic' levels of verse – a scheme which owes much to Jakobson's concept of parallelism. Jury Lotman's 'On Some Principal Difficulties in the Structural Description of a Text' (*Linguistics*, no. 121, 1974, pp. 57–63) deals with the problem of relating the 'static' description of a poem's mechanism to the 'dynamic' interaction of its parts, and provides a useful supplement to Jakobson's model of space, time and the linguistic sign (dealt with in Part III above, pp. 184–97). John Hollander, another delegate at the 1958 conference, is best known for his work on poetry and music, and his collection *Vision and Resonance. Two Senses of Poetic Form* (1975, Oxford: Oxford University Press) contains a rich diversity of perspectives upon poetic form – aural, visual, historical, situational. It would be unfairly parochial to claim that Hollander's originality carries the influence of anyone in particular; rather, his work shows that the spirit of the 1958 conference was kept productively alive through the poststructuralist era. Yet another Indiana veteran, Edward Stankiewicz, has continued to produce detailed studies of poetic form and poetics. His 'Poetic and Non-Poetic Language in their Interrelation' (in *Poetics, Poetyka, Poetika*, 1961, ed. D. Davie, Warsaw: Polish Scientific Publishers) is an intriguing reconsideration of the underlying principles of Jakobson's Indiana paper.

For an adaptation of Jakobson's poetics to the various historical, literary and cultural contexts of post-sixteenth-century English poetry see my own *A Linguistic History of English Poetry* (1993, London: Routledge). Barbara Herrnstein Smith's *Poetic Closure. A Study of How Poems End* (1968, Chicago: University of Chicago Press) should be read as a brilliant counterpoint to Jakobson's concept of the autonomy of poetic language: Smith examines poetic closure as in effect a token of poetry's structural difference from other discourses. Paul Werth, in 'Roman Jakobson's Verbal Analysis of Poetry' (*Journal of Linguistics*, 12, 1976, pp. 21–73) follows Culler's anti-Jakobson line, but extends his critique into the issue of how we might use the projection principle to distinguish between good and bad poems: the fact that he chooses a self-evidently bad poem (by McGonagall) as an example tends to short-circuit his argument.

David Lodge's *The Modes of Modern Writing. Metaphor, Metonymy*

and the Typology of Modern Literature (1977, London: Edward
Arnold) is a justly celebrated projection of Jakobson's metonymy–
metaphor model into the sphere of fictional and non-fictional
prose. One of Jakobson's allies among the post-1970s, post-practi-
cally everything generation of critics is Derek Attridge, and in
*Peculiar Language. Literature as Difference from the Renaissance to James
Joyce* (1988, London: Methuen) he considers the relation between
Jakobson's model of sound and meaning and Joyce's taste for
onomatopoeia. Attridge was one of the key participants in the
1986 conference on 'The Linguistics of Writing' at Strathclyde
University (selected papers published as *The Linguistics of Writing*,
1987, Manchester: Manchester University Press). The conference
was explicit in its claim to foreground the major changes that
had taken place in the uneasy relationship between literary studies and linguistics since Indiana, 1958. Jakobson's paper, and its
assumptions about the literariness of literature, is, as one would
expect, given special prominence in many of the Strathclyde
papers. If one can discern a mood or consensus from such a
diffuse collection, then the Strathclyde conference signalled a far
less dismissive attitude to Jakobson than was evident in the 1970s.
Attridge, in his respectfully titled paper, 'Closing Statement:
Linguistics and Poetics in Retrospect', is cautiously even-handed:
'the six-factor diagram is a masterly piece of theoretical rhetoric'
designed to make any doubts about 'The existence of an inherent
property of poetic language ... fade in the bright sunlight of
Jakobson's apodictic prose' (p. 26).

An intriguing, widely praised and finally inconclusive reading
of Jakobson's theory of poetics and linguistics will be found in
Julia Kristeva's *Desire in Language: A Semiotic Approach to Literature
and Art* (1980, New York: Columbia University Press; relevant
section reprinted in Lodge, 1988). Kristeva considers the origins
of Jakobson's theories in the political and aesthetic cauldron of
the Russian Revolution and Futurism, stressing his association
with Xlebnikov and Majakovskij. In brief, she seems to share
Bakhtin's argument that poetry (unlike the novel) freezes and
distorts any proper engagement with the historical process:
'Poetic discourse measures rhythm against the meaning of language structure and is thus always eluded by meaning in the
present while continually postponing it to an impossible time to
come' (Lodge, p. 238). She calls for a (Bakhtinian) 'historical
epistemology of linguistics' and a 'semiology' which moves

beyond 'simple linguistic studies' to a consideration of the meta-languages of social interaction. Her thesis is yet another contribution to the new paradigm.

Jakobson has been commemorated in a number of collections. The best, in my view, is *Language, Poetry and Poetics. The Generation of the 1890s: Jakobson, Trubetzkoy, Majakovskij* (1987, ed. K. Pomorska *et al.*, Amsterdam: Mouton) The pieces by Chvany, Vallier, Pomorska, Matejka and Toman are of particular theoretical and historical interest. *Roman Jakobson. Echoes of His Scholarship* (1977, ed. D. Armstrong and C. H. Van Schoonveld, Lisse: Peter de Ridder Press) is detailed and scholarly – Umberto Eco's essay brilliantly contextualises Jakobson's work within the broader field of semiotics. *A Tribute to Roman Jakobson, 1896–1982* (1983, Amsterdam: Mouton) contains illuminating anecdotes and reminiscences by his friends and colleagues from the USA and beyond; and Morris Halle's (ed.) *Roman Jakobson. What He Taught Us* (1983, *International Journal of Slavic Linguistics and Poetics*, 27, supplement) does so on a more modest scale. Krystyna Pomorska's *Jakobsonian Poetics and Slavic Narrative* (1992, Durham, N.C.: Duke University Press) contains a combination of her own work and accounts of Jakobson's influence and objectives.

Bibliography

Abrams, M. H. (1953) *The Mirror and the Lamp. Romantic Theory and the Critical Tradition*, Oxford: Oxford University Press.

Armstrong, D. and Van Schoonveld, C. H. (eds) (1987) *Roman Jakobson. Echoes of his Scholarship*, Lisse: Peter de Ridder.

Auden, W. H. (1966) *Collected Shorter Poems 1927-57*, London: Faber.

Austin, J. L. (1962) *How To Do Things With Words*, London: Oxford University Press.

Bakhtin, Mikhail (1968) *Rabelais and his World*, Cambridge, Mass.: Harvard University Press (first published in 1940).

—— (1973) *Problems of Dostoyevsky's Poetics*, Ann Arbor: Michigan University Press (first published in 1929).

—— (1975) *Voprosy literatury i éstetiki*, Moscow, reprinted in *The Dialogic Imagination* (1981) Austin, Tex.: University of Texas Press.

Bakhtin, Mikhail and Medvedev, P. N. (1978) *The Formal Method in Literary Scholarship*, Baltimore: Johns Hopkins University Press (first published in 1928).

Barthes, Roland (1967) *Elements of Seminology*, London: Cape (first published in 1964).

—— (1970) *S/Z*, Paris: Seuil.

—— (1977) 'The Death of the Author', in *Image Music, Text*, New York: Hill & Wang. Reprinted in Lodge (1988).

Blake, William (1966) *The Complete Writings*, ed. G. Keynes, London: Oxford University Press.

Bradford, Richard (1992) *Silence and Sound. Theories of Poetics from the 18th Century*, New Jersey and London: Associated University Presses.

—— (1993a) *The Look of It. A Theory of Visual Form in English Poetry*, Cork: Cork University Press.

—— (1993b) *A Linguistic History of English Poetry*, London: Routledge.

Brogan, T. V. F. (1981) *English Versification 1570-1980. A Reference Guide with a Global Appendix*, Baltimore: Johns Hopkins University Press.

Brown, Edward J. (ed.) (1971) *Modern Soviet Writers*, London: Oxford University Press.

Chatman, Seymour (1956) 'Robert Frost's "Mowing": An Inquiry into Prosodic Structure', *Kenyon Review*, 18, 421-38.

Chomsky, Noam (1957) *Syntactic Structures*, The Hague: Mouton.

Clark, K. and Holquist, M. (1984) *Mikhail Bakhtin*, Cambridge, Mass.: Harvard University Press.

Culler, Jonathan (1975) *Structuralist Poetics. Structuralism, Linguistics and the Study of Literature*, London: Routledge & Kegan Paul.

—— (1980) '*Fabula* and *Syuzhet* in the Analysis of Narrative', *Poetics Today*, 1:3, 27–37.

Derrida, Jacques (1975) 'The Purveyor of Truth', *Yale French Studies*, 52, 31–113.

—— (1977) *Of Grammatology*, trans. G. Chakravorty Spivak, Baltimore: Johns Hopkins University Press.

Donne, John (1971) *The Complete English Poems*, ed. A. J. Smith, London: Penguin.

Dryden, John (1668) 'Essay of Dramatic Poesie' in *Essays of John Dryden* (1926), ed. W. P. Ker, vol. I, Oxford: Oxford University Press.

Eagleton, Terry (1983) *Literary Theory. An Introduction*, Oxford: Basil Blackwell.

Eisenstein, Sergei (1938) *The Film Sense*, reprinted in *The Modern Tradition: Backgrounds of Modern Literature* (1965), ed. R. Ellmann and C. Feidelson Jr, New York: Oxford University Press.

Ejxenbaum, Boris (1922) *Melodika Stixa*, Petrograd.

Eliot, T. S. (1917a) 'Reflections on *Vers Libre*', in *Twentieth Century Poetry* (1975), ed. G. Martin and P. N. Furbank, Milton Keynes: Open University Press.

—— (1917b) 'Tradition and the Individual Talent', in Martin and Furbank (1975).

—— (1969) *The Complete Poems and Plays*, London: Faber.

Erlich, Victor (1955) *Russian Formalism: History-Doctrine*, The Hague: Mouton.

Felman, Shoshana (1977) 'Turning the Screw of Interpretation', *Yale French Studies*, 55/6, 94–207.

Fenollosa, Ernest (1919) *The Chinese Written Character as a Medium for Poetry*, ed. Ezra Pound, in *Prose Keys to Modern Poetry* (1962), ed. K. Shapiro, New York: Harper & Row.

Fillmore, C. J. (1973) 'May We Come In?', *Semiotica*, 9, 1–15.

Fish, Stanley (1980) *Is there a Text in this Class? The Authority of Interpretive Communities*, Cambridge, Mass.: Harvard University Press.

Fowler, Roger (1966) 'Structural Metrics', *Linguistics*, 27, 49–64.

—— (1981) *Literature as Social Discourse*, London: Batsford.

Freud, Sigmund (1900) 'The Interpretation of Dreams', in *Standard Edition* (1953), vols IV and V, London: Hogarth Press.

—— (1908) 'Creative Writers and Day Dreaming', in *Standard Edition* (1959), vol. IX, London: Hogarth Press.

—— (1920) 'Beyond the Pleasure Principle', in *Standard Edition* (1955), London: Hogarth Press.

Galan, Frantisek (1985) *Historic Structures: The Prague School Project, 1928–1946*, London: Croom Helm.

Gascoigne, George (1575) 'Certayn Notes of Instruction concerning the Making of Verse or Rhyme in English . . .', in *The Complete Works of*

George Gascoigne (1907–10), ed. J. Cunliffe, Cambridge: Cambridge University Press.

Gross, Harvey (1964) *Sound and Form in Modern Poetry*, Ann Arbor: University of Michigan Press.

Halle, Morris (ed.) (1983) *Roman Jakobson: What He Taught Us. International Journal of Slavic Linguistics and Poetics*, 27, supplement.

Halle, Morris and Keyser, Samuel J. (1971) *English Stress: Its Growth, and its Role in Verse*, New York: Harper & Row.

Hawkes, Terence (1977) *Structuralism and Semiotics*, London: Methuen.

Holenstein, Elmar (1974) *Roman Jakobson's Approach to Language*, Bloomington, Ind.: Indiana University Press.

Hollander, John (1975) *Vision and Resonance. Two Senses of Poetic Form*, London: Oxford University Press.

Husserl, Edmund (1970) *Logical Investigations*, New York: Humanities Press (first published in 1913).

Jakobson, Roman (1949) 'Notes on General Linguistics: Its Present State and Crucial Problems', New York, Rockefeller Foundation, mimeograph.

—— (1966) *Selected Writings IV. Slavic Epic Studies*, The Hague: Mouton.

—— (1971a) *Selected Writings I. Phonological Studies*, The Hague: Mouton.

—— (1971b) *Selected Writings II. Word and Language*, The Hague: Mouton.

—— (1978a) *Selected Writings V. On Verse, its Masters and Explorers*, The Hague: Mouton.

—— (1978b) *Six Lectures on Sound and Meaning*, Cambridge, Mass.: MIT Press.

—— (1980) *Selected Writings III. Poetry of Grammar and Grammar of Poetry*, The Hague: Mouton.

—— (1982) *Selected Writings VI. Early Slavic Paths and Crossroads*, The Hague: Mouton.

—— (1985) *Selected Writings VII. Contributions to Comparative Mythology. Studies in Linguistics and Philology*, ed. S. Rudy, The Hague: Mouton.

—— (1985) *Verbal Art, Verbal Sign, Verbal Time*, Minneapolis, Minn.: University of Minnesota Press.

—— (1987) *Language in Literature*, ed. K. Pomorska and S. Rudy, Cambridge, Mass.: Harvard University Press.

Jakobson, Roman, Fant, C. G. M. and Halle, M. (1952) *Preliminaries to Speech Analysis*, Cambridge, Mass.: MIT Press.

Jakobson, Roman and Halle, Morris (1956) *Fundamentals of Language*, The Hague: Mouton.

Jakobson, Roman and Pomorska, Krystyna (1983) *Dialogues*, Cambridge: Cambridge University Press.

Jakobson, Roman and Waugh, Linda R. (1979) *The Sound Shape of Language*, Bloomington, Ind.: Indiana University Press.

Jakubinskij, Lev (1921) 'Otkuda berutsja stichi' *Kniznyj ugol*, no. 7, 23.

Johnson, Barbara (1979) 'The Frame of Reference', in *Psychoanalysis and the Question of the Text*, ed. G. Hartman, Baltimore: Johns Hopkins University Press.

Johnson, Samuel (1779) 'Milton', in *Lives of The English Poets*, reprinted in *Oxford Anthology of English Literature* (1973) vol. II, ed. F. Kermode, J. Hollander *et al.*, London: Oxford University Press.

Jones, Peter (ed.) (1972) *Imagist Poetry*, London: Penguin.

Kiparsky, Paul (1975) 'Stress, Syntax and Metre', *Language*, 51, 576–616.

—— (1977) 'The Rhythmic Structure of English Verse', *Linguistic Enquiry*, 8, 189–247.

—— (1983) 'Roman Jakobson and The Grammar of Poetry', in *A Tribute to Roman Jakobson 1896–1982*, Amsterdam: Mouton.

Kristeva, Julia (1980) *Desire in Language: A Semiotic Approach to Literature and Art*, New York: Columbia University Press.

Labov, W. (1972) *Sociolinguistic Patterns*, Pennsylvania: University of Pennsylvania Press.

Lacan, Jacques (1949) 'The Mirror Stage', in *Ecrits. A Selection* (1977), trans. A. Sheridan, New York: Norton.

—— (1953) 'The Function and Field of Speech and Language in Psychoanalysis' (originally entitled, 'Discourse at Rome'), in *Ecrits. A Selection*, trans. A. Sheridan, New York: Norton.

—— (1957) 'The Insistence of the Letter in the Unconscious', reprinted in Lodge (1988).

—— (1976) 'Seminar on "The Purloined Letter"', *Yale French Studies*, 48, 38–72.

Levin, S. R. (1962) *Linguistic Structures in Poetry*, Janua Linguarum, no. 23, The Hague: Mouton.

—— (1971) 'The Conventions of Poetry', in *Literary Style. A Symposium*, ed. Seymour Chatman, London: Oxford University Press.

Lévi-Strauss, Claude (1968) *L'Origine des manières de table*. vol. III of *Mythologiques*, Paris: Plon.

—— (1972) *Structural Anthropology*, London: Penguin.

Lodge, David (ed.) (1972) *Twentieth Century Literary Criticism. A Reader*, London: Longman.

—— (ed.) (1988) *Modern Criticism and Theory. A Reader*, London: Longman.

Lowell, Amy (1920) 'Some Musical Analogies in Modern Poetry', *Musical Quarterly*, 6, 127–57.

Merquior, J. G. (1986) *From Prague to Paris. A Critique of Structuralist and Poststructuralist Thought*, London: Verso.

Milton, John (1968) *Paradise Lost*, ed. A. Fowler, London: Longman.

Mukarovsky, Jan (1934) 'Art as a Semiotic Fact', in *Aesthetic Function, Norm and Value as Social Facts* (1970), Ann Arbor: University of Michigan Press.

—— (1940) 'O jazyce básnickém' in *Kapitoly z ceské poetiky* (1948), vol. I, 78–128.

Ohmann, R. (1971) 'Speech Acts and the Definition of Literature', *Philosophy and Literature*, 4, 1–19.

Peirce, C. S. (1931–58) *Collected Papers*, ed. C. Hartshorne, P. Weiss and A. Burks, Cambridge, Mass.: Harvard University Press.

Pomorska, Krystyna (1968) *Russian Formalist Theory and its Poetic Ambiance*, The Hague: Mouton.

—— (1992) *Jakobsonian Poetics and Slavic Narrative. From Pushkin to Solzhenitsyn*, Durham, N.C.: Duke University Press.

Pomorska, Krystyna *et al.* (eds) (1987) *Language, Poetry and Poetics. The Generation of the 1890s: Jakobson, Trubetzkoy, Mcjakovskij, Proceedings of the First Roman Jakobson Colloquium at MIT Oct. 5–6, 1984*, Amsterdam: Mouton.

Pratt, Mary Louise (1977) *Toward a Speech Act Theory of Literary Discourse*, Bloomington, Ind.: Indiana University Press.

Ransom, John Crowe (1938) 'Criticism Inc.', reprinted in Lodge (1972).

Riffaterre, Michael (1966) 'Describing Poetic Structures: Two Approaches to Baudelaire's "Les Chat" ', *Yale French Studies*, 36–7, 200–42.

Rudy, Stephen (1987) 'Jakobson-Aljagrov and Futurism', in *Language, Poetry and Poetics*, ed. K. Pomorska *et al.*, Amsterdam: Mouton.

Saintsbury, George (1906–10) *A History of English Prosody from the 12th Century to the Present Day*, London: Macmillan.

Sangster, Rodney B. (1982) *Roman Jakobson and Beyond: Language as a System of Signs*, Amsterdam: Mouton.

Saran, F. L. (1907) *Deutsche Verslehre*, Munich: C. H. Beck.

Saussure, Ferdinand de (1959) *Course in General Linguistics*, trans. W. Baskin, New York: McGraw-Hill.

Scholes, Robert (1974) *Structuralism in Literature. An Introduction*, New Haven: Yale University Press.

Searle, John (1969) *Speech Acts*, Cambridge: Cambridge University Press.

Sebeok, Thomas A. (1960) *Style in Literature*, Cambridge, Mass.: MIT Press.

Shklovsky, Victor (1965) 'Art as Technique', in *Russian Formalist Criticism*, ed. L. T. Lemon and M. J. Reis, Lincoln, Nebr.: University of Nebraska Press.

Sievers, Eduard (1912) *Rhythmisch-melodische Studien: Vortrage und Aufsatze*, Heidelberg: Carl Winter.

Starobinski, J. (1979) *Words upon Words: The Anagrams of Ferdinand de Saussure*, New Haven: Yale University Press.

Steiner, Peter (1984) *Russian Formalism. A Metapoetics*, Ithaca: Cornell University Press.

Stempel, W. D. (ed.) (1972) *Texte der Russischen Formalisten II*, Munich: Fink.

Trager, George L. and Smith, Henry Lee Jr (1951) *An Outline of English Structure*, Studies in Linguistics Occasional Papers no. 3, Norman, Okla.: Battenburg Press.

Trubetzkoy, Nikolaj (1931) 'Die phonologischen Systeme', *Travaux du Cercle Linguistique de Prague*, 4, 96–116.

Tynjanov, Jurij (1924) 'Rhythm as the Constructive Factor of Verse', originally part of *Problema Stixotvornoga jazyka*, reprinted in *Readings in Russian Poetics. Formalist and Structuralist Views* (1978), ed. L. Matejka and K. Pomorska, Ann Arbor: University of Michigan Press.

Vallier, Dora (1987) 'Jakobson as Poet: Pre-figure of a Linguist', in *Language, Poetry and Poetics*, ed. K. Pomorska, Amsterdam: Mouton.

Verrier, Paul (1909) *Essai sur les principes de la métrique anglaise*, Paris: Libraire Universitaire.

Waugh, Linda R. (1976) *Roman Jakobson's Science of Language*, Lisse: Peter de Ridder Press.

Weaver, Mike (1971) *William Carlos Williams. The American Background*, Cambridge: Cambridge University Press.

Webb, Daniel (1769) *Observations on the Correspondence between Poetry and Music*, London.

Wellek, René (1949) *Theory of Literature*, London: Cape.

Whitman, Walt (1965) *The Collected Writings*, ed. E. W. Allen and S. Bradley, New York: New York University Press.

Williams, William Carlos (1948) 'On Measure: Statement for Cid Corman', in *Selected Essays*, New York: New Directions.

—— (1962) *Pictures from Brueghel and Other Poems*, New York: New Directions.

—— (1991) *Collected Poems* vols I and II, New York: New Directions.

Wimsatt, W. K. and Monroe Beardsley (1946) 'The Intentional Fallacy', *Sewanee Review*, 54, reprinted in Wimsatt's *The Verbal Icon*, Lexington: Kentucky University Press.

Wordsworth, William (1984) *The Oxford Authors*, ed. S. Gill, Oxford: Oxford University Press.

Xlebnikov, Velimir (1989) *Collected Works of Velimir Xlebnikov*, trans. P. Schmidt, ed. R. Vroon, Cambridge, Mass.: Harvard University Press.

Index